Beyond Formalism ▶

Beyond Formalism

▶▶▶▶▶▶▶▶▶▶▶▶▶▶▶▶▶

Naming and Necessity for Human Beings

JAY F. ROSENBERG

Temple University Press

Philadelphia

Temple University Press, Philadelphia 19122
Copyright © 1994 by Temple University. All rights reserved
Published 1994
Printed in the United States of America

∞ The paper used in this publication meets the minimum requirements of
American National Standard for Information Sciences—Permanence of
Paper for Printed Library Materials, ANSI Z39.48-1984

Library of Congress Cataloging-in-Publication Data
Rosenberg, Jay F.
    Beyond formalism : naming and necessity for human beings / Jay F.
Rosenberg.
      p. cm.
    Includes bibliographical references and index.
    ISBN 1-56639-118-0
    1. Onomasiology. 2. Language and languages—Philosophy. 3.
Knowledge, Theory of. 4. Logic. I. Title.
P325.5.O55R67 1994
121'.68—dc20   93-12691

▶ TO THE MEMORY OF MY PARENTS

MOTTO *If you send your concepts to spend the night with Procrustes, you should not be surprised when, the next morning, they come back all the same size.*

CONTENTS

PREFACE *xi*
▶ Dialectical Preliminaries *1*
1 ▶ Essential Properties, Thought-Experiments, and Modal Intuitions *6*
2 ▶ Rigid Designators, Proper Names, and Possible Worlds *28*
3 ▶ Referential Alternatives: Names and Descriptions *57*
4 ▶ Theoretical Desiderata for Nominal Reference *86*
5 ▶ Idiolectic Sense, Confluence, and Isonymy *109*
6 ▶ Reference and Belief in Epistemological Perspective *135*
7 ▶ Logical Analysis in Epistemological Perspective *159*
8 ▶ Roots and Roles of Logical Form *183*
NOTES *199*
WORKS CITED *225*
GENERAL INDEX *229*
NAME INDEX *239*

PREFACE

I BEGIN with a brief personal history: Some twenty years ago, when Saul Kripke's "Naming and Necessity" was first published in Harman and Davidson's anthology, *Semantics of Natural Language*, like most philosophers, I found it both brilliant and stimulating. Unlike most philosophers, however, I also thought it was largely *wrong*. Kripke's essentialist modal theses struck me as quirky and implausible, and while his critique of a particular interpretation of "Descriptivism"—that is, the thesis that the referent of a proper name is determined by way of an associated (descriptive) sense—was plainly on target, the specific version of Descriptivism that he had singled out for criticism seemed both deliberately and unnecessarily naive. Meanwhile, Kripke's own adumbrations of an alternative "causal-historical" picture of proper names and natural kind sortals pointed toward the sort of theory that would inevitably disconnect the ostensible semantics of such expressions ("direct reference") from their roles and modes of functioning in contexts of individual understanding and interpersonal communication.

It also seemed to me obvious where things had gone wrong. Kripke's *first* brilliant achievement had been the development of a formal (model theoretic) semantics for systems of quantified modal logic with identity. What he had now done, in essence, was to transform key elements of his ingenious formalisms into substantive metaphysical views and philosophical theses regarding aspects of natural languages. Once those views and theses had been disentangled from allegiance to the formal archetypes that inspired them, I thought, they would themselves be subjected to appropriate critical scrutiny and, fairly soon (now that, thanks to Kripke, the issues had been so well joined), they would in turn give way to a family of more defensible philosophical convictions. But that wasn't what happened.

What happened was rather that a surprisingly large number of philosophers simply *adopted* the new Kripkean ideas, images, and idioms root and branch. Instead of being treated simply as the latest story, one still in need of substantial improvement, they became the phenomena to be saved. The quirky essentialist theses became *premisses* in ("Twin Earth" style) thought-experiments, mobilized in support of a wide variety of claims, and the causal-historical picture of "direct reference" became the subject of a series of epicyclic refinements and modifications which continues unabated today.[1]

There, as far as I was concerned, the matter rested. I had my own philosophical agenda,[2] and while it indeed required me to say something about *representation,* the account which emerged funded its own claims of (relative) necessity epistemologically and located the significant stratum of extensional word-world (token-object) regularities at a level of analysis *below* that occupied by explicitly meta-level semantic notions. Such Kripkean images and idioms as "possible worlds" and "rigid designators" proved to be simply *irrelevant* to the stories I was engaged in telling, and so, while their popularity spread and epicycles accumulated, I personally gave them little attention.[3]

In 1989, I stepped down from the chair of the Chapel Hill department. As they customarily do in the case of a retiring chairperson, the University of North Carolina bestowed a semester's research leave upon me—presumably to get me out of town and facilitate an orderly transfer of power without the necessity of staging a coup. I had the good luck to be able to combine this leave with a term as an Alexander von Humboldt Research Fellow, thereby freeing myself from teaching and administrative duties for an entire year. In an extraordinarily fortuitous consilience of circumstances, as all this was taking shape, my friend and philosophical colleague Peter Bieri, together with the psychologist Eckart Scheerer, was busily organizing a year-long project at the Center for Interdisciplinary Research in Bielefeld, Germany,[4] on the topic "Mind and Brain". Discerning a superb opportunity to hobnob with my fellow wizards, both foreign and domestic, in what was, after all, my wife Regina's home town, I promptly signed on as a project member. My plan was to participate in the ongoing collective interdisciplinary activities as a philosopher of mind, while simultaneously privately thinking and writing primarily about the role of "intuitions" in philosophical reasoning.

It was approximately at this point, however, that my subconscious, an undisciplined and insubordinate character, grabbed me by the scruff of the neck and said, roughly, "Oh no you don't! You've been walking around being inarticulately irritated by Kripke's views for almost twenty years. *This* year, you're going to think through your differences and disagreements and *write them down*!" In the end, my subconscious and I struck a bargain. I was allowed to think—and even to write something—about the role of intuitions in philosophical reasoning, but I had to use a detailed discussion of my quarrels with various of Kripke's reasonings and conclusions regarding names and modalities as an expository vehicle. The present book is the product of these compromises.

In a sense, then, this book has been twenty years in the making. It has, however, been only two years in the writing, and for those two years, some quite specific thanks are in order: to the University of North Carolina, and especially Gillian Cell, then Dean of the College of Arts and Sciences, for the initial post-chairmanship released time; to the Alexander von Humboldt Foundation of Bonn–Bad Godesburg, Germany, for support as a Research Fellow during 1989–1990; to the Center for Indisciplinary Research (ZiF) of Bielefeld, Germany, for providing a superb research environment, as close to ideal conditions as one could reasonably hope for; and to the Institute for the Arts and Humanities of the University here in Chapel Hill, for an appointment as a Faculty Research Fellow during the fall semester of 1991, which enabled me to complete final preparation of a finished manuscript.

A number of colleagues also deserve appreciative mention at this point: for especially helpful discussions among my co-residents at the ZiF, Peter Bieri and David Rosenthal; for insights gathered on the road, Isaac Levi and Mike McKinsey in one natural language, and Andreas Kemmerling and Anton Koch in another; and, for spirited last-minute arguments which inspired at least twenty-five pages of additional manuscript, Ruth Marcus and George Bealer. Jerry Postema, my successor as Department Chair, has earned my gratitude by biting various unpalatable fiscal bullets; Paul Ziff, by plying me with vodka and inspiration; and, by spending much more of their own valuable time in reading, commenting on, and otherwise reacting to my manuscript-in-progress than they should have (much to my profit and education), my colleagues in Chapel Hill: Dorit Bar-On, Keith Simmons, Simon Blackburn, and especially Bill Lycan (who even sacrificed a precious sliver of his own research leave). As usual, Bill doesn't believe a word of it, but he sure keeps me honest. The book is *much* better (and somewhat longer) than it would have been, had not Bill, who seems to have read *everything*, politely but firmly insisted that I really *should* take a look at certain significant ancillary texts.

It is likely to be quite a while before I set myself to writing another book. Much to my amazement, on my last birthday I turned fifty. Since I completed my last book five years ago, both my parents have died, and so too have the two philosophers who had been my mentors, guides, and inspiration throughout the whole of my academic career, Wilfrid Sellars and David Falk. My daughter, Leslie, has graduated from Georgetown University (*magna cum laude*!), and my stepson, Glen, is most of the way through his university education as well. The family-in-residence is down to me, my dear wife, Regina, and one nineteen-year-old cat (Torquata).[5] Recently I was struck by the realization that I have now been teaching and writing philosophy here in Chapel Hill for longer than most of my present students, including doctoral students, have been alive. (My fantasy life, curiously enough, remains largely unaffected by such realizations.) This is, in fact, my twenty-sixth year on the faculty of the University of North Carolina; I have been here over half my life. The time seems auspicious for an extended reflective pause.

The most important lesson that I have perhaps learned during my twenty-five years in this business is that things are always more complicated than I think they are.[6] Stories that satisfied me twenty, ten, or even five years ago have largely lost their persuasive charms. I've been around long enough to have discovered where the edges are frayed and the joints loose. What doesn't come completely unraveled usually at least leaks. Although they are expressed a tad more tentatively than has formerly been my wont, the stories that I tell in this book are no exception. They, too, are leaky, and I know it. What makes them nevertheless worth telling, I hope, is that they are rather *less* leaky than the stories that I suggest they should replace.

My personal daemons appear for once to be somewhat in tune with the *Zeitgeist*. That is, it is getting harder for everyone to find his or her intellectual way about in the old *Geisteswissenschaften* nowadays. On the one hand, there is such a clamoring proliferation of *insistent* voices—black, female, gay, African, Asian, Islamic, Hispanic, native American. On the other, there is the French Surrender—the curious "postmodern" idea that everything is a text, that texts are either about nothing or about themselves, and that no one person's reading is or can be any better than anyone else's. That this sort of thing is taken seriously is hard enough to understand; that it bids fair to become the new orthodoxy boggles what is left of the mind.[7]

A philosopher is supposed to be a lover of wisdom, but you can't be a lover of wisdom if there isn't any wisdom. The bottom line of "postmodernism" seems to be that there isn't any wisdom. An aspiring philosopher (a "philosopher wannabe") must then presumably choose between remaining in academia as a merely clever dilettante or packing it in completely and seeking honest work, say, as a fry cook or a ditch digger. It does give one pause.

I intend to pause. For the moment, I still believe that there is wisdom, but I do agree that it is getting unusually hard to find. Wisdom is what the *logos* says, when you listen to it carefully and aright, but nowadays, if the *logos* has not actually taken a vow of silence, then it is certainly at least more difficult to hear among all those clamoring *insistent* voices. My own best hope for hearing it, I have decided, is first to stop talking myself. For a time, therefore, I intend to devote myself mostly to listening. I'm not sure what will come of that, but if I do think I hear anything worth repeating, I will certainly let you know.

Chapel Hill, N.C.
December 1991–December 1992

Beyond Formalism

Dialectical Preliminaries

FEW EVENTS have affected the insular world of academic philosophy in recent years as much as Saul Kripke's revolutionary 1970 Princeton lecture series "Naming and Necessity".[1] Kripke's rethinking of central notions in the philosophy of language and his redrawing of the modal landscape have been received by the analytic community with almost unprecedented alacrity, and his expository idioms—for example, "rigid designators" and "possible worlds"—are now widely and enthusiastically wielded as shiny new tools of the analytical trade.

Sociologically, so to speak, the phenomenon is not difficult to explain. Kripke's forthright essentialism and his spirited defense of "metaphysical necessity" ("necessity in the highest degree") could only be received as liberating by a generation of philosophers accustomed to working within the extensionalist strictures established by Quine's similarly influential 1950 essay "Two Dogmas of Empiricism"[2]. A professional competence to render verdicts on what *must be* or *cannot be*, a modal high ground claimed by philosophers from Plato to Hegel, suddenly seemed once again to be within reach.

This appearance, however, is deceptive. Quine's critique of traditional modal essentialisms was directed specifically against a concept of necessity rooted in the notion of meaning. His discred-

1

ited "necessary truths" were, in the first instance, *analytic* truths, that is, sentences "true by virtue of the meanings of the words composing them", and thus, crucially, truths knowable *a priori*. What was ultimately wrong with the notion of *de re* modality, on this account, was that it presupposed and relied upon a theory of *meaning* which, Quine argued, could not be reconciled with the (behavioristic) constraints of a healthy philosophical naturalism.

Kripke's strategy for coming to terms with Quine's critique of essentialism, however, was not to attempt to rehabilitate the repudiated theory of meaning. What Kripke proposed instead was rather to decouple the notions of *de re* necessity and aprioricity. On his view, what can be known *a priori* are at best only *conditional* necessities: "If this table is made of wood, then it is necessarily made of wood", "If water is H_2O, then water is necessarily H_2O", "If Hesperus is identical to Phosphorus, then it is necessary that Hesperus is identical to Phosphorus". The corresponding essentialist *unconditional* necessary truths, however, we know only *a posteriori,* on the basis of the various specific experiences that *de facto* license us to assert the antecedents of such conditionals. The essentialist high ground claimed by the mainstream philosophical tradition and disavowed by Quine, in other words—a material modal knowledge *a priori*—thus remains inaccessible to Kripke and his epigones as well.

Never having been myself a participant in the Quinean flight from intensional idioms, I have always viewed the Kripkean modal renaissance with a certain skeptical detachment. I remain, indeed, deeply unconvinced that Kripke's analytical tools are as sharp and effective as they have widely been taken to be or that the edifice of theories and theses that has been erected with their aid can in fact withstand prolonged and careful critical scrutiny. One proximate aim of the present study is to attempt to explain and vindicate my continued reluctance to align myself with this new metaphysical order.

Dialectical Preliminaries 3

As Quine's "Two Dogmas of Empiricism" is the conspicuous dialectical contrary to Kripke's essentialism, Russell's "On Denoting" is the *prima facie* antithesis to his account of nominal reference. In this instance, it is clear that the favorable reception generally accorded Kripke's trenchant critique of "Descriptivism" was well and properly deserved. It is less clear, however, that the widespread uncritical extension of such enthusiasm to Kripke's *positive*, "causal-historical", picture of the referential functioning of proper names was equally merited, and a second proximate aim of this study is, indeed, to provide a critical counter-voice and sketch an alternative to this new linguistic order.

Methodologically viewed, Kripke and Russell are in fact close cousins. Many of Kripke's first intellectual achievements, like Russell's, were consummated on the orderly conceptual playing fields of mathematical logic, and, again like Russell's, his subsequent contentive philosophical views bear significant traces of this earlier history. Kripke's "Naming and Necessity" stands in the same relation to his model-theoretic semantics for quantified modal logic that Russell's "On Denoting" and "Lectures on Logical Atomism" do to the formal system of *Principia Mathematica*. In each instance, the philosophy is in essence driven by the formalism. Elements of the formal system are treated as paradigms for understanding specific aspects of natural language use, and systematic ontological commitments are subsequently shaped by the tacit supposition that natural language thus understood effectively mirrors the metaphysical structure of a reality that it semantically represents.

"Naming and Necessity" thus also provides a useful point of entry to a more abstract methodological reflection on the appropriate relationships among natural languages, mathematical formalisms, and philosophical commitments. The ultimate aim of this essay is consequentially to engage such general themes. To do so responsibly, however, I need, so to speak, an explicit place to stand. The dialectical underpinning upon which this study is erected is the methodical exploitation of the fact that we are epistemologically *situated* beings. The world is epistemically present to us, initially and paradigmatically, in terms of perceptual *takings as*. These are "propositional" representational episodes, functionally embodying aspects of (demonstrative) "reference" and (conceptual) "classification". It follows that the world that is present to us always has us *in* it and so is necessarily present only *in perspective*, that is, from a determinate spatio-temporal point of view. A central conviction which animates my inquiries here is that a proper appreciation of this fact imposes *epistemic* constraints on admissible philosophical accounts of modal and semantic notions. My interrogations of Kripke's texts, in turn, are shaped by my understanding of these constraints.

The central significance of such observations for questions of reference and necessity emerges gradually during this essay, their full import becoming clear only in the later chapters, after considerable groundwork has been laid. The movement of the essay itself is from a specific engagement with Kripke's texts and the views regarding necessity, reference, and belief there endorsed to a general consideration of the epistemology of dominant contemporary modes of philosophical theorizing and a correlative exploration of the role of logical representations *per se* in the behavioral economy of situated beings.

In the course of this movement, I offer critical objections to various of Kripke's views and theses, sometimes in my own voice and sometimes in the less cautious voice of the Rival, a useful hypothetical character with definite and articulate epistemocentric philosophical opinions. Where I propose and defend substantial alternatives to Kripke's views, however—for example, in the extended development of an "epistemic" account of nominal reference in the systematic place occupied by both "descriptivism" and Kripke's own "causal-historical" picture—the voice is always my own.

In an important sense, however, the specific views and theses in terms of which my dialectical confrontation with Kripke proceeds are secondary matters. What this essay is primarily about is the confrontation itself and the methodological and metaphilosophical issues and problems that it enables me to thematize. From this perspective, Kripke's texts and topics have the function of a case study. What commends them to our attention is not their independent plausibility or implausibility, but their relationships to determinate symbolic formalisms, their illustrative use of thought experiments, and their passing commentaries on the epistemic role and probative force of modal and other logical intuitions in philosophical reflection.

1
Essential Properties, Thought-Experiments, and Modal Intuitions

I WANT to open these explorations by considering Kripke's account of *essential properties*. My aim is not only to understand what sort of account this is, i.e., how Kripke arrives at and argues for judgments regarding accidental and essential properties, but also to examine how one might engage critically an account of the sort Kripke advances.

I begin the story in an epistemological tone of voice. The claim

(1) Gold is yellow,

Kripke notes, has historically been advanced as an example of an *a priori* truth, something we know "prior to" and "independently of" specific experience. Kripke is initially concerned to challenge this purported epistemic status and to establish that, if (1) is in fact true, its truth is nevertheless not something we know *a priori*. To this end, he proposes a thought-experiment:

> Suppose there were an optical illusion which made the substance appear to be yellow; but, in fact, once the peculiar properties of the atmosphere were removed, we would see that it is actually blue. Maybe a demon even corrupted the vision of all those entering the gold mines . . . , and thus made them believe that this substance was yellow, though it is not. (118)

Here, according to Kripke, we have the description of a situation in which, contrary to our present beliefs, (*a*) gold is not yellow and, indeed, (*b*) gold never was yellow. If we were to discover tomorrow that atmospheric conditions or corrupting demons have continuously been producing the envisioned effects, claims Kripke, we would not conclude that there is no gold or that what we took to be gold was not in fact gold. Rather, we would conclude that gold only *appears* (and always has appeared) to be yellow, but that it has turned out that gold is actually blue. We would conclude, that is, that (1) expresses what has proved to be a *mistaken belief* about the color of gold. Thus, Kripke concludes, even if gold really is yellow, as it appears to be and as we now believe it to be, *that* gold is yellow is not something we know *a priori*. Being yellow is not "part of the concept" of gold. Our present belief (1) rather derives from our various experiential encounters with gold, and further such experiences and matter-of-factual discoveries could show that belief to be false; (1) is empirically defeasible.

We will return to Kripke's account of (1) shortly. First, however, I want to begin the exploration of the new instruments Kripke introduces in "Naming and Necessity" for dealing with traditional questions of modality and identity: the idea of a rigid designator, a strategy of argument by counterfactual stipulation, and a causal-historical account of the reference of proper names and other designators.

What linked these three instruments into a functioning unit was the further centripetal notion of a *possible world*. Kripke introduces the notion of a rigid designator, for example, by telling us that a rigid designator is an expression which designates the same object "in every possible world"(48). A possible world, in turn, is "given" by a counterfactual description.

> A possible world is *given by the descriptive conditions we associate with it*. (44)

> 'Possible worlds' are *stipulated*, not *discovered* by powerful telescopes. (44)

There are, however, constraints on those descriptive specifications suitable for "stipulating" possible worlds. Not just any subjunctive supposition will do. A *sine qua non* condition is that such a stipulation be framed in our current language "with *our* meanings and *our* references".

> When I say that a designator is rigid, and designates the same thing in all possible worlds, I mean that, as used in *our* language it stands for that thing, when *we* talk about counterfactual situations. I don't mean, of course, that there mightn't be counterfactual situations in which the other possible world's people actually spoke a different language. One doesn't say that 'two plus two equals four' is contingent because people might have spoken a language in which 'two plus two equals four' meant that seven is even. . . . [We may even be] describing a possible world or counterfactual situation in which people, including ourselves, did speak in a way different from the way we speak. But still, in describing that world, we use *English* with *our* meanings and our references. It is in this sense that I speak of a rigid designator as having the same reference in all possible worlds. (77–78)

What these remarks imply is that, when "stipulating" a possible world, we need to hold fixed the references of any *rigid* designators we use in describing that world. Correlatively, then, our confidence in the conclusions we propose to draw from consideration of such a counterfactual stipulation extends no further than our ability to conform to this constraint, and so, *inter alia*, our ability to recognize which of the designators we have used in that stipulation are in fact rigid designators.

But now it may well seem that we are traveling in a circle, for to identify these rigid designators, we will need to determine which of the expressions we have used in the stipulative specification of *that* possible world in fact designate the same object in *every* possible world. In other words, we have so far characterized rigid designators in terms of possible worlds, possible worlds in terms of admissible counterfactual descriptions, and the admissibility of a counterfactual description in terms of rigid designators. This may well provoke some echoes.

Recall, for example, Quine's "Two Dogmas of Empiricism". Analyticity was to be explained as truth by virtue of meaning, more specifically, as derivability from logical truths upon substitution of synonyms for synonyms. Synonymy, in turn, was to be explained in terms of substitutivity *salve veritate* in all contexts, including modal ones, and specifically in contexts of necessity. And necessity, of course, was to be explained in terms of the analyticity of certain biconditionals. The critical movement in "Two Dogmas", in other words, was similarly circular: from analyticity to synonymy, from synonymy to necessity, and from necessity back once again to analyticity.

As Quine recognized, what one needed to break out of this circle was a bit of epistemology. In particular, one needed a non-arbitrary strategy for *establishing* synonymies. One needed for there to be a fact of the matter concerning the synonymy or non-synonymy of two expressions (whether in the same or in different languages), and so for there to be a *method of inquiry* for determining in specific cases what that fact of the matter in fact was. Quine, as is well known, claimed that we couldn't have the requisite bit of epistemology, at least that there could be no non-arbitrary *empiricist* strategy for establishing term synonymies—hence the indeterminacy of translation, the inscrutability of reference, ontological relativity, and all that. I've argued elsewhere[1] that Quine was wrong about this, but that isn't currently to the point. What *is* now to the point is that, in order to break out of Kripke's circle of elucidations, we might suppose, one also needs a bit of epistemology. It is puzzling, therefore, to discover that, at the crucial moment, Kripke explicitly rules out the relevance of epistemological considerations to questions of contingency and necessity.

But doesn't Kripke's thought-experiment regarding the discovery of odd atmospheric conditions or corrupting demons also supply a description of a *possible world* in which gold is not yellow? That is, doesn't this thought-experiment, if successful, suffice to secure not only an *epistemic* status for the claim expressed by (1), namely, that it is not known *a priori,* but also a *modal* status for that claim, namely, that it is contingent? The thought-experiment surely at least describes a possible state of the *actual* world, a way that the world *might be* (might yet prove to be), and, we recall, such discoveries would entitle us to conclude both that gold is not yellow, and that gold never was yellow. But does this suffice to demonstrate that we can satisfactorily describe a *possible* world in which gold isn't yellow? One of the most striking features of Kripke's views is that his answer here is "No". Securing an *a posteriori* epistemic status for a given proposition has *no implications at all* regarding the question of its modal status, its necessity or contingency.[2]

The alternative philosophical strategy that lies closest to hand at this point would be to *couple* modality to epistemology and let the necessities fall where they may. Thus one might begin in a pragmatist vein by affirming both that

Whatever is accepted *a posteriori* is defeasible (revisable)

and that

Whatever is defeasible (revisable) is contingent

and conclude straightaway that there are no necessary *a posteriori* truths. I in fact find this sort of epistemically constrained account of modality quite congenial, but rather than claim it straightaway as my own, I shall attribute it, at least temporarily, to a character whom I'll call "the Rival". Kripke's way of treating such modal notions as necessity and contingency, then, is not the Rival's epistemic way. Among the things we need to discover is *why* it isn't and, of course, what it is instead.

Let me therefore turn from Kripke's discussion of gold's color to another of his illustrations, the question of the material composition of a specific table. The sentence

(2) This table is made of wood,

Kripke tells us, an appropriate table having been indicated by suitable pointing gestures, *does* express a necessary truth. We *cannot*, he claims, describe a possible world in which this table—this *very* table, as Kripke frequently puts it—would be and would always have been made, for example, of ice.

In particular, Kripke is convinced that the (material) *substance* of which a material object is composed—as well as its (material) origins—is one of its essential properties.[3] To the extent that he offers us an *argument* for the necessity of (2), it rests initially on successive instantiations of just such a general premise:

(I.0) For any object, x, and for any "kind of stuff" (material), S, if x is made (composed) of S, then x is *necessarily* made of S.

(I.1) For any "kind of stuff", S, if the table is made of S, then the table is *necessarily* made of S.

(I.2) If the table is made of wood, then the table is necessarily made of wood.

(2) The table *is* made of wood.

(I.3) The table is necessarily made of wood.

Given her epistemological inclinations with regard to modal matters, the Rival, we may suppose, is not likely to be moved by this argument. We can rather expect to find her responding somewhat along these lines:

Of course I grant that *if* (I.0) is true, then so is (I.3). Logic is logic, and the argument given is formally valid as it stands.

But one person's modus ponens is another's modus tollens. I am equally convinced that (I.0) *isn't* true, and, what's more, I can produce an equally valid argument in support of that conclusion. It goes like this: (2) is empirically defeasible; whatever is defeasible is contingent; hence, (I.3) is *false*. Since, however, (2) is true, it follows that (I.2) is false, likewise that (I.1) is false, and hence that (I.0) is false.

One of the especially seductive features of Kripke's new apparatus of "possible worlds" was that it gave the illusion of containing resources for resolving such conflicts between prior convictions regarding modal matters.[4] Thus, confronted with the Rival's disagreement, Kripke's strategy is to transpose the subjunctive question regarding the table in the actual world, "Could this table ("this very table") have been (originally) made of ice?", into an indicative question phrased in terms of "possible worlds": "Can we stipulate or describe or imagine a possible world in which this (very) table *is* (originally) made of ice?" And although our tenacious Rival is inclined to answer this question, too, in the affirmative:

> Here's the stipulation you're looking for:
>
> [S] "Consider a possible world in which this (very) table is (originally) made of ice."

Kripke is now evidently prepared to offer *reasons* for concluding that she has failed to deliver the goods:

> We could conceivably discover that, contrary to what we now think, this table is indeed made of ice from the river. But suppose that it is not. Then, though we can imagine making a table out of another block of wood or even from ice, identical in appearance with this one, and though we could have put it in this very position in the room, it seems to me that this is *not* to imagine *this* table as made of wood or ice, but rather it is to

imagine another table, *resembling* this one in all external details, made of another block of wood, or even of ice. (113–114)

Now Kripke does acknowledge a contingency in the *neighborhood* of (2). Given a certain "epistemic situation", he says, the table might have *turned out* to have been made of ice, or indeed of anything else. But, contrary to expectations, this truth does not imply the contingency of (2). Rather,

> . . . it means simply that there might have been *a table* looking and feeling just like this one and placed in this very position in the room, which was in fact made of ice. In other words, I (or some conscious being) could have been *qualitatively in the same epistemic situation* that in fact obtains, I could have the same sensory evidence that I in fact have, about *a table* which was made of ice. (142)

According to Kripke, however, that would not be a possible world in which *this* table is made of ice. That would be a possible world in which *another, different*, table—qualitatively quite like this one—is made of ice.

> *This* table itself could not have had an origin different from the one it in fact had, but in a situation qualitatively identical to this one with respect to all the evidence I had in advance, the room could have contained *a table made of ice* in place of this one. (142)

Kripke's analytical apparatus thus evidently requires *inter alia* that we draw a sharp distinction between two species of thought-experiment. On the one hand, there are thought-experiments in which we consider in what ways we might (still, here and now) be mistaken about the actual world. Call these *Type E* (*epistemic*) thought-experiments. In a Type E thought-experiment, we do not, so to speak, venture beyond the actual world. Nothing in such an epistemic thought-experiment involves us in the counterfactual stipulation of a possible world (numerically) *different from* the actual world. On the other hand, there are thought-experiments in which we suppose ourselves to be right about the *actual* world—we stipulatively fix the truths about the actual world to be what we take them to be—and then consider in what ways the world *could have been* different, for example, how its history could have been different from its actual history. Call these *Type M (metaphysical)* thought-experiments. A metaphysical thought experiment does involve us in the counterfactual stipulation of possible worlds, worlds *different from* (having a different history from) the actual world.[5]

Kripke's response to the Rival's skepticism regarding his substance essentialism is to argue that she is making one of two characteristic errors:

either she is confusing Type E and Type M thought-experiments,

or she is wrong about *which* Type M thought-experiment she is performing, that is, she is actually performing a different Type M thought-experiment from the one she *takes* herself to be performing.

What in either case the Rival has not succeeded in doing, however, is to stipulate or describe or imagine a possible world, (numerically) different from the actual world, in which *this* table is (originally) made not of wood but of ice. Either she has imagined our discovering, in the *actual* world, that this table *never was* made of wood, i.e., that, contrary to what we believe, the table is indeed (and always has been) made of ice from the river—and that is a Type E thought-experiment—or she has imagined a possible world, different from the actual world, in which *some other* table, one made of ice and qualitatively indistinguishable from this one, occupies the (epistemic-evidential) position occupied in the actual world by this table made of wood—and, although that is indeed a Type M thought-experiment, it is the wrong one. The fact that one is able to imagine a possible world containing some *other* table has no consequences at all regarding the truth or falsehood of modal claims about *this* table.

But have we really made any progress here? For what underwrites Kripke's evident confidence in *these* assertions? The Rival claims, after all, to be imagining a possible world in which *this very table*, not some other one, is originally made of ice. That, after all, is what her stipulation [S] *stipulates*. What warrants Kripke's conviction that, whatever thought-experiments the Rival may successfully consummate, the crucial Type M thought-experiment, one that would establish or confirm the contingency of (2), will not be among them? By Kripke's own lights, after all, possible worlds are stipulated, not discovered by powerful telescopes. Why, then, can't the Rival simply stipulate that, in the possible world that *she* is considering, it is *that very table* that is made of ice, and not some other one?

As far as I can see, Kripke's answer can only be that the Rival isn't imagining the possible world she claims to be imagining because she *can't be* imagining such a possible world. She can't be imagining it, in turn, because there *is* no such possible world; that is, no such world is possible. In other words, Kripke must hold that the Rival's stipulative description of what she *purports* to imagine is contradictory or incoherent. But why is this so? Why, because a thing's (original) material composition is one of its essential properties, of course. What reveals that the stipulation [S] is contradictory or incoherent, in other words, is the fact that it is inconsistent with a *necessary* truth, namely, that the table ("this very table") is (originally) made of wood. It is only because he already accepts (I.0), in short, that Kripke finds the Rival's stipulation [S] inadmissible. But now it is painfully clear that invoking the apparatus of possible worlds has yielded, and indeed can yield, no argumentative advance on the intuitive general essentialist convictions with which Kripke begins.

If Kripke regards (2) as necessary and accepts (I.1) and (I.2), then, this can only be on the grounds of a *prior* and *independent* judgment to the effect that an object's material composition is one among its essential properties (whereas, for example, a substance's color is not), that is, on the grounds of a prior and independent commitment to the truth of (I.0). The framework of Kripke's "Naming and Necessity" gives us nothing more. Specifically, the necessity of (2) is in no way a *consequence* of Kripke's new analytical apparatus. His only argument for it rests on the assumption (I.0), and (I.0) in turn is not a thesis *for* which Kripke offers any cogent arguments at all. It is a thesis *from* which he argues. It is a prior conviction which is controlling his critique of the "possible world" counterfactual stipulations offered by his skeptical Rival, a critique that could create the appearance, but only that, of giving his necessity thesis independent theoretical support.

Parallel observations pertain to several of Kripke's other claims regarding essential qualities. His ostensible argument for the thesis that Queen Elizabeth's (familial) origins, her parents, could not have differed from those from which she actually came, for example, throws the role of such prior independent judgments into especially sharp relief. Here, too, Kripke begins by conceding the *epistemological* points regarding discoveries which could still, here and now, be made.

> Could she, let's say, have been the daughter instead of Mr. and Mrs. Truman? There would be no contradiction, of course, in an announcement that . . . , fantastic as it may sound, she was indeed the daughter of Mr. and Mrs. Truman. I suppose there might even be no contradiction in the discovery that—it seems very suspicious on either hypothesis that she has a sister called Margaret—that these two Margarets were one and the same person. . . . At any rate, we can imagine discovering all of these things. (112)

Next Kripke stipulates the availability of the relevant empirical antecedent as a true premiss (i.e., assumes that we are right about the actual world): "But let us suppose that such a discovery is not in fact the case. Let's suppose that the Queen really did come from these parents" (112). Finally, he invokes the apparatus of "possible worlds": "[Can] we imagine a situation in which it would have happened that this very woman came out of Mr. and Mrs. Truman?" His answer, predictably, is "No".

> How could a person originating from different parents, from a totally different sperm and egg, be *this very woman*? One can imagine, *given* the woman, that various things in her life could have changed. . . . One is given, let's say, a previous history of the world up to a certain time, and from that time it diverges considerably from the actual course. This seems to be possible. . . . But what is harder to imagine is her being born of different parents. It seems to me that anything coming from a different origin would not be this object. (113)

However plausible these remarks might strike one as being, their plausibility should not blind us to the absence here of any *argument* for the necessity of origins. The exercise of stipulating possible worlds does not require that one explain *how* a person originating from different parents (i.e., parents other than King George VI and Queen Elizabeth *nee* Lady Elizabeth Bowes-Lyon) could be this very woman (i.e., Queen Elizabeth II), but only that one satisfactorily describe a situation in which that would be the case.

Interestingly enough, the first sentence of this quotation is one of the few places in which the text of the *book Naming and Necessity* diverges from that of the published *essay* "Naming and Necessity". In its original incarnation, the sentence read: "What right would you have to call this baby from completely different parents—in what sense would she be—*this very woman*?"

It is not difficult to understand why Kripke has altered the text at just this point. The unacceptable suggestion of the original wording, of course, was that we here face a problem of "transworld identification", that we must somehow *earn* the right, in describing some possible world, to call the baby "this very woman". But this suggestion runs precisely counter to Kripke's steady insistence that possible worlds need *not* be described purely qualitatively, but rather may be given by counterfactual stipulations *using* the designators available to us in *this* world:

> [We] do not begin with worlds (which are supposed somehow to be real, and whose qualities, but not whose objects, are perceptible to us), and then ask about criteria of transworld identification; on the contrary, we begin with the objects, which we *have*, and can identify, in the actual world. We can then ask whether certain things might have been true of the objects. (53)

Kripke's supposition that our current beliefs regarding the Queen's parentage are in fact true, in other words, can be put to *use* in his argument only if he has available the requisite additional (tacit) *conditional* premiss to the effect that

> *If* this very woman (i.e., Queen Elizabeth II) came from specific parents (e.g., George VI and the former Elizabeth Bowes-Lyon), *then* it is necessary that she came from those parents.

Now one can produce a Kripkean argument for this requisite premiss, analogous to the earlier argument for (I.2), namely:

> (II.0) For any object, x, and for any "origins", O, if x came from O, then x *necessarily* came from O.

> (II.1) For any "origins", O, if this very woman (i.e., Queen Elizabeth II) came from O, then it is necessary that she came from O.

> (II.2) *If* this very woman (i.e., Queen Elizabeth II) came from specific parents (e.g., George VI and the former Elizabeth Bowes-Lyon), *then* it is necessary that she came from those parents.

Once again, however, the reasoning takes as its point of departure a prior and independent modal conviction, a prior and independent commitment to the truth of (II.0). What Kripke leaves us with, therefore, is only the bare appeal to the prior judgment with which his ostensible argument regarding Queen Elizabeth concludes: "It seems to me that anything coming from a different origin would not be this object". In short, plausible or implausible, like (I.0), (II.0) is not a thesis for which Kripke argues but a prior conviction from which he argues.

One of Kripke's most exciting and controversial theses is that

> [statements] representing scientific discoveries about what [some] stuff *is* are not contingent truths but necessary truths in the strictest possible sense. It's not just that it's a scientific law, but of course we can imagine a world in which it would fail. Any world in which we imagine a substance which does not have these properties is a world in which we imagine a substance which is not [that stuff], provided these properties form the basis of what that substance is. (125)

Kripke's illustrative case is the elementhood and atomic number of gold. Both

(4) Gold is an element

and

(5) Gold has atomic number 79

he claims, are not merely "physically necessary" truths, but full-fledged "metaphysically necessary" truths, "necessary truths in the strictest possible sense". His ostensible argument, as before, invokes the notion of "possible worlds" in a Type M thought-experiment:

> [Consider] a possible world. Consider a counterfactual situation in which, let us say, fool's gold or iron pyrites was actually found in various mountains in the United States, or in areas of South Africa and the Soviet Union. Suppose that all the areas which actually contain gold now, contained pyrites instead, or

some other substance which counterfeited the superficial properties of gold but lacked its atomic structure. Would we say, of this counterfactual situation, that in that situation gold would not even have been an element (because pyrites is not an element)? It seems to me that we would not. We would instead describe this as a situation in which a substance, say iron pyrites, which is not gold, would have been found in the very mountains which actually contain gold and would have had the very properties by which we commonly identify gold. But it would not be gold; it would be something else. One should *not* say that it would still be gold in this possible world, though gold would then lack the atomic number 79. It would be some other stuff, some other substance. (124)

Here, for a change, even the Rival will agree with Kripke. But this is not because he has finally produced a cogent argument in support of one of his fundamental substantive essentialist theses. It is rather because he has produced a series of *trivially* necessary truths. Of course, what was found in the mountains in *this* possible world would not be gold, because this possible world is explicitly stipulated to be one in which what was found in the mountains *isn't* gold. We are explicitly enjoined, that is, to "suppose that all the areas which actually contain gold now, contained . . . some *other* substance" (124, my emphasis), and it would be a straightforward contradiction to say *both* that those areas (exclusively) contain gold *and* that they contain (exclusively) some other substance, that is, some substance other than gold.[6]

But does this go any distance toward showing that we cannot stipulate or imagine or describe a possible world in which *gold* isn't an element or doesn't have atomic number 79? Obviously not. The counterfactual stipulations relevant to the necessity or contingency of (4) and (5) would need to begin quite differently, say:

Consider a possible world in which all the areas which now actually contain *elemental* gold contained *non-elemental* gold instead.

or

> Consider a possible world in which all the areas which now actually contain Au^{79} instead contained a variety of gold having atomic number 82.

Kripke would doubtless object that there can *be* no such "possible worlds", that such counterfactual stipulations are contradictory or incoherent. Not only is the possible world that he has described not a case in which gold might not have been an element, he argues, but (except in the epistemic sense of 'possible') there can be no such case.

> Given that gold *is* this element [with atomic number 79], any other substance, even though it looks like gold and is found in the very places where we in fact find gold, would not be gold. It would be some other substance which was a counterfeit for gold. In any counterfactual situation where the same geographical areas were filled with such a substance, they would not have been filled with gold. They would have been filled with something else. (125)

But, once again, this string of trivial, *analytic* necessary truths:

> Any other substance [i.e., any substance *other than gold*], even though it looks like gold . . . would not be gold,

> In any counterfactual situation where the same geographical areas [that are now filled with gold] were filled with such a substance [i.e., a substance *other than gold*], they would not have been filled with gold,

adds no support to Kripke's substantive necessity claims. The trivial fact that we cannot coherently imagine or describe a counterfactual situation in which some element or compound (stipulated to be) *other than gold* is (simultaneously stipulated to be) gold is utterly irrelevant to the question of whether one can stipulate a possible world in which *gold* is (stipulated to be) a

22   Chapter 1

non-elemental substance or a substance with an atomic number other than 79. Once again, the theoretical apparatus of possible worlds, counterfactual stipulations, and Type M thought-experiments drops out of the picture, and we are left with only prior convictions.

We have now confirmed that each of Kripke's specific unconditional essentialist necessity claims depends upon an intuitive *general conditional* essentialist principle. In each case, the principle is instantiated in such a way that its antecedent becomes an empirical, *a posteriori*, truth, and its consequent is then detached by modus ponens as the desired unconditional claim of "metaphysical necessity". If we search for textual or argumentative support for these general conditional essentialist principles themselves, however, we will be disappointed. In each instance, all we will find is that Kripke simply appeals to his prior convictions regarding such matters, to "how it seems to him", or, to invoke a more fashionable phrase, to his "modal intuitions".

It is not obvious that Kripke would find this a *defect* in his presentation, for he evidently takes such intuitions to have considerable probative force: "[Some] philosophers think that something's having intuitive content is very inconclusive evidence in favor of it. I think it is very heavy evidence in favor of anything, myself. I really don't know, in a way, what more conclusive evidence one can have about anything, ultimately speaking." (42). It is not entirely clear how these remarks are properly to be understood. The notion that intuitions function as *evidence* initially suggests that Kripke takes them to play a role in the epistemology of modal theorizing analogous to the role played by *measurements* or *observations* in the case of matter-of-factual, empirical theorizing, but the analogy strikes me as a dubious one. We can, of course, also interpret the notion of "evidence" less literally, and understand Kripke as holding only that modal intuitions function as the best sort of *good reasons* that can be given in support of theoretical or systematic modal principles. This may well prove to be a defensible view, but it plainly needs some defending.

It remains unclear, for example, why the fact that one finds oneself with an immediate and unreflective inclination to accept a given modal claim is *any sort of reason at all* for believing that claim to be correct. The case of perception provides a useful contrast. Here it is quite possible to explain *why* the fact that *I find myself* with an immediate and unreflective inclination to believe, for example, that there is a cubical red object on a triangular blue table in the center of the room is a *good reason* for me to believe that there is a cubical red object on a triangular blue table in the center of the room. That is, there is a (relatively) straightforward story that can be told regarding how any being possessing my sort of sensory and language-learning capacities can come to be "calibrated", so to speak, as a *reliable indicator* of the colors and shapes of objects in its vicinity. It is far from obvious that the ostensible probative force of modal intuitions allows of being backed in a similar way by analogous explanatory arguments.

Such questions regarding the evidential or probative force of modal (and other) intuitions will gradually gravitate toward the center of our attention. At this stage of my explorations, however, I want to stress only the limited point that assigning even a strong presumptive probative force to intuitions is no help at all when the question at issue is how to adjudicate among *conflicting* intuitions—and this in turn arguably suggests that intuitions as such may, contra Kripke, play only a very minor epistemic role in philosophical theorizing.

In this regard, Hilary Putnam's now-classic "Twin Earth" thought-experiment, originally advanced in support of the conclusion that "meanings aren't in the head", provides an instructive case study.[7] Putnam describes Twin Earth as differing from Earth only in that, wherever we on our planet encounter instances of the natural kind *water*, that is, H_2O, inhabitants of Twin Earth encounter some quite different chemical compound, XYZ.

On Putnam's account, XYZ is *phenomenally* indistinguishable from H_2O, but—although they also *call* it 'water'—the scientifically and technologically more primitive natives of Twin Earth ("Twin Earthlings") lack any analytical chemical and physical techniques adequate to distinguish XYZ *compositionally* from H_2O.

Putnam, in other words, proposes to describe a possible world in which some distinct chemical compound XYZ occupies, so to speak, the natural-kind station occupied on Earth by H_2O, and he concludes, on the basis of this thought-experiment, that "meanings aren't in the head". The argument runs essentially as follows:

(TE1) What's "in the head" of an Earthling when she uses the word 'water' can be identical to what's "in the head" of a Twin Earthling when *she* uses the word 'water'. Suppose it is.

(TE2) H_2O is water, and XYZ isn't water.

(TE3) Since, when an Earthling uses the word 'water' she's referring to H_2O, and hence to *water*, what the Earthling means by 'water' is *water*.

(TE4) But since, when a Twin Earthling uses the word 'water', she's referring to XYZ, and hence *not* to water, what the Twin Earthling means by 'water' *isn't* water.

(TE5) Thus, since the Earthling word 'water' and the Twin Earthling word 'water' differ in meaning, while what's "in the head" of the Earthling is, *ex hypothesi*, identical to what's "in the head" of the Twin Earthling, meanings aren't in the head. QED

The key premiss in this argument is clearly (TE2), and what supports (TE2) are precisely Kripkean intuitions about the necessity attaching to the constitutive or compositional discoveries made by the sciences about such natural substances as gold and water. Kripke himself puts the case this way:

It certainly represents a discovery that water is H_2O. We identified water originally by its characteristic feel, appearance and perhaps taste, (though the taste may usually have been due to the impurities). If there were a substance, even actually, which had a completely different atomic structure from that of water, but resembled water in these respects, would we say that some water wasn't H_2O? I think not. We would say instead that just as there is a fool's gold there could be a fool's water; a substance which, though having the properties by which we originally identified water, would not in fact be water. And this, I think, applies not only to the actual world but even when we talk about counterfactual situations. If there had been a substance, which was a fool's water, it would then be fool's water and not water. (128)

The last sentence here, of course, is another one of those irrelevant *trivially* necessary truths that we have already encountered in Kripke's discussion of gold. The balance of the passage, however, is precisely an appeal to "intuitions" of the sort that we have found characteristic of Kripke's defense of each of his essentialist theses.

Not only are conflicting intuitions possible here, however, but, viewed from a different angle, Putnam's Twin Earth thought-experiment brings out quite nicely what they are likely to be. For, despite Kripke's contrary conviction ("I think not"), it is clearly possible to regard Putnam as having described a state of affairs in which there would be *two kinds of water*. H_2O would still be water, but XYZ would *also* be water, although a different kind of water. On this view, what it is to be water is, roughly, to be whatever stuff occupies a certain phenomenal natural kind station, and it is always possible that a single such phenomenal natural kind station is, in fact, occupied by more than one (compositional) natural kind structure.[8] 'Water' thus would mean the same thing in English and Twin English, namely *water,* and meanings, although they needn't be, still could be "in the head". Correlatively, however, the logical form of the discovery we report by asserting that "water is H_2O" (i.e., of a "theoretical identification"), on this account, would *not* be "F = G" (e.g., "water = H_2O"), which is incompatible with the conjunction of "F = H" (e.g., "water = XYZ") and "G ≠ H", but rather that of a more complicated claim to the effect that the phenomenal properties of water can be explained by positing H_2O in the *role* of water—a claim compatible with the claim that the phenomenal properties of water can *also* be explained by positing XYZ in the role of water.[9] We'll have occasion to return to these considerations later, but it's important to notice, before we proceed, that 'water' is an *everyday* term—not one, so to speak, "owned" by some scientific, linguistic, or philosophical theory. That is why the competing intuitions here initially have, so to speak, epistemic parity. Everyday beliefs, I suggest, are simply noncommittal when it comes to the question of whether there can or cannot be more than one *kind* of water.

The epistemic point is not that this alternative style of account is clearly preferable to Kripke's or, conversely, that his account is clearly preferable to any account of this sort. The point is that, *qua intuition*, the Putnamian-Kripkean conviction that XYZ, if there were such stuff, wouldn't be (another kind of) water, since water is necessarily H_2O, is epistemologically on a par with the contrary conviction that water isn't necessarily H_2O, since XYZ would also be (a different kind of) water. Both convictions are plainly possible,[10] and neither is *obviously* initially more plausible than the other. Each intuition, in turn, harmonizes with a distinct family of more abstract general convictions regarding modal sentences, empirical knowledge, natural kinds, referential discourse, scientific theories, and so on, in their diverse interrelationships. This is the sort of thing that is traditionally called a "philosophical system", and each intuition could, I suppose, be said to "support" the philosophical system into which it naturally "fits". But if such contrary intuitions can have equal probative force, then the probative force of the intuitions *as such*, considered in isolation from any prior systematic philosophical convictions, must surely be nil. What will be epistemically significant with regard to a philosophical system will not be the fact that it is "supported by intuitions". *Every* such system will initially be equally supported by, so to speak, *its* intuitions. What will be epistemically significant will be the success of the system as a whole in telling a coherent story that diminishes our philosophical puzzlements.

My leading critical idea, if you like, is that Kripke's philosophical system fails on this score. It fails, I shall argue, primarily because it leaves the *epistemology* of its own main concepts and contentions utterly mysterious. Like other views inspired by logico-mathematical achievements—Descartes, Leibniz, Frege, and Russell come to mind—it turns out to be a philosophical system befitting omniscient beings, where epistemological considerations essentially fall by the wayside, but ill suited for understanding the various epistemic accomplishments (*vis-à-vis* our knowledge, for example, of modalities, references, and natural kinds) of the particular sort of *situated* and *perspectival* spatio-temporal creatures that we actually are. Therein, of course, lies a long tale, but our first task is to command a proper survey of Kripke's views. I want consequently to turn next to the concepts and the case that lie at the heart of those views—proper names, rigid designators, and the (putatively) necessary identity of Hesperus and Phosphorus.

2
Rigid Designators, Proper Names, and Possible Worlds

IN CONTRAST to the argumentative lacunae that collapse his case for "essential properties" into mere appeals to "modal intuitions", in the matter of the necessary identity of Hesperus and Phosphorus, Kripke *seems*, at least on the face of it, to be better off. Here, for the first time, the third item in his analytical toolbox, the notion of a rigid designator, comes explicitly into play, and here he purports to offer an argument in support of the indispensable *conditional* premiss from which he derives his conclusion of necessary identity. What I want next to suggest, however, is that this too is mere appearance. In actuality, I believe, Kripke is *logically* no better off in this case than in those we have already canvassed.

It is important first, however, to be clear just what it is that I propose to raise questions about. Kripke himself distinguishes three theses in this neighborhood:

> (T1) that identical objects are necessarily identical; (T2) that true identity statements between rigid designators are necessary; (T3) that identity statements between what we call 'names' in actual language are necessary. (T1) and (T2) are (self-evident) theses of philosophical logic independent of natural language. They are related to one another, although (T1) is about objects and (T2) is metalinguistic. ((T2) roughly 'follows' from (T1), using substitution of rigid designators for universal quantifiers. . . .) From (T2) all that strictly follows about

so-called 'names' in natural language is that *either* they are not rigid *or* true identities between them are necessary. Our intuitive idea of naming suggests that names are rigid. (4, numbering altered)

Now I am certainly not foolish enough to set myself against "self-evident theses of philosophical logic", and I consequently have not the least inclination to deny, for example, either that

F1: $(x)(y)(x=y \to \Box x=y)$

is a *theorem* of standard quantified modal logics with identity, or that, according to standard set-theoretic semantics for such formal systems, the formula F1 comes out *true-in-all-models*. These metalogical claims, I presume, are what Kripke intends us to understand by his thesis (T1), that identical objects are necessarily identical, and *if* that is what (T1) asserts, then I, of course, have no quarrel with it at all.

Nor do I wish to quarrel with a certain thesis that one might easily confuse with Kripke's thesis (T2), namely,

(T2*) True identity statements between *individual constants* are necessary.

That is, if the vocabulary of some standard quantified modal logic with identity contains, in addition to bindable variables ('x', 'y', etc.), individual constants ('a', 'b', etc.) as substituends for such variables, then, from F1, one may indeed derive

F2: $a=b \to \Box a=b$

and, if 'a=b' is true (in some *model, M*), then '$\Box$ a=b' will also be true (*in M*). This, too, I am prepared to acknowledge as a "self-evident truth of philosophical logic".

About Kripke's thesis (T2), however, I am considerably less clear. Unlike 'individual constant', which denotes a relatively well understood category of formal syntax, 'rigid designator' is a Kripkean term of art, nor is it synonymous with any predicate of the syntactic theory of formal systems, since, according to his thesis (T3), items of a *natural* language can properly be classified as rigid designators.[1] Once (T2) has been carefully distinguished from (T2*), the question of how we are to understand thesis (T2) and, in particular, how we are to understand the very idea of a "rigid designator" may appropriately be raised, and I do, indeed, intend to raise it. I am not, in any event, prepared to accept (T2) as either a "truth of philosophical logic" or a "self-evident" *anything* without considerable further discussion. Providing that discussion is one of the items on my agenda in this chapter.

The other principal item on that agenda, of course, is Kripke's thesis (T3), that identity statements between (proper) names in a natural language are necessary. By Kripke's own lights, thesis (T3) is neither a truth of philosophical logic (*simpliciter*) nor, given the tradition of widespread philosophical belief in "contingent identities", is it in any obvious sense intuitively self-evident. Thesis (T3) turns on substantive issues in the philosophy of language and on specific arguments regarding the necessity of individual natural-language claims, and there is consequently much at stake here with which one at least *might* quarrel. In due course, I shall in fact quarrel with some of it. First, however, we must better appreciate what Kripke's views in this region of the philosophical terrain come to, and how he proposes to defend them. And that brings us to Hesperus and Phosphorus. Let me begin, then, by recalling just how Kripke's *argument* regarding Hesperus and Phosphorus goes.

> <i> [We], using the names as we do right now, can say in advance that if Hesperus and Phosphorus are one and the same then in no other possible world can they be different. <ii> We use 'Hesperus' as the name of a certain body and 'Phosphorus' as the name of a certain body. <iii> We use them as names of those bodies in all possible worlds. <iv> If, in fact, they are the *same* body, then in any other possible world we have to use

them as a name of that object. <v> And so in any other possible world it will be true that Hesperus is Phosphorus. (104)

I want to take a slow and careful look at this passage, for it is, in fact, the *only* instance of Kripke's offering an argument in support of the sort of conditional premiss that we have found to be an indispensable step in each of his demonstrations of "metaphysical necessity". Recent history has demonstrated amply enough that the passage strikes many philosophers as entirely plausible upon a first (superficial) encounter, but a *detailed* scrutiny of the reasoning here, a disciplined attempt to render it logically tight and rigorous, is comparatively hard to find. Such a proper examination of the passage is, unfortunately, a rather tedious and pedantic business, but if we are interested in a *rationally defensible* appraisal of the cogency of Kripke's argumentation and conclusions, there is really no alternative. With apologies in advance for the drudgery, then, I shall set to work.

The first thing we need to notice is that Kripke actually advances *two* conclusions in the passage, a main conclusion and a subsidiary conclusion, neither of which is precisely the *ultimate* conclusion at which he is aiming, namely, that if Hesperus and Phosphorus are identical, then they are necessarily identical. The main conclusion of this argument is formulated in <i>; the subsidiary conclusion, in <v>.

The main conclusion is also a conditional: If Hesperus and Phosphorus are identical ("one and the same") in the *actual* world, then Hesperus and Phosphorus are identical in all *other* possible worlds.[2] From this, of course, the desired *ultimate* conclusion follows in short order: If Hesperus and Phosphorus are identical both in the actual world and in all other possible worlds, then they are identical in all possible worlds. And this, in turn, by the "definitional" equivalence of 'necessary' and 'true in all possible worlds', should lead to the sought modal conditional:

Chapter 2

(HP) If Hesperus = Phosphorus, then it is necessary that Hesperus = Phosphorus.

The subsidiary conclusion <v> states, in essence, the *consequent* of the main conclusion <i>: Hesperus and Phosphorus are identical in "any other possible world", that is, in all possible worlds distinct from the actual world. It is surely plausible, then, to suppose that Kripke is arguing for his *main* conclusion by "conditional proof", the tacit hypothesis that Hesperus is identical with Phosphorus in the *actual* world being discharged by "conditional introduction" in the move from <v> to <i>. Making this tacit hypothesis explicit and rearranging the steps in logical order, then, we arrive at the following *skeleton* argument:

(a) Hesperus and Phosphorus are identical (in the actual world). [hypothesis for conditional proof]

. . .

(g) Hesperus and Phosphorus are identical in all *other* possible worlds.

(h) Hesperus and Phosphorus are identical *both* in the actual world *and* in all other possible worlds.[from (a) and (g)]

(i) Hesperus and Phosphorus are identical in *all* possible worlds.[from (h)]

(j) If Hesperus and Phosphorus are identical (in the actual world), then they are identical in *all* possible worlds. [from (a)–(i) by conditional proof]

(HP) If Hesperus = Phosphorus, then it is necessary that Hesperus = Phosphorus.[from (j)]

What remains, then, is to fill in the missing steps between (a) and (g). As the introductory clause of sentence <i> suggests, the derivation of (g) from (a) is supposed to be mediated by considerations regarding the way in which we "right now" use the *names*

'Hesperus' and 'Phosphorus'. What Kripke proposes is that "such terms as 'Hesperus' and 'Phosphorus', when used as names, are rigid designators" (102).

The work of filling in the steps linking (a) and (g) is ostensibly done in sentences <ii> through <iv> of the original passage. These missing steps address the *semantics* of the terms 'Hesperus' and 'Phosphorus' and so, in these steps, unlike the steps in the skeleton we have already reconstructed, those terms will be *mentioned* as well as *used*. The significance of this fact will increasingly intrude on our considerations.

Sentence <ii> begins by specifying that the *terms* or *expressions* 'Hesperus' and 'Phosphorus' are in fact *used*—that is, used by us right now, in the actual world—*as names* (of "certain bodies").

<ii> We use 'Hesperus' as the name of a certain body and 'Phosphorus' as the name of a certain body.

Temporarily adopting a convenient quasi-formal *patois*, what <ii> evidently says is:

(b1) ($\exists x$) We *use* 'Hesperus' *as a name of* x in the actual world.

(b2) ($\exists x$) We *use* 'Phosphorus' *as a name of* x in the actual world.

The transition from <ii> to <iii>, in turn, clearly depends upon an additional (tacit) premiss to the effect that terms or expressions that we use in the actual world as names are rigid designators. This, of course, is precisely what Kripke has proposed. Call it "Kripke's rigidity thesis":

(KRT) For every object x and for every natural-linguistic expression E, if, in the actual world, *we use* E *as a name* of x then, in the actual world, E *rigidly designates* x.

Together with (b1) and (b2), then, (KRT) straightforwardly yields:

(c1) (∃x) 'Hesperus' rigidly designates x in the actual world.

(c2) (∃x) 'Phosphorus' rigidly designates x in the actual world.

When we turn to <iii>, however, the logical waters begin to grow rather murky.

<iii> We use them as names of those bodies in all possible worlds.

The notion of a rigid designator was, of course, introduced as the notion of an expression that "designates the same object in all possible worlds".[3] The *prima facie* difficulties, however, in proceeding directly from (c1) and (c2) to some reading of <iii> along the lines of

($d1_a$) (∃x) 'Hesperus' designates x in all possible worlds.

($d2_a$) (∃x) 'Phosphorus' designates x in all possible worlds.

are considerable. First, Kripke's sentence <iii> does not speak of an expression's *designating* an object in all possible worlds, but rather returns to the idiom of *our using* an expression *as a name of* an object ("body") in all possible worlds. Second, ($d1_a$) and ($d2_a$) have dropped the *restrictive* phrase "in the actual world". These observations are, in fact, two sides of one coin. If we take our cue from (KRT) and regard talk of using an expression as a name as consequently more or less *interchangeable* with talk of that expression's being a rigid designator, then what <iii> should be understood as saying is not ($d1_a$) and ($d2_a$), but rather something like

($d1_b$) (∃x) 'Hesperus' *rigidly* designates x in all possible worlds.

($d2_b$) (∃x) 'Phosphorus' *rigidly* designates x in all possible worlds.

That is, one natural way of interpreting <iii> is as generalizing what (c1) and (c2) claim about the way the expressions 'Hesperus' and 'Phosphorus' function referentially in the *actual* world to a claim about the referential functioning of those expressions in every possible world. The problem with this interpretation, however, is that it renders <iii> plainly false.

Kripke says very little explicitly about how to understand (single) quotation marks, that is, about what sort of thing a *word* or *expression* or *term* is and how such items are properly individuated. The picture implicit in the text, however, is pretty clearly one according to which such natural-linguistic items as proper names are individuated purely syntactically or inscriptionally, as strings of (ink, graphite, chalk, etc.) marks or (in Sellarsian terminology) as "sign-designs".[4] It is, consequently, an entirely contingent matter which sign-designs are referentially "hooked up" with which objects. Premisses (b1) and (b2) and, correlatively, (c1) and (c2), that is, all have the modal status of contingent truths.

That much, in fact, Kripke does say explicitly: "There might be a possible world in which, a possible counterfactual situation in which, 'Hesperus' and 'Phosphorus' weren't names of the things they in fact are names of" (102–103). Here Kripke is evidently treating the terms 'Hesperus' and 'Phosphorus' simply as sign-designs, individuated according to purely inscriptional criteria. The possible world that he envisages is presumably precisely one in which those (syntactical) sorts of inscriptions aren't referentially (semantically) "hooked up", as they are in our own actual world, with the planet Venus.[5] What follows from these observations, then, is that, whatever "N rigidly designates X" means, that is, whatever

> (RD) (The expression) N designates (the same object) X in all possible worlds

means, it *cannot* be understood as meaning (or even as having the same truth conditions as):

> (EW) For every possible world, W, it's true in W that (the expression) N designates (the object) X.

I shall return to this observation shortly. First, however, we still face the problem of finding an acceptable reading of sentence <iii>. The moral of our most recent considerations appears to be that "actual world" restriction introduced in <ii> needs to be carried along as an indispensable feature of that interpretation. This, in turn, suggests something along the lines of:

> (d1) (∃x) In the actual world, 'Hesperus' designates x in all possible worlds.
>
> (d2) (∃x) In the actual world, 'Phosphorus' designates x in all possible worlds.

These are peculiar turns of phrase, to be sure, but, in the interest of getting on with business, let us nevertheless provisionally adopt them as parsings of Kripke's <iii> and turn to the extraordinarily puzzling matter of sentence <iv>:

> <iv> If, in fact, they are the *same* body, then in any other possible world we have to use them as a name of that object.

Sentence <iv> is syntactically rather a mess.[6] The first thing we need to do is to locate the grammatical antecedents of its various pronouns. The occurrence of 'them' here is plainly an anaphoric descendent of its occurrence in <iii>,

> <iii> We use *them* as names of those bodies in all possible worlds,

whose own antecedent, in turn, occurs in <ii>,

> <ii> We use 'Hesperus' as the name of a certain body and 'Phosphorus' as the name of a certain body.

It consequently refers to the terms or expressions 'Hesperus' and 'Phosphorus'. The ultimate pronominal antecedent of 'they', a descendent of 'those bodies' in <iii>, also originally occurs in <ii>. It is, in fact, the "certain bodies" that we use the expressions 'Hesperus' and 'Phosphorus' to name. That is, not to be coy about it, 'they' here refers to Hesperus and Phosphorus. If we make these substitutions, what <iv>, in first approximation, says is:

<iv*> If, in fact, Hesperus and Phosphorus are the *same* body, then in any other possible world we have to use 'Hesperus' and 'Phosphorus' as a name of that object.

The sense of the antecedent of <iv*> is unproblematic. It clearly amounts to: "If Hesperus and Phosphorus are identical (in the actual world). . . ." But what are we to make of its consequent? It appears that we are going to have to be a little coy after all, for we still need to locate a grammatical antecedent for 'that object'.

What object is "*that* object"? Well, if the antecedent of <iv*> is *true*, that is, if Hesperus *is* identical to Phosphorus, this question will have *many* correct answers, among them "(the object) Hesperus", "(the object) Phosphorus", and "the planet Venus". But if the antecedent of <iv*> is *false*, that is, if Hesperus is *not* identical to Phosphorus, the question will have *no* correct answers. If Hesperus is not identical to Phosphorus, that is, the nominal expression 'that object' will apparently designate nothing at all. What we seem to need, to put it in semi-formal *patois*, is something along the lines of

<iv⁺> *If* there is an object, O, such that Hesperus and Phosphorus are both identical to O (in the actual world), *then* in any other possible world we have to use 'Hesperus' and 'Phosphorus' as a name of O,

where the occurrence of the variable 'O' in the consequent of the conditional *somehow* also gets bound by the particular quantifier

38 *Chapter 2*

appearing in its antecedent, but just in case that antecedent is true. On the face of it, however, this makes no sense at all.

But surely I am being unreasonably obtuse here. Surely we *understand* Kripke well enough. So, in any event, the immediate objection is likely to run. But the awkward fact of the matter, I am convinced, is that we do *not* understand Kripke well enough. For look at where we now stand, that is, where the effort to reconstruct *carefully* Kripke's (only) argument for the necessary identity of Hesperus and Phosphorus has so far brought us:

(a) Hesperus and Phosphorus are identical (in the actual world). [hypothesis for conditional proof]

(b1) ($\exists$x) We use 'Hesperus' *as a name of* x in the actual world.

(b2) ($\exists$x) We use 'Phosphorus' *as a name of* x in the actual world.

(KRT) For every object x and for every natural-linguistic expression E, if, in the actual world, we *use* E *as a name* of x then, in the actual world, E *rigidly designates* x.

(c1) ($\exists$x) 'Hesperus' rigidly designates x in the actual world [viz. Hesperus].

(c2) ($\exists$x) 'Phosphorus' rigidly designates x in the actual world [viz. Phosphorus].

(d1) ($\exists$x) In the actual world, 'Hesperus' designates x in all possible worlds [viz. Hesperus].

(d2) ($\exists$x) In the actual world, 'Phosphorus' designates x in all possible worlds [viz. Phosphorus].

. . .

(g) Hesperus and Phosphorus are identical in all *other* possible worlds.

(h) Hesperus and Phosphorus are identical *both* in the actual world *and* in all other possible worlds.[from (a) and (g)]

(i) Hesperus and Phosphorus are identical in *all* possible worlds.[from (h)]

(j) If Hesperus and Phosphorus are identical (in the actual world), then they are identical in *all* possible worlds. [from (a)–(i) by conditional proof]

(HP) If Hesperus = Phosphorus, then it is necessary that Hesperus = Phosphorus. [from (j)]

(d1) and (d2) correspond to Kripke's sentence <iii>; (g) corresponds to sentence <v>. In whatever way sentence <iv> is properly to be understood, the *logical job* that it must do is to bridge the inferential gap between (a)–(d2) and (g)–(HP). Since the consequent of <iv> *prima facie* says something, not about Hesperus and Phosphorus, but about 'Hesperus' and 'Phosphorus', however, it is difficult to see how <iv> alone could do the job. At best, <iv> might carry us as far as something like:

(f*) 'Hesperus' and 'Phosphorus' designate the same object in every other possible world,

and we will still need to perform a sort of "semantic descent" to arrive at (g).

But then haven't I thereby just settled the question of how properly to interpret Kripke's sentence <iv>? Recall that <iv> is a conditional, whose antecedent amounts to "If Hesperus and Phosphorus are identical (in the actual world)...." If we are going to use <iv> validly to arrive at something like (f*), then something like (f*) will *a fortiori* need to occur as the consequent of that conditional, and <iv> itself, therefore, will say something like:

(e*) If Hesperus and Phosphorus are identical (in the actual world), then 'Hesperus' and 'Phosphorus' designate the same object in every other possible world.

(f*) will then follow from (a) and (e*) by modus ponens, and, in turn, (g) will follow from (f*) by some sort of "disquotational" principle.[7] This would indeed be an elegant and straightforward solution to our interpretive difficulties. Unfortunately, it is not an acceptable solution. For (f*) as it stands, lacking a suitable "actual world" restriction, appears to be *false*, for the same reasons that ($d1_b$) and ($d2_b$) proved to be false. As we have noted, Kripke makes it quite clear that we can imagine possible worlds in which, for example, 'Hesperus' designates Hesperus but 'Phosphorus' does *not* designate Phosphorus.[8]

But, even if these matters could be responsibly tidied up and such difficulties legitimately set aside (a question to which I shall return), I want to suggest that we are now in the position to see that there is something problematic about Kripke's proceedings here. The proximate conclusion for which Kripke is arguing, we recall, is a conditional:

(H) If Hesperus and Phosphorus are identical in the actual world, then they are identical in *all* possible worlds.

Temporarily bracketing our interpretive difficulties, his argument, reduced to its most skeletal form, in essence runs as follows:

(A) Hesperus and Phosphorus are identical in the actual world. [factual premiss]

(B) 'Hesperus' and 'Phosphorus' designate the same object in the actual world. [(A), "semantic ascent"]

(K) (Expressions used as) proper names are rigid designators. [hypothesis]

(C) 'Hesperus' designates the same object [viz. Hesperus] in all possible worlds. [from (K)]

(D) 'Phosphorus' designates the same object [viz. Phosphorus] in all possible worlds. [from (K)]

(E) If 'Hesperus' and 'Phosphorus' designate the same object in the actual world, then 'Hesperus' and 'Phosphorus' designate the same object in all possible worlds.

(F) 'Hesperus' and 'Phosphorus' designate the same object in all possible worlds. [(B), (E), modus ponens]

(G) Hesperus and Phosphorus are identical in all possible worlds. [(F), "semantic descent"]

(H) If Hesperus and Phosphorus are identical in the actual world, then Hesperus and Phosphorus are identical in all possible worlds. [(A)–(G), conditional proof]

Step (E), we should notice, is *another* conditional. It is, indeed, the metalinguistic counterpart of the conclusion, (H), that the argument aims to secure. But what justifies the introduction of this new conditional at this point in the reasoning? Does it follow from what has come before it? I cannot see that it does.

Kripke's thesis is evidently that the object language conditional (H) and the meta-language conditional (E) stand or fall together. One cannot consistently accept one of them and not the other. But, for all Kripke has yet shown, one *can* consistently accept *neither,* and if (E) should prove to be problematic, then so too, to that extent, will (H) be.

In the preceding chapter, I argued that Kripke's justificatory reasonings in support of various essentialist claims each depended upon the prior acceptance of a general conditional essentialist principle unsupported by independent arguments. One thing we have now discovered, I suggest, is that something analogous is true of his reasoning in support of the necessary identity of Hesperus and Phosphorus, although at one remove.

His direct reasoning in support of that modal conclusion, like his reasoning in support of the essentialist claims canvassed earlier, appeals to a specific conditional premiss:

> (HP) If Hesperus = Phosphorus, then it is necessary that Hesperus = Phosphorus.

Rather than deriving this premiss from a corresponding intuitive general principle, also framed as an object-language conditional, however, Kripke's reasoning here takes a metalinguistic detour, with (HP) being justified in essence by an appeal to a metalinguistic counterpart (framed in the idiom of "possible worlds"):

> (E) If 'Hesperus' and 'Phosphorus' designate the same object in the actual world, then 'Hesperus' and 'Phosphorus' designate the same object in all possible worlds.

It is when we inquire into the justification of (E) that we encounter the *unsupported* prior general principles upon which Kripke's necessity thesis rests. For the only plausible, non-question-begging justification of (E) will treat it as derivable from a general *metalinguistic* conditional, along the lines of:

> (2PN) If two (expressions used as) *proper names* designate the same object in the actual world, then they designate the same object in all possible worlds,

together with the (matter-of-factual?) premiss

> (HPN) 'Hesperus' and 'Phosphorus' are (used as) proper names.

The epistemic pedigree of (2PN), in turn, can be traced to the conjunction of Kripke's rigidity thesis,

> (K) (Expressions used as) proper names are rigid designators,

with another general metalinguistic conditional

(2RD) If two *rigid designators* designate the same object in the actual world, then they designate the same object in all possible worlds.

With (HPN), (2RD), and (K), then, the justificatory *reasoning* is at an end. We have again arrived at the point at which "intuitions"—now including "linguistic intuitions" as well as "modal intuitions"—unavoidably come into play. That is, as I proposed at the outset, Kripke is logically no better off in this case than in those canvassed in the preceding chapter.

He may, however, be rather worse off. For to get even this far, we should recall, we have had to bracket and simply ignore a goodly number of interpretative difficulties. Having now highlighted the central role of (HPN), (2RD), and (K) in Kripke's reasoning, we can begin to bring those difficulties into sharper focus.

One item that was explicitly put on our agenda was the question of how to understand the very notion of a rigid designator, as it appears in (2RD) and (K). Given that

(RD) (The expression) N designates (the same object) X in all possible worlds

cannot be interpreted as

(EW) For every possible world, W, it's true in W that (the expression) N designates (the object) X,

we are surely owed a *positive* story about how we *are* to interpret it. How *should* we understand the notion of a rigid designator? If we adhere to the "possible worlds" idiom, our only option appears to be to regard *designation* as a *triadic* relation obtaining among a linguistic expression, an object, and a (possible) world. Lapsing temporarily into a quasi-formal notation, we can represent the form of a designation statement on this account by something like "Des(N,X,W)", which we might read as "(Expression) N designates (object) X *at* (world) W", in order not to confuse it with "It's true *in* W that N designates X". The latter claim, in turn, must be understood on this interpretation as implicitly containing *another*, tacit or suppressed, reference to possible worlds, namely, the world or worlds, W_i, at which N designates X, for example: $T_w[Des(N,X,W_i)]$.

The fundamental problem with this proposal, as I see it, is that an appeal to such a notion of a triadic designation relation gives us precious little help in *understanding* the notion of rigid designation. At best, it simply allows us to express our puzzlement in a new notation. We seem to have reached a dead end. We can assess Kripke's unsupported premises (2RD) and (K) only if we can first understand them, and we can understand them along the present lines only if we can make some sort of *literal* sense of a triadic designation relation obtaining among bits of language, objects, and possible worlds. But, when the language in question is *English* (or some other natural language), this is something that Kripke and his epigones have not yet adequately told us how to do. Indeed, the notion that designation might be a *triadic* relation in the first place is hardly mentioned, much less subjected to explicit scrutiny. Rather, what is perhaps clear enough in the corresponding *formalisms* tends simply to go unremarked in substantive philosophical discussions, and when Kripke turns to his explicit exploration of the way in which proper names in our *natural* language are related to their referents, triadic relations are nowhere in evidence at all. Nor is this especially surprising, for 'possible world' is a term of art which has no clear counterpart in everyday discourse.[9] It is appropriate to inquire, then, whether there is not perhaps *another* strategy for understanding the notion of rigid designation. When we do so, our attention naturally falls on the "intuitive test" for rigidity that Kripke outlines on pages 48–49 of *Naming and Necessity*.

The gist of Kripke's "intuitive test" is this: an expression, E, is rigid if the result of substituting it into the sentence frame

"No-one/nothing other than———could have been———" expresses what is (intuitively) a truth; it is non-rigid (or "flaccid") if the substitution yields an (intuitive) falsehood. Thus, Kripke tells us, since

(nn) No-one other than Richard Nixon could have been Richard Nixon

is true—equivalently, "Someone other than Richard Nixon might have been Richard Nixon" is false—the designator 'Richard Nixon' is rigid, whereas the designator 'the President of the U.S. in 1970' is flaccid, since "someone else (e.g., Humphrey) might have been the President in 1970, and Nixon might not have" (49) and so the sentence

(np) No-one other than the President of the U.S. in 1970 could have been the President of the U.S. in 1970

expresses a falsehood.

But if this is what rigidity amounts to, then the thesis, (K), that our ordinary proper names *are* rigid designators immediately becomes dubious. Kripke evidently believes it plausible to suppose that all our ordinary proper names will yield (intuitive) truths when substituted into the sentence frame "No-one/nothing other than———could have been———". Paul Ziff, in contrast, disagrees:[10]

> Is it true that no one other than Nixon might have been Nixon? What's so unusual about him? Perhaps no one other than Fidel might have been Fidel. But Nixon has no special qualities. Is what I am saying intelligible? Of course it is. Consider such remarks as these: 'Do you know what made Hitler such a monster? He was dropped on his head as a baby. Hitler wouldn't have been Hitler if that hadn't happened. . . .' 'Hilbert wouldn't have been Hilbert but for an altogether fortuitous combination of genes effected by Otto and Maria Hilbert.' And so 'Nixon might not have been Nixon had some-

one given him adequate moral instruction in his youth. . . . Contrary to Kripke's thesis that names are always rigid designators any given name is a nonrigid designator on Kripke's "intuitive test."(217)

What Ziff is pointing out is that, when Kripke's sentence frame is instantiated with ordinary proper names, the resulting claim *normally* does not have the sense of a (trivial) negated assertion of possible identity,

(nns) $\neg \Diamond (\exists x)(x \neq \text{Nixon} \mathbin{.\&.} x = \text{Nixon})$,

but rather has the force of denying that its subject necessarily possesses unique and interesting special characteristics. Consequently, if *intuitive* (pre-theoretical) truth or falsehood is what is to be determinative of or criterial for rigidity, most, if not all, ordinary proper names will *fail* to be rigid.

This objection, of course, would hardly render Kripke speechless, and I shall shortly want to consider his obvious reply. First, however, we need to look briefly at some implications of the fact that the most straightforward attempt to transpose the English sentence (nn) into familiar *symbolic* resources apparently issues in a *trivially* necessary truth. One useful way of exploring those implications is by asking what issues from an analogous attempt to transpose the ostensibly *contrasting* English sentence (np) into symbolic form. What is immediately evident is that there are two ways of symbolizing (np). There is the version which assigns the modality its so-called "narrow-scope" reading:

(npn) $(\exists !x)[(Px \mathbin{\&} \neg \Diamond (\exists !y)(y \neq x \mathbin{.\&.} Py)]$

One and only person, x, was (in fact) the President of the U.S. in 1970 and it could not have been the case that some [one and only] *other* person, y (≠x), was the President of the U.S. in 1970.

But there is also the so-called "wide-scope" reading of the modality:

(npw) ¬◊[(∃!x)(Px .&. (∃!y)(y ≠ x .&. Py))]

It could not have been the case that: One and only person, x, was the President of the U.S. in 1970 and one and only *other* person, y (≠x), was [also] the President of the U.S. in 1970.

And while (npn) is apparently indeed the symbolic counterpart of an intuitive falsehood, (npw) appears to be as trivially necessary a *truth* as (nns).

A properly careful formulation of Kripke's "intuitive test" would need to acknowledge the possibility of such scope ambiguity. It would look, that is, something like this:

> An expression, E, is rigid if the result of substituting it into the sentence-frame "No-one/nothing other than———could have been———" *always* expresses what is (intuitively) a truth; it is non-rigid ("flaccid") if *there is a reading* of the substitution on which it expresses an (intuitive) falsehood.

What these considerations call to our attention is that *one* difference between such ordinary proper names as 'Richard Nixon' and such ordinary descriptive phrases as 'the President of the United States in 1970' reflected in Kripke's "intuitive test" is the fact that ordinary descriptive phrases are *scope-ambiguous* referring expressions (i.e., sentences containing them can be ambiguous between wide-scope and narrow-scope readings), whereas ordinary proper names are *scope-unambiguous* referring expressions (i.e., sentences containing them are never analogously ambiguous). But having noted this, I suggest, it is no longer clear that this is not the *only* difference between ordinary proper names and descriptive phrases that is captured by the intuitive test.

Kripke insists, of course, that the distinction between rigid and flaccid designation is not *itself* a scope distinction (see, for example, pages 11–12 of *Naming and Necessity*), and I am not proposing to contest *that* claim. But it does not follow that the dichotomous classification of referring expressions imposed by the "intuitive test" (formulated with proper care) cannot be *explained* exclusively and entirely in terms of the notion of scope—in particular, in terms of the distinction between scope-ambiguous and scope-unambiguous referring expressions. It at least requires further argument to establish a connection between scope-unambiguity and the "possible worlds" notion of rigidity needed for the necessity argument or between scope-ambiguity and flaccidity—and, as far as I can see, such an additional argument is nowhere forthcoming.[11]

How would Kripke respond to Ziff's suggestion that what the sentence

> (nn) No-one other than Richard Nixon could have been Richard Nixon

is used to say, in its customary acceptation, is arguably false? The obvious reply, surely, is that, as Ziff proposes to interpret (nn), the second occurrence of the expression 'Richard Nixon' is *not* (being used as) *a proper name*.

Given the central place of the premisses

> (K) (Expressions used as) proper names are rigid designators

and

> (HPN) 'Hesperus' and 'Phosphorus' are (used as) proper names

in Kripke's reasoning, it is clear that the cogency of that reasoning in general turns crucially on what it is for an expression to be (used as) a proper name. Making this observation explicit, in fact, opens the door to additional interpretations of Kripke's text, interpretations which may finally point a way past the interpretive difficulties we encountered when we earlier attempted to formulate his argument with full rigor and in detail.

Kripke's views are blessed with many excellent apologists. One useful way to develop an alternative interpretation of his text is by engaging in a dialogue with one of the best and most articulate of them. I shall call him simply "The Apologist".[12]

The Apologist begins by distinguishing between two conclusions for which Kripke might be arguing:

(KC1) If the identity sentence 'Hesperus is Phosphorus' is true, then it is necessarily true.

(KC2) If Hesperus and Phosphorus are identical, then Hesperus is necessarily identical to Phosphorus.

(KC1) is a (metalinguistic) conclusion about the modal status of a sentence of English; (KC2), a conclusion about the necessity of the identity of objects in the world.

Up to this point, I have taken Kripke to be aiming at (KC2). That is, I have understood him as treating the terms 'necessary' and 'necessarily' functionally, as logicians are characteristically wont to do, as *sentence operators* at the object-language level. I consequently interpreted his talk of "metaphysical necessity" as addressed (affirmatively) to traditional questions regarding modality *de re*. Corresponding to this (object-language) necessity operator was a theoretical (metalinguistic) *predicate*, 'true in all possible worlds'. On this interpretation, (KC1) as it stands is *strictly speaking* an imprecise rendering of

(KC1*) If the identity sentence 'Hesperus is Phosphorus' is true in the actual world, then it's true in all possible worlds.

In any event, the Apologist interprets Kripke as going after (KC1*)—and I certainly agree that Kripke *also* wants to establish (KC1*). As I read him, indeed, his (only) *argument* for (KC2)

50   Chapter 2

precisely and indispensably relies on (KC1*). In contrast to the Apologist, I think Kripke wants more, but there is enough to talk about without belaboring that question.

The Apologist's version of Kripke's *argument* for (KC1*) is refreshingly direct:

> (k1) English names (names as we use them) are rigid designators.
>
> (k2) (Our English names) 'Hesperus' and 'Phosphorus' are rigid designators. [from k1]
>
> (rp) [A rigid designator designates the same individual in every possible world.]
>
> (k3) 'Hesperus' (our name, used as we actually use it) designates the same individual in every possible world. [from k2, rp]
>
> (k4) 'Phosphorus' (our name, used as we actually use it) designates the same individual in every possible world. [from k2, rp]
>
> (k5) 'Hesperus' and 'Phosphorus' designate the same object in the actual world. [hypothesis for conditional proof]
>
> (k6) 'Hesperus' and 'Phosphorus' designate the same object in every possible world. [from k3, k4, and k5]
>
> (k7) If 'Hesperus' and 'Phosphorus' designate the same object in the actual world, then 'Hesperus' and 'Phosphorus' designate the same object in every possible world. [k5–k6, conditional proof]

To be sure, (k7) isn't precisely (KC1*), but, given that

> The identity sentence 'Hesperus is Phosphorus' is true in any possible world just in case 'Hesperus' and 'Phosphorus' designate the same object in that world,

it's surely close enough to allow us to get on with business.[13]

The argument is apparently valid. As usual, our challenge is to understand and assess the truth of its premisses. Like Kripke, the Apologist is *using* the notions of "rigid designation" and "possible worlds". How does he propose that we interpret them?

The key to the Apologist's interpretive strategy lies in the parenthetical phrases sprinkled among the argument's first four steps. For the crux of his interpretation is that Kripke's rigidity thesis (and its specific applications) is a thesis about what the Apologist calls *English names,* that is, expressions with which a certain *use* is already associated. The Apologist, that is, proposes to distinguish the *English name* 'Hesperus' ('Phosphorus') from the *sign-design* 'Hesperus' ('Phosphorus'). My earlier interpretive difficulties, he adds, arose from conflating the two.

What led me to talk of sign-designs in the first place, we may recall, was my desire to find a consistent reading of Kripke's use of *single quotes.* To me, it just seemed obvious that, whatever the positive criteria were to which Kripke would have us appeal in locating and individuating the referents of the single-quoted expressions 'Hesperus' and 'Phosphorus', if there was to be any hope of making such remarks as "There might be a possible world in which, a possible counterfactual situation in which, 'Hesperus' and 'Phosphorus' weren't names of the things they in fact are names of" (102-103) come out true, those criteria *couldn't* include facts about our actual use of those expressions or about what, as used by us, they actually named. When, two pages later, I found Kripke writing: "We use 'Hesperus' as the name of a certain body and 'Phosphorus' as the name of a certain body. We use them as names of those bodies in all possible worlds" (104), then I quite naturally assumed that these quoted expressions were to be understood in the same way, as being used to talk about linguistic items *individuated* purely "syntactically",

prescinding from "semantic" considerations regarding actual use and *de facto* reference.[14]
In response to the (mistaken) suggestion that we elucidate

(RD) (The expression) N designates (the same object) X in all possible worlds

by generalizing actual relationships between name-tokens and named objects across possible worlds, the Apologist replies that there are clearly *no* generalizations to other possible worlds to be had from actual instances of *sign-designs* and their referents. The correct interpretation of (RD) must understand it as instantiating the thesis that our *English names* differ from (our English) descriptions in that their referents remain the same across possible worlds. At root, the Apologist says, it's a claim about how items belonging to a linguistic category of ours, viz. (proper) names, function semantically—like mere tags, with no descriptive content.

This is a potentially helpful remark. It suggests that the professed *rigidity* of proper names is actually supposed to be a consequence of a more fundamental fact about them, and it further suggests what this presumptive more fundamental fact is supposed to *be:* that proper names refer to objects *directly,* i.e., in a manner not in any essential way mediated by descriptive concepts.

The theme broached here is unquestionably a central one in Kripke's thinking. It certainly deserves a thorough discussion, and in due time I will give it one. For the moment, however, I want to postpone that discussion, for we still have some minor unfinished business.

As I understand the Apologist, his interpretive strategy requires *inter alia* that, as Kripke uses them, single-quotation marks are functionally *ambiguous*. Sometimes they are used to talk about the *sign-designs* 'Hesperus' and 'Phosphorus', and sometimes they are used to talk about the *English names* 'Hesperus' and 'Phosphorus'. The obvious question at this point becomes: how are these two uses of single quotes related? More generally, how shall we understand the relationship between sign-designs and names? Sign-designs, we recall, are individuated purely structurally (syntactically). How are *names* individuated?

The only possible answer appears to be: semantically. And *if* names are expressions that "refer directly", 'semantically', in turn, can only mean: in terms of their referents. That is, the (English) *name* 'Hesperus' will be the sign-design 'Hesperus' *used* (as we use it) *to refer to the planet Venus*. On this reading, a semantic relation to a determinate object is built into the very identity conditions of a *name*. Since the only semantic relation available is presumably that of designation (reference, denotation), what apparently follows is that, whereas

The *sign-design* 'Hesperus' designates Venus

says something at best contingently true,

The English name 'Hesperus' designates Venus

in contrast, expresses a necessary truth, and

'Hesperus' designates Venus

is just plain ambiguous—and indeed, *doubly* so, since the sense of the term 'designates' will need to shift according to whether it is being predicated of sign-designs or of names. This seems an unpalatable result.

Rather than drawing such conclusions, what the Apologist ingeniously and consistently proposes at this point instead is that we should no longer think of *designation* as a two-place relation between *names* and objects named—nor even, as I earlier suggested, as a three-place relation among sign-designs, objects, and worlds. We must rather replace (dyadic or triadic) talk of the designation *of names* by appeals to what is in essence a *four-place* relation, obtaining among a sign-design, an object, and *two* (perhaps identical) possible worlds, for example:

Des('Hesperus',W_i,O,W_j),

read: "The sign-design 'Hesperus', used as it is used in the possible world W_i, designates the object O in possible world W_j." (In my terminology, W_i is a world *in* which it's true that W_j is a world *at* which 'Hesperus' designates O. In what follows, I'll restrict W_i to @, the actual world.[15])

Curiously enough, however, on this understanding, talk of names *as such* drops out of the Apologist's picture altogether, and the rigidity thesis turns out to be about sign-designs after all. Extending our current quasi-formal *patois* (and supposing, as usual, that the relevant objects exist in all the relevant worlds), the full-dress version of the rigidity thesis applied to "our name 'Hesperus'", for example,

(k3) 'Hesperus' (our name, used as we actually use it) designates the same individual in every possible world

becomes:

(k3*) (O)[Des('Hesperus',@,O,@)→(W)(Des('Hesperus',@,O,W))],

where the antecedent ties down the sign-design 'Hesperus' to our *de facto* use of it (in the actual world) to designate whatever it does (at the actual world).

But now the dialectic has once again confronted us with the problem of understanding a "higher-polyadicity" designation relation. If designation is a four-termed relation obtaining among sign-designs, objects, and pairs of "worlds", what relation is it? Correlatively, if an expression, N, (of our actual language) is a rigid designator just in case it satisfies the schema

(O)[Des(N,@,O,@) → (W)(Des(N,@,O,W))],

what reason do we have to believe that those expressions we use (in English) as proper names are *in this sense* rigid designators?

This brings us around again to the Apologist's, and Kripke's, "intuitive Millianism", the idea that our proper names are "mere tags" which "refer directly" to the objects they denote.[16] For whatever story the Apologist will want to tell about his four-place *designation* relation, he will presumably want it to be compatible with the conviction that a *semantic relation* of "direct reference" obtains between proper names and their nominata, indeed, that just this is what it *means* for an expression to *be* (used as) a proper name. The thorough discussion of "direct reference" promised above, it appears, can no longer be postponed.

The next four chapters of this study are devoted to precisely that discussion, not only of Kripke's "intuitive Millianism", but of its alternatives as well. I shall contend that, at just this point in the dialectic, the fact of our inescapable *epistemic situatedness* comes significantly into play. My critical claim will be that a philosophical naturalist—that is, one who denies ontological standing for *primitive* semantic or intentional properties or relations—will have no way of funding an account of ordinary proper names as "referring directly" which is compatible with their playing the roles in our communication, inquiry, and thought that they actually do. In particular, I shall argue that Kripke's own "causal-historical picture", which offers the best hope for naturalizing "direct reference", cannot be sustained from an epistemic point of view, and I shall sketch out an alternative story about proper names of my own. That, briefly put, is my score for the music still to come.

As I remarked above, Kripke's views are blessed with many excellent apologists. Unfortunately, they all too often frame their apologetics in terms of the very Kripkean notions for which I here have been seeking elucidations—rigid designators, possible worlds, (expressions used as) proper names [as opposed to "mere" sign-designs], designation (denotation), "direct reference", and the like. The present Apologist is better than most, but when we look *carefully* at his interpretive proposals and arguments and subject such expository idioms as "(English) names" and "designates" to *detailed* critical scrutiny, what we find is that he has ultimately not offered us a significant advance in clarity and understanding over Kripke's original text.

A *careful* and *detailed* critical look at Kripke's original text is what this chapter has been about. In the process, I have indeed, as one colleague has put it, "made very heavy weather" of certain points and "belabored" others. But that is as it should be. *Any* philosophical work—including the present study, of course—should be able to withstand the challenge of just that sort of "heavy weather" and "belaboring". Despite the efforts of his excellent apologists, however, for the reasons I have given and reasons still to come, I am not *yet* convinced that Kripke's work ultimately can do so.

3
Referential Alternatives: Names and Descriptions

WHAT IS shaping Kripke's views regarding proper names? What is it that gives rise to the very idea (which we have not yet discovered how properly to understand) that names are "rigid designators"? One influential factor, of course, is the paradigm provided by a certain formalism, quantified modal logic with identity, and its associated set-theoretic semantics. An equally significant and influential factor, however, is the *failure* of a certain traditional philosophical account of the referential functioning of proper names—Descriptivism.

Compactly formulated, Descriptivism holds that a relation of *reference* obtaining between a (proper) name and an object is derivative from relations of *satisfaction* obtaining (uniquely) between that object and one or more descriptions. The description or descriptions are said to constitute the *sense* of the proper name, and an object, x, *uniquely satisfies* a description, 'ø', just in case the sentence 'x, and only x, is ø' is true. Kripke formulates this theory and its consequences in the form of six theses (64–65; 71):

[T1] To every name or designating expression 'X', there corresponds a cluster of properties, namely the family of those properties ø such that A believes 'øX'.

[T2] One of the properties, or some conjointly, are believed by A to pick out some individual uniquely.

[T3] If most, or a weighted most, of the ø's are satisfied by one unique object y, then y is the referent of 'X'.

[T4] If the vote yields no unique object, 'X' does not refer.

[T5] The statement, 'If X exists, then X has most of the ø's' is known *a priori* by the speaker.

[T6] The statement, 'If X exists, then X has most of the ø's' expresses a necessary truth (in the idiolect of the speaker).

The "vote" in [T4] adverts not to an election held among several persons but only to the idea that some properties in the group picked out in [T1] may be more important than others for determining the referent at issue.[1] In what follows, I shall speak instead of "a weighted assessment of the ø's".

The first thing we need to notice is that [T1]–[T6] formulate Descriptivism as an account of *speaker's* reference, that is, as yielding an answer the question, "To what or whom does (a speaker) *A* refer by (A's use of) the name or designating expression 'X'?" Kripke has little explicitly to say about how Descriptivism might be formulated as a theory of *semantic* reference, that is, as answering the question, "To what or whom does the name or designating expression 'X' (itself) refer?" Such a theory must presumably build on an account of speaker's reference, and there are various ways in which it might do so. The most fruitful course now, I would propose, is to leave the matter of semantic reference as unfinished business and devote our immediate efforts rather to commanding a suitable view of speaker's reference. Since this dialectical strategy is *prima facie* open to immediate objections, however, we need first to pause at this point for a rather lengthy digression.

The distinction between speaker's reference and semantic reference is in the first instance at home in certain contexts of *false belief*. What I have in mind here is the sort of traditional Donnellan-style² scenario in terms of which the distinction originally took shape, for example:

> *Jacques:* (looking at a tall red-haired man in one corner of the room) "That fellow over there drinking a martini is wearing a particularly handsome Armani suit."
>
> *Bartender:* (glancing toward a short balding man in a different corner, who happens to be the only person *actually* drinking a martini) "You think so? I'd call it a rather shabby off-the-rack department store number."
>
> *Jacques:* (gesturing appropriately) "I was talking about the tall red-haired man in that corner."
>
> *Bartender:* "Oh him. *He's* drinking a Gibson. But you're right about the suit. It is nice, isn't it?"

Motivated by such examples, Donnellan was led to distinguish a "referential" from an "attributive" use of definite descriptions:

> A speaker who uses a definite description attributively in an assertion states something about whoever or whatever is the so-and-so. A speaker who uses a definite description referentially in an assertion, on the other hand, uses the description to enable his audience to pick out whom or what he is talking about and states something about that person or thing. (RDD, 285)

In *Naming and Necessity,* Kripke provides in passing (25, n3) an analogous example employing proper names which he elaborates upon, however, only elsewhere, in his own more extended discussion of semantic and speaker's reference:[3]

> Two people see Smith at a distance and mistake him for Jones. They have a brief colloquy: "What is Jones doing?" "Raking the leaves." "Jones," in the common language of both, is a name of Jones; it *never* names Smith. Yet, in some sense, on this occasion, clearly both participants in the dialogue have referred to Smith, and the second participant has said something true about

the man he referred to if and only if Smith was raking the leaves (whether or not Jones was). (SRSR, 263)

Kripke's inclination is to assimilate the distinction between semantic reference and speaker's reference to the Gricean distinction[4] between what a speaker's *words* mean on a given occasion and what *he* (the speaker) means, in saying those words, on that occasion. This latter distinction, in turn, Kripke interprets as *pragmatic,* rather than semantic.[5] What the speaker means in saying certain words—which Kripke also, misleadingly I think, identifies with Grice's "conversational implicature"—does not derive from "the conventions of our language" (together with the general intention of a speaker to adhere to them), but from "various further special intentions of the speaker, together with various general principles, applicable to all human languages regardless of their special conventions. (Cf. Grice's "conversational maxims.")" (SRSR, 263). Analogously, the semantic referent of a non-indexical designator "will be given by a *general* intention of the speaker to refer to a certain object whenever the designator is used. The speaker's referent is given by a *specific* intention, on a given occasion, to refer to a certain object" (SRSR, 264).

On Kripke's view, then, Donnellan's distinction between attributive and referential uses applies to all non-indexical referring expressions, whether descriptions or names, and amounts to a pragmatic distinction between "simple" cases, in which a speaker's specific referential intention simply coincides with his general one, and "complex" cases, in which the two intentions are distinct, but *believed* by the speaker to determine the same object.

> In the "simple" case, the speaker's referent is, *by definition,* the semantic referent. In the "complex" case, they may coincide, if the speaker's belief is correct, but they need not.... Donnellan's "attributive" use is nothing but the "simple" case, specialized to

definite descriptions, and . . . the "referential" use is, similarly, the "complex" case. (SRSR, 264)

The nerve-center of Kripke's discussion of speaker's reference and semantic reference, then, is the notion of a speaker's *intending to refer to a specific object*. Analogously, Michael Devitt speaks in this context of a speaker's *having a particular object in mind*. In the first Donnellan scenario, for instance, one can say that, when he used the descriptive phrase 'that fellow over there drinking a martini', Jacques *intended to refer* to the tall red-haired man drinking a Gibson; that was who he *had in mind*. Similarly, in Kripke's scenario, his two speakers *intended to refer* to the person raking the leaves, and, since that person was in fact Jones, it was Jones whom they *had in mind*. What I want next to argue is that such remarks admit of two possible interpretations, but that neither of them offers any significant *explanatory* advance on questions of reference.

On the first of these interpretations, the concept of speaker's reference is *prior* to that of "intending to refer" or "having in mind", and the latter notions are ultimately to be explained in terms of it. On this account, the point of the remarks about Jacques' referential intentions or state of mind is simply to stress the fact that his linguistic performance is most usefully characterized in terms of speaker's reference rather than semantic reference. Whatever is in the cocktail glass, *Jacques* was talking about the tall red-haired man. Mention of a martini enters into the linguistic episode, so to speak, only *per accidens,* as an ostensible feature of the situation that is supposed to help Jacques' audience recognize or pick out the object of his discourse. On this interpretation, talk specifically about Jacques' referential *intentions* or whom he *has in mind* is adventitious and dispensable. One could instead simply say that, when Jacques used the descriptive phrase 'that fellow over there drinking a martini', although the *phrase* referred to a man drinking a martini, *Jacques* was referring to the tall red-haired man drinking the Gibson. Thus interpreted, talk about "intentions to refer" or "having in mind" is interchangeable with talk about speaker's reference and semantic reference and ultimately presupposes both notions. It consequently cannot coherently be supposed to belong to their analysis or explanation.

On the second interpretation, in contrast, appeals to intentions to refer or having in mind are offered precisely *as* ostensibly explanatory remarks. On this understanding, Jacques' "intending to refer to the tall red-haired man drinking the Gibson" (Jacques' "having *him* in mind") is an *occurrent episode* that is part of what causally occasions his public linguistic performance. According to this view, it is precisely the fact that the etiology of his linguistic performance appropriately incorporates just such an episode that explains *how and why* the speaker, Jacques, succeeds in referring to a tall red-haired man drinking a Gibson, despite the fact that the descriptive phrase he employs is rather true of (denotes, scmantically refers to) a man drinking a martini.

Before we proceed to examine this would-be explanatory story in more detail, it is worth noting that the notions of "intending to refer" and "having in mind" are sufficiently labile to allow us *also* to say, correctly, that when he used the descriptive phrase in question, Jacques intended to refer to (and had in mind) a man drinking a martini. The point of *this* remark would be to stress the fact that the semantic reference of Jacques' descriptive phrase is indeed to a man drinking a martini, and the fact that, from another perspective, it is *not* an accident that Jacques employed a descriptive phrase with just that semantic reference. The word 'martini' was not, for example, a case of misspeaking or a slip of the tongue. Falsely believing the tall red-haired man to be drinking a martini, 'martini' was what Jacques *meant* to say.

It follows, *inter alia*, that the notion of "speaker's reference" is potentially ambiguous. The question "To whom did Jacques refer?", in other words, may embody an ambiguity analogous to one which arguably infects the question "What did X see?"

Consider a case where, for example, Bruno has mistaken a bush for a bear. Here, one can correctly say that, in one sense, what Bruno saw was a bear. Bruno, namely, had an *of-a-bear* visual experience. "A bear" is Bruno's *own* answer to the question "What did you see?" One can also, however, *equally* correctly say that, in another sense, what Bruno saw was a bush. His visual experience was (causally) *occasioned* by a bush; and there was nothing else there in his physical surroundings—and in particular, no bears there—to *be* seen.[6]

On this model, there is a sense of 'see' which is ontologically noncommittal and independent of the etiology of the perceptual act and actual contents of the perceiver's environment, and another sense of 'see' which is entirely determined by the etiology of that act and the contents of that environment. Analogously, one could hold that there is *a* sense of "speaker's reference" which is descriptively noncommittal and independent of the actual semantic meaning of the referring expression employed and also that there is *another* sense of "speaker's reference" according to which it is entirely determined by the semantic meaning of the referring expression employed.

Whatever our final verdict on this question, what I want next to suggest is that positing occurrent episodes of "intending to refer" or "having in mind" will appear to shed light on linguistic referring in the first place only if such an episode is tacitly or implicitly treated as being itself, in all essential respects, a *case* or *instance* of (*non*-linguistic) referring. That is, an episode of "intending to refer" or "having in mind" must be regarded as itself instantiating intentional or semantic relations, not between sounds or inscriptions and objects in the world, but between "mental items" and the world.

Appeals to "intentions to refer" or "having in mind" in the second, would-be explanatory sense, in other words, belong to the long philosophical tradition that proposes to elucidate the notion of someone's *talking about* X in terms of the notion of someone's *thinking of* X ("meaning X", etc.) But the hard fact of the matter has always been that the intentional or referential aboutness of thought is no less in need of theoretical elucidation than the intentional or referential aboutness of speech.[7]

The notion that the semantic properties of public representations (e.g., words) are ultimately to be explained and understood in terms of private intentional acts performed by individual persons (speakers and hearers), I would argue, is the confused offspring of what are essentially two truisms:

(a) There are intentional states of persons, and inner episodes in which those states are implicated, that are prior *in the order of causes* to intelligent public speech.

(b) The semantic properties of natural linguistic items must ultimately be explained and understood in terms of the states and activities of language-using organisms.

The explanatory states and activities adverted to in (b) can be identical to the intentional states and episodes adverted to in (a), however, only if what is here prior in the order of causes is also prior in the order of understanding, and that is simply not the case. Indeed, unless we are prepared to endorse an utterly mysterious ontology along the lines of the Scholastic-Cartesian system of formal and objective "modes of being", the *only* coherent model we have for a person's thinking of (meaning, intending to refer to, having in mind) someone or something, X, is the model of mental *representations*—"inner pictures" or "inner speech"—and even here we must take some care, for this model, too, admits of being handled in different ways.

One representationalist strategy, for example, proposes to understand speaker's linguistic reference as a *derivative* semantic relation, obtaining between public items (words) and things in the world (objects), that is, as derivative from *another* semantic relation—say, "designating", "aboutness", or simply "standing for"—which obtains between "inner" particulars ("mental words") and things in the world. *If* one has identified the explanatory states and activities of (b) with the semantic states and episodes of (a), however, one is left with no further explanatory option at this point but to regard designation, aboutness, or standing for, in turn, as a *primitive* semantic or intentional relation between mental items and things in the world—and primitive intentional relations are, unfortunately, ontologically no less mysterious than the Cartesian modes of being that mental representations were introduced in an effort to avoid.[8]

An ontologically more promising representationalist strategy, in contrast, will reject the identification of the states and activities of (b) with the states and episodes of (a). On this reading, an inner state or episode is understood to possess specific semantic properties by virtue of its being decomposable into elements or aspects which play roles in a person's rational behavioral economy *analogous* to those played by the corresponding bits of public language. On this strategy, although posterior in the order of causes, public linguistic representations will nevertheless be prior in the order of understanding in the sense that

(c) The semantic properties of *all* representations must ultimately be explained and understood in terms of the publicly accessible states and activities of language-using organisms (considered in extension, as items in the natural order).

On neither representationalist strategy, however, does an appeal to "intending to refer", "having in mind", or some comparable inner state or episode *as such* provide any elucidation of the possibility of semantic relationships between representing items and represented objects. The first strategy simply exchanges an unexplicated overt relation of reference for an unexplicated covert relation of designation, aboutness, or standing for; the second insists that any elucidation of representation, overt or covert, must be constructed from certain public, extensional materials—surely a reasonable naturalistic constraint on philosophical theorizing here *in general*—but, until it is supplemented by a specific theoretical proposal, its appeals to inner states or episodes remain uninformative.

What these considerations imply is that the only *useable* notions of "intending to refer" and "having in mind" turn out to be simply *applications* of the notion of linguistic reference *per se* to items of an "inner" representational system, a "language of thought". And what follows from this observation, I submit, is that what I earlier called the second, ostensibly explanatory, strategy for interpreting such idioms collapses, in the final analysis, into the first. That is, the basic structure of a correct philosophical account of the reference of "inner" tokens will simply *echo* the basic structure of a correct philosophical account of the reference of "public" tokens, *whatever* that turns out to be.[9]

In particular, precisely the Descriptivist strategy itself has traditionally been "moved inside" as a proposed account of the referential aboutness of *thoughts*. I began this digression by remarking that Kripke formulates Descriptivism as an account of *speaker's* reference, that is, as yielding an answer to the question, "To what or whom does (a speaker) *A* refer by (A's use of) the name or designating expression 'X'?" Kripke himself, we observed, proposed to treat the contrast between semantic and speaker's reference, *inter alia*, in terms of a contrast between general and specific "intentions to refer", but what the intervening discussion has shown is that, on the *only* plausible model for "intending to refer" (or "having in mind"), a strict analogue to the question of speaker's reference arises for the "inner" names or designating expressions of a "language of thought". To answer *that* question, however, there is no alterative but to tell a story within which, at most, only the speaker's beliefs can play a role.[10] There are good expository reasons, therefore, to take Kripke's formulation of Descriptivism at its face value, as a theory of *speaker's* reference, and to proceed to explore his objections and alternatives to it in those terms. For sooner or later, *any* collective story of "conventional", semantic, *shared* reference will need to appeal to *some* distributive account of *individual* referential achievements, to which the contrast between "inner" and "public" states or episodes will be, at best, epiphenomenal.[11]

Kripke proposes, then, to challenge Descriptivism, understood as a theory of speaker's reference and characterized by his six theses, along two main lines. The first line of attack is internal. It suggests that such Descriptivist theories often, or even characteristically, violate a non-circularity condition:

(C) For any successful theory, the account must not be circular. The properties which [enter into the weighted assessment] must not themselves involve the notion of reference in such a way that it is ultimately impossible to eliminate. (71)

The second line is external. It proposes that central consequences of Descriptivism are at odds with a variety of robust, intuitively plausible *counterfactual* claims in which proper names occur, and that, roughly, our initial confidence in the truth of those claims is sufficient to undermine the credibility of Descriptivism as a theory of proper names. The two lines of criticism occasionally interact, when, for example, it is Descriptivist attempts to meet a specific external challenge that give rise to violations of condition (C).

The heart of the Descriptivist theory, as Kripke has formulated it, lies in the first four theses. Theses [T1]–[T4] purport to explain in what relationship(s) between signs and the world (proper names and objects) reference *consists* or, at least, how the reference of a proper name is determined or *fixed*. Theses [T5] and [T6], in contrast, address epistemological and modal *consequences* of the theory proper, respectively the epistemological and modal status of specific conditional claims containing a given proper name. It is these consequences that Kripke undertakes, in the first instance, critically to engage.

In addressing [T6], for example, Kripke argues that " 'Moses exists' means something different from 'the existence and uniqueness conditions for a certain description [or family of descriptions] are fulfilled' " (59), for

> if we speak of a counterfactual case where no one did indeed do such and such, say, lead the Israelites out of Egypt, does it follow that, in such a situation, Moses wouldn't have existed? It would seem not. For surely Moses might have just decided to spend his days more pleasantly in the Egyptian courts. He might never have gone into either politics or religion at all; and in that case maybe no one would have done any of the things that the Bible relates of Moses. That doesn't in itself mean that in such a possible world Moses wouldn't have existed. (58)

Similarly, claims Kripke, [T5] is undermined by its failure to respect the distinction between a completely fictitious story, one whose events *and characters* are imaginary, and a fictitious story about a real person. "In the latter case, it seems to me that a scholar could say that he supposes that, though Moses did exist, the things said of him in the Bible are substantially false" (66–67). The cogency of such a scholarly pronouncement, however, belies the suggestion that we know *a priori* that if the biblical stories are substantially false, then Moses did not exist or, equivalently, that, if Moses *did* exist, then the biblical stories are substantially true, which in essence is what [T5] requires. Modifying the Descriptivist theory to address this problem by requiring only that one believe that Moses is the person of whom *the Bible relates* that such and such is true, in turn, threatens a vicious regress, "because how do we know whom the Bible is referring to? The question of our reference is thrown back to the question of reference in the Bible" (68).

Kripke's critique of the heart of the Descriptivist theory,

theses [T1]–[T4], is brisk and straightforward. [T1] can be understood, so to speak, purely definitionally. It merely directs our attention, for each proper name, 'X', and person, A, to a specific property or set of properties, ø, the property or properties believed by A to be true of the referent of 'X', and so is not *per se* disputable. Theses [T2]–[T4], in contrast, advance specific claims regarding the *nature* of these properties and their *role* with respect to the constituting or fixing of relations of reference, and it is these claims that Kripke proposes to challenge.

Thesis [T2]—that one of the associated descriptions, or some conjointly, are believed to pick out some individual uniquely—Kripke suggests, is simply false, and he describes a number of situations, any one of which would serve as a counterexample to it.

> [M]ost people, when they think of Cicero, just think of *a famous Roman orator,* without any pretension to think either that there was only one famous Roman orator or that one must know something else about Cicero to have a referent for the name. (81)

> [T]he man in the street . . . may use the name 'Feynman'. When asked he will say: well he's a physicist or something. He may not think that this picks out anyone uniquely. I still think he uses the name 'Feynman' as a name for Feynman. (81)

Even when, however, some description that a speaker is likely (or at least able) to produce when queried *does* succeed in picking out someone uniquely, Kripke surmises, it typically does so in a manner which at least runs the risk of generating a violation of condition (C).

> Let's say, for example, that we know that Cicero was the man who first denounced Catiline. . . . [T]here is a problem, because this description contains another name, namely 'Catiline'. We must be sure that we satisfy the conditions in such a way as to avoid violating the noncircularity condition here. In particular,

> we must not say that Catiline was the man denounced by Cicero. . . . [W]e had better add some other conditions in order to satisfy the uniqueness condition. (81)
>
> If we say Einstein was 'the man who discovered relativity theory', that does pick someone out uniquely; but it may not pick him out in such a way as to satisfy the noncircularity condition, because the theory of relativity may in turn be picked out as 'Einstein's theory'. (82)

In the case of Thesis [T3]—that if most, or a weighted most, of the associated descriptions are satisfied by one unique object, then that object is the referent of the name—Kripke focuses on the example of the reference of the proper name 'Kurt Gödel', supposing Gödel to be (correctly) believed to be the person who discovered and proved the incompleteness of elementary arithmetic. He proceeds to argue that [T3] gives the wrong answer to the question of reference in a certain counterfactual situation. To this end, he provides a (type-E) thought-experiment:

> Imagine the following blatantly fictional situation. . . . Suppose that Gödel was not in fact the author of this theorem. A man named 'Schmidt', whose body was found in Vienna under mysterious circumstances many years ago, actually did the work in question. His friend Gödel somehow got hold of the manuscript and it was thereafter attributed to Gödel. On the view in question, then, when our ordinary man uses the name 'Gödel', he really means to refer to Schmidt, because Schmidt is the unique person satisfying the description, 'the man who discovered the incompleteness of arithmetic'.[12] . . . [S]ince the man who discovered the incompleteness of arithmetic is in fact Schmidt, [according to T3] we, when we talk about 'Gödel', are in fact always referring to Schmidt. But it seems to me that we are not. We simply are not. (83–84)

Finally, suggests Kripke, the falsehood of [T4]—that if the weighted assessment of properties yields no unique object, the name does not refer—is a corollary of various cases he has already discussed. [T4], in fact, has two subcases. On the one hand, the weighted assessment may fail to yield a unique object by issuing in a description that is satisfied by more than one object. The Cicero and Feynman examples fit this model. On the other hand, the assessment may fail to yield a unique object by issuing in a description that is not satisfied by any object at all. To show this, Kripke offers a radicalization of the Gödel example:

> Suppose . . . no one had discovered the incompleteness of arithmetic—perhaps the proof simply materialized by a random scattering of atoms on a piece of paper—the man Gödel being lucky enough to have been present when this improbable event occurred. Further, suppose arithmetic is in fact complete. . . . So even if the conditions are not satisfied by a unique object the name may still refer. (86)

A substantial piece of the argument is simply missing from the original text here, but Kripke clearly intends to endorse the conclusion that, even if these peculiar counterfactual conditions were satisfied, and thus even if the various beliefs we entertained about him were *radically* false, when we used the name 'Kurt Gödel', just as we would, in the Schmidt case, be referring to Gödel (rather than to Schmidt), so too, in this case, we would still be referring to Gödel (rather than failing to refer at all).

Considered as appeals to our pre-theoretical commonsense convictions, to our "intuitions", Kripke's examples are indeed telling. For surely we *do* believe that (although it is false) it *makes sense* to suppose that Kurt Gödel did not actually discover and publish the proof of the incompleteness of arithmetic. Surely we *do* believe that one can think of the famous Roman orator Cicero (or the famous physicist Feynman), and refer to him, while having no substantive beliefs about him beyond the belief that he was a famous Roman orator (a scientist). And if we believe these specific claims (and many other relevantly similar specific claims)—as we surely do—then we cannot consistently *also* believe that Descriptivism, as Kripke has characterized it, is a correct general account of the reference of proper names.

This leaves us with two options: Either it is only Descriptivism *as Kripke has formulated it* which fails to give an acceptable general account of the reference of proper names, or *no* version of Descriptivism *can* satisfactorily give such an account. Kripke, naturally enough, arrives at the latter conclusion. He is convinced, indeed, that "the whole picture given by this theory of how reference is determined seems to be wrong from the fundamentals" (93). He proposes, therefore, to present a "better picture", and he begins with an example:

> Someone, let's say, a baby, is born; his parents call him by a certain name. They talk about him to their friends. Other people meet him. Through various sorts of talk, the name is spread from link to link as if by a chain. A speaker who is on the far end of this chain, who has heard about, say Richard Feynman, in the market place or elsewhere, may be referring to Richard Feynman even though he can't remember from whom he first heard of Feynman or from whom he ever heard of Feynman. He knows that Feynman is a famous physicist. A certain passage of communication reaching ultimately to the man himself does reach the speaker. He then is referring to Feynman even though he can't identify him uniquely. (91)

Descriptivist theories are "Fregean" insofar as they imply that each proper name is affiliated with a (descriptive) *sense* through which the referent of the name is determined. The traditional alternative to a Fregean theory of proper names is a "Millian" account, according to which a proper name has *only* a referent and *no* sense, a "denotation" but no "connotation". Proper names, the Millian story has it, are "mere labels" or "tags". Kripke's picture is fundamentally Millian, but Kripke attempts to take into account precisely what a literal reading of 'label' or 'tag' leaves puzzling, namely, the fact that, unlike actual tags or labels, which must be (physically) attached to what they label or tag, proper names can be used *in absentia*. Kripke's response to this puzzle, in essence, is to insist that proper name tokens *are* (physically) attached to the items they name. They are connected to those items by historical series of causal transactions, the links in diverse chains of (speaker-hearer) communication. Reference is a *natural*, causal-historical, relation between bits of language and bits of the world.[13]

As Kripke himself insists, his "better picture" is far from being a fully articulated *theory* of proper name reference. To begin with, it is plain that

> not every sort of causal chain reaching from me to a certain man will do for me to make a reference. There may be a causal chain from our use of the term 'Santa Claus' to a certain historical saint, but still the children, when they use this, by this time probably do not refer to that saint. So other conditions must be satisfied in order to make this into a really rigorous theory of reference. (93)

Again, not every communicative transaction in which a proper name passes from speaker to hearer qualifies as a link of the appropriate sort.

> When the name is 'passed from link to link', the receiver of the name must, I think, intend when he learns it to use it with the same reference as the man from whom he heard it. If I hear the name 'Napoleon' and decide it would be a nice name for my pet aardvark, I do not satisfy this condition. (Perhaps it is some such failure to keep the reference fixed which accounts for the divergence of present uses of 'Santa Claus' from the alleged original use.) (96–97)

It is clear, then—and Kripke agrees—that the "better picture" that he has sketched, in its present schematic form, does not purport to *eliminate* the notion of reference: "[O]n the contrary, it takes the notion of intending to use the same reference as a given. There is also an appeal to an initial baptism which is explained in terms either of fixing a reference by a description, or ostension" (97). What is not so clear is why Kripke is prepared so sanguinely to endorse these observations about the story he has been telling when, earlier, the mere possibility that the Descriptivist might be unable to complete *his* story without violating the non-circularity condition (C) was repeatedly cited as evidence that the theory was fatally and fundamentally flawed.

Condition (C), we recall, requires that a successful theory not be circular. Particularized to the "cluster-of-properties" Descriptivist account, this general constraint took the form of a requirement that the properties used to determine reference not themselves ineliminably involve the notion of reference. On Kripke's view, in contrast, reference is not determined by descriptive properties but by the existence of a sequence of historical *reference-transmitting* communicative events causally linking a present use of a proper name to initial *reference-fixing* or "baptismal" events (in which, typically, the referent itself is causally implicated). Particularized to such a causal-historical theory, the non-circularity condition must take the form of the requirement that the theory's central and fundamental notions of an event's being reference-fixing or reference-transmitting can be analyzed or explained in ways that do not themselves ineliminably involve the notion of reference. What I want to suggest, however, is that there is absolutely no reason to believe that Kripke's story *can* be told in a way that satisfies the non-circularity condition thus understood.

Kripke himself periodically invokes to this end the notion of a reference-preserving *intention*, an "intention to refer", as if it were the well-understood first step toward such an explanation or analysis. In particular, the notion emerges, as we have seen, as part of the story of a *proper* communicative link: the hearer must intend to use the name with the same reference as the speaker from whom he hears it.

It seems clear enough that Kripke's suggestion is meant to invoke the idea of an "intention to refer" in the second, would-be explanatory, sense discussed earlier. Kripke's talk of intentions to refer here is not simply a surrogate for or interchangeable with talk about speakers' references but is rather supposed to advert to a (causal) factor *determinative* of (future) speakers' references. Yet, even if we assume, for the sake of argument, that the notion of such a referential intention *qua* causally mediating "inner episode" can itself be satisfactorily explicated without an appeal to the semantic properties of public linguistic episodes, the occurrence of such intentions, I want next to argue, would be neither necessary nor sufficient for the transmission of a proper name reference across a communicative link.

To focus our considerations, suppose that Helmut has acquired his ability to use the previously unfamiliar names 'Moritz Schlick' and 'Otto Neurath' by listening to Heidi deliver a marvelously detailed lecture about the Vienna Circle and the main figures of the early Positivist movement. He is so captivated by Heidi's stories, in fact, that he immediately resolves to tell them to his roommate Reinhold (who, like Helmut, had never heard of Schlick or Neurath or any of these matters before). On the picture suggested by Kripke's remarks, at some point in this scenario, "when he learns to use the name" 'Moritz Schlick' and in order later successfully to communicate the name to Reinhold, Helmut must entertain a certain reference-preserving intention. But at what point? *When* is Helmut supposed to form the relevant semantic intention, and what specifically is it supposed to look like?

Taken at face value, "intentions to refer" are *metalinguistic* intentions. It seems reasonable to conclude, for instance, that only a hearer who was in command of the concept of reference *per se* could form an intention (henceforth) to refer by a newly encountered name to that item to which a speaker was referring by *her*

76   Chapter 3

use of that name. While listening to Heidi's lecture, for example, Helmut might explicitly (perhaps even consciously) form an intention that he could publicly express by saying something like:

> [I1] I shall henceforth use the name 'Moritz Schlick' to refer to the person to whom *she* (Heidi) has been referring during this lecture whenever *she* has used the name 'Moritz Schlick'.

Not only would this be a very peculiar thing for Helmut to do; it is also difficult to see what the *point* of his doing so might be.

If, analogously to Kripke's deciding that the newly encountered name 'Napoleon' would be a nice name for his pet aardvark, Helmut had instead been utterly uninterested in what Heidi had to say *about* Schlick, but sufficiently charmed by the sound of 'Moritz Schlick' to decide that it would be a nice name for *his* pet aardvark,[14] then we can perhaps usefully imagine Helmut's explicitly forming a special ("baptismal") intention to *that* effect:

> [I2] I shall henceforth use the name 'Moritz Schlick' to refer to my pet aardvark.

It is easier to see that there might here be work for a special referential intention to do, since Heidi had obviously not been referring to any aardvark at all, much less to Helmut's own pet. What is not at all clear, however, is that Helmut's proceeding to use the name 'Moritz Schlick' with the *same* reference as Heidi requires anything like a similar special metalinguistic intention.

On the contrary, if Helmut just sticks to the substance of Heidi's narrative, it seems that he will *automatically*, so to speak, be referring to Moritz Schlick when telling Reinhold Heidi's stories, quite independently of any special intent or resolve (tacit or explicit) on his part. In these proceedings, the notion of Helmut's "intentions to refer" seems to be completely idle. Indeed, Helmut's reference to Schlick in this case appears to be robust enough to survive some rather radical misunderstandings on his part. It seems intuitively plausible, for example, that the stories he tells Reinhold are stories about the historical figures Moritz Schlick and Otto Neurath—even if Helmut himself mistakenly believes that Heidi's narrative was entirely fictional.[15]

What separates this case from our earlier first Donnellan scenario, where the notion of intentions to refer originally found an apparently useful point of purchase, is that there is no issue here of *two descriptions,* one which does and one which does not fit a specific object. The epistemic role imputed to intentions to refer is, in the first instance, to explain *disparities* between a speaker's reference and the semantic reference of the referring expression that the speaker employs. In the case of a pure Donnellan scenario, the disparities in question are differences of descriptive content, differences between what is *said to be* true of a specific object and what *is* true of that object. If Helmut's retelling remains true to the content of Heidi's narrative, however, there is no analogous disparity to explain. In particular, there can be no question here of Helmut's using the name 'Moritz Schlick' with a different *descriptive sense* from that with which Heidi used it, for, on the view we are presently examining, proper names do not have such descriptive senses to begin with.

Suppose, nevertheless, that Helmut *does* explicitly, even consciously, form some such intention as [I1]. Then it should also make sense to suppose that, later (e.g., shortly after telling Heidi's stories to his roommate Reinhold), Helmut recalls this earlier intention and *legitimately* proceeds to worry about whether or not he had successfully carried it out. *Had* he, while telling Reinhold the stories, in fact (always) used the name 'Moritz Schlick' to refer to the person to whom Heidi had been referring when *she* used that name (while delivering the lecture)? He had certainly *intended* to do so—but had he *succeeded* in doing so? Perhaps, quite inadvertently, he had once or twice referred to someone else, to someone other than the person to whom Heidi had been referring. (And, if so, then to what or whom will poor *Reinhold* be referring when later—even with only all the best Kripkean referential intentions—he tells Heidi's stories to someone else ?)

Obviously such worries are silly. Assuming that he successfully reproduces Heidi's narrative, Helmut runs no risk of *inadvertently* referring to someone other than the persons to whom Heidi referred. Determinate referential intentions exemplified by the general form of [I1], whether tacit or explicit, I conclude, would not be necessary for successful proper name reference transmission over a communicative link.

Neither, however, would such referential intentions be *sufficient* to ensure that proper name reference is preserved over such a communicative transaction. Alter the example so: Helmut is so concerned to do justice to Heidi's splendid lecture that he consciously and explicitly frames a whole family of Kripkean communicative intentions—not only separate individual referential intentions on the model of [I1] for *each* of the proper names used by Heidi, but also a *general* intention to faithfully recount Heidi's stories to Reinhold. Otherwise, everything remains as it was—except that we shall now further suppose that Helmut has an exceedingly poor memory. In consequence, when he finally comes to recount Heidi's stories to Reinhold, we find Helmut saying things like "Moritz Schlick compared our epistemic situation to that of sailors who must continuously rebuild their ship while at sea" and "Otto Neurath was shot by an enraged student on the steps of the university library". Quite consistently and systematically, in fact, Helmut attributes to someone he *calls* 'Moritz Schlick' the views, accomplishments, and experiences of Otto Neurath, and he attributes to someone he calls 'Otto Neurath' the views, accomplishments, and experiences of Moritz Schlick.

Here, it seems clear enough, Helmut has in fact *confused* Schlick and Neurath. But what does this mean? I want to suggest that there are two distinct things that it might mean. On the one hand, it might mean that Helmut has acquired a large number of *false beliefs* about both Schlick and Neurath. On this view, speaker's reference and semantic reference coincide. When Helmut uses the name 'Moritz Schlick', he is referring to Moritz Schlick; when he uses the name 'Otto Neurath', to Otto Neurath. Helmut's sincere endorsement of the sentence "Moritz Schlick compared our epistemic situation to that of sailors who must continuously rebuild their ship while at sea", then, will be compelling evidence that Helmut believes *of Moritz Schlick* that *he* compared our epistemic situation to that of such sailors. Since this is true not of Schlick but of Otto Neurath, Helmut's belief will be false—and thus analogously for almost all the beliefs Helmut undertakes to express by using sentences containing the names 'Moritz Schlick' and 'Otto Neurath'.

On the other hand, however, that Helmut has confused Schlick and Neurath might mean that the *speaker's* references of (Helmut's usings of) the names 'Moritz Schlick' and 'Otto Neurath' here *diverge* from the *semantic* references of those names. In particular, one might conclude from the *systematic* character of his confusion that when Helmut uses the name 'Moritz Schlick', *he* is referring to Otto Neurath; when he uses the name 'Otto Neurath', to Moritz Schlick. Correlatively, on this view, Helmut's utterances containing the name 'Moritz Schlick' would not express false beliefs about Moritz Schlick but rather true beliefs about Otto Neurath. To be sure, Helmut explicitly *intended* to use the names 'Moritz Schlick' and 'Otto Neurath' to refer to the persons to whom Heidi referred when *she* used those names during her lecture. But, if and when they do exist, such semantic intentions are not "self-fulfilling". In this instance in particular, on the present view, owing to his poor memory, Helmut has failed to carry out his referential intentions.

I want modestly to suggest that we here confront a case in which our "pre-theoretical intuitions" regarding speaker's reference—i.e., regarding who it is that Helmut is *talking about*—might be thought to yield no single, determinate verdict.[16] On the first view, when he uses the name 'Moritz Schlick', Helmut is talking about Moritz Schlick, but is confused about what he thought and did. On the second view, when he uses the name 'Moritz Schlick', Helmut is talking about Otto Neurath, but is confused about *his name*. *Both* views are plainly possible and both, I submit, are at least *equally* "intuitive".

But if the second of these views could be coherently accepted, it follows that, just as they proved not to be necessary, determinate referential intentions of the general form of [I1] would also not be sufficient for the successful transmission of a proper name reference over a communicative link. On the second view, what determines our intuitive verdicts regarding Helmut's references is not the names he uses but rather what Helmut says to Reinhold *about* the persons he calls 'Schlick' and 'Neurath'—i.e., the descriptive statements containing the names 'Moritz Schlick' and 'Otto Neurath' which Helmut actually endorses. Kripke's causal-historical picture has no room for such a connection between the descriptive *contents* of the statements a speaker makes and the referents of the proper names that the speaker thereby uses.

I conclude, then, that Kripke's occasional gestures in the direction of "intentions to refer" do nothing to address the sort of circularity that threatens his own causal-historical "better picture". As yet, that is, we have *no* reason to believe that the notions of a reference-fixing (baptismal) event and a reference-preserving communicative transaction central to that picture can be explained or elucidated in ways that do not themselves ineliminably involve the notion of reference.

Such cases as Helmut's will arguably pose a central problem for any elaboration of the basic causal-historical picture. Devitt, for example, develops a version of the causal theory which proposes to explain designational reference (roughly Donnellan's "referential use", but generalized to include proper names as well as descriptions) in terms of what he calls "d-chains": "There are three different types of link in a d-chain: groundings, which link

Referential Alternatives 81

the chain to an object; abilities to designate [which may be exercise by individual speakers]; communication situations in which abilities are passed on or reinforced (reference borrowings)" (D, 129). "Grounding" events—Devitt's theoretical extension and elaboration of Kripke's "initial baptisms"—include a person's *perception* of an object which thereby becomes a (possible) designatum (for him). Although sooner or later we will also need to examine the role of such perceptual encounters, our present concern is with Devitt's "reference borrowings". Consonant with a wish to avoid circularities, he takes one aim of a theory of designation to be "to distinguish (in nonsemantic terms) the semantically significant d-chains from other causal connections between singular terms and the world" (D, 129). Cases like Helmut's pose a special problem for such a theory, I suggest, because their divergence from paradigmatically normal cases of speaker-hearer communication lies entirely in what happens *subseqent to* the communicative event *per se*, i.e., despite the fact that *all the normal non-semantic causal processes and connections up to and including that event are in place.*

Devitt's own account of reference borrowing, in fact, appears to entail just this consequence.

> In reference borrowing *the act of perceiving a designation of the object by the term* plays the role for the borrower that the earlier act of perceiving the object played for a person present at a grounding: it grounds the term in the object.... A person hears the expression of a thought containing what is in fact a designational term. He comes to have thoughts as a result, thoughts including representations based on the designational term he heard.... Since the speaker's term was in fact a designational term, it had underlying it a representation grounded in an object. The reference-borrower, by coming to have these thoughts on the strength of this utterance, gains the benefit of that grounding. He gains an ability to designate that object.... He has mental representations which are of the object in virtue

of being causally linked via his act of borrowing to the object. (D, 137)

In the present case, Heidi is the speaker; Helmut is her audience; and all the conditions for a successful reference borrowing appear to be fulfilled. *Ex hypothesi* there is nothing problematic about Heidi's linguistic performances. She produces utterances including designations of Moritz Schlick by 'Moritz Schlick' and designations of Otto Neurath by 'Otto Neurath', and we may also suppose that Helmut perceives them, for there is nothing amiss with Helmut's *perceptual* abilities. Nor would it be incorrect to say that, as a result of hearing Heidi's lecture, Helmut gains the ability to talk (and think) about Moritz Schlick and Otto Neurath. On *any* view of the matter, that is, the *stories* Helmut proceeds to tell Reinhold are stories about Schlick and Neurath, and, in telling them, Helmut presumably gives expression to his *thoughts* about Schlick and Neurath. The problem, however, is that none of this yields a verdict about the *specific* references of the terms 'Moritz Schlick' and 'Otto Neurath' in Helmut's individual utterances or, for that matter, of the various individual "inner" representational counterparts of those terms in the thoughts we may suppose those utterances express. None of this tells us *which* of Helmut's thoughts and utterances are about Schlick and which are about Neurath—for *all* of those thoughts and utterances are hooked up through Helmut's perceptions of Heidi's performances *both* with d-chains grounded in Schlick *and* with d-chains grounded in Neurath.

Although Devitt discusses a variety of mistakes and confusions, none of them has all the features of this example. The closest he comes is a case in which someone—let me, for convenience, call him 'Cato'—who already believes (correctly) that 'Nana' is the name of Devitt's cat, and so possesses an ability to designate Nana, comes to utter the sentence "Nana is black" by virtue of perceiving *another* (black) cat, Jemima, who is, however, *introduced* to him *as* Nana, i.e., with the accompanying demonstrative utterance "This is Nana". Nana herself, we are to suppose, is not black. As a result of this introduction, Cato is led to identify the black cat that he sees as Nana, i.e., to form a perceptual judgment having the content: *that cat is Nana*.

> Any thought associated with 'Nana' resulting from this identification will contain a token grounded in the object designated by 'that cat', that is, in Jemima. So the thoughts expressed by ["Nana is a cat" and "Nana is black"], hence, those statements themselves, contain tokens grounded in Jemima. However, since the tokens of 'Nana' in [those statements] result partly from the person's earlier ability, they are also grounded in Nana. (D, 143–144)

Devitt's own strategy for dealing with this and similar examples is to introduce[17] a notion of *partial* designation and, correlatively, a notion of *partial truth*. On his view, in other words, when Cato utters the sentences "Nana is a cat" and "Nana is black", the tokens of 'Nana' in those utterances "partially designate both cats". Since both Nana and Jemima are cats, the first utterance is true, but the second is "only partially true" (D, 144). And since Cato may proceed to pass on his confusions to others, as it were, in attenuated form (and for further similar reasons), Devitt in fact concludes that he will need to "refine the notions of partial designation and partial truth into notions of *degrees of designation* and *degrees of truth*" (D, 147).

Devitt makes a valiant effort to cloak these strategies with a mantle of plausibility, but to my ear they have the hollow ring of a counsel of despair. He suggests that "our basic intuitions", "the reflections of folk semanticists" include only

> one strong one: the "total performance" involves elements of truth and falsity. I capture this: in its speaker meaning ["Nana is black"] is partially true and partially false; in its conventional one it is false. (D, 145)

On the contrary I would argue that, more strongly than they do any specific claims about the "total performance" in this or that complex case of mistake or confusion, "the reflections of folk semanticists" plainly support the fundamental intuition that what someone has said on a given occasion will be either true or false or perhaps neither true nor false, but in *no* sense will it be *both true and false*. Nor should we suppose that "folk semantics" will supply a determinate verdict for every conceivable thought-experiment. Sometimes we just don't know *what* to say.[18] But sometimes the most "strongly intuitive" answers to questions about the reference of 'Nana' in an utterance of "Nana is black" and, correlatively, about the truth-value of what is said, will depend on the *details* of the circumstances in which the utterance occurs.

If, for instance, Jemima is still on the perceptual scene, Cato is most likely to be talking about *her*. This will be the case, for instance, whenever he is disposed to answer the question "What cat are you talking about?" with some form of the demonstrative "That cat over there." Since Jemima *is* black, what is said on such an occasion will be true. If, on the other hand, some time has elapsed since the misleading introduction of Jemima as Nana and Jemima herself is no longer perceptually available, the most plausible interpretation of Cato's utterance is likely to be quite different. Since he mistakenly believes that the cat to whom he was recently introduced was Devitt's cat Nana, and since the cat to whom he was introduced was in fact black, Cato now mistakenly believes *Nana* to be black. His utterance "Nana is black" expresses precisely this false belief *about Nana*—as his answer "Why, Michael Devitt's cat Nana, of course" to the question "What cat are you talking about?" confirms.[19]

The case of Helmut, however, brackets such potential complications. Helmut comes to his abilities to think and talk about both Moritz Schlick and Otto Neurath in exactly the same way and, indeed, at the same time, by hearing Heidi's lectures. There is no question of "contamination" of a pre-existing referential ability by later misleading events, and no question of alternative referents being supplied by concurrent perceptions. If we take our cue from Devitt, it would appear that the best a causal-historical account can do with Helmut's later utterances "Moritz Schlick compared our epistemic situation to that of sailors who must continuously rebuild their ship while at sea" and "Otto Neurath was shot by an enraged student on the steps of the university library" would be to say something like: *each* name, 'Moritz Schlick' and 'Otto Neurath' partially designates Schlick and partially designates Neurath, and everything that Helmut says to Reinhold is consequently partially true and partially false. While this may not strictly speaking be a *reductio* of causal theories, I submit that it is at least peculiar enough to motivate us to seek a different alternative to Descriptivism.

In fact, what such cases show us, I think, is that, although Kripke's examples are intuitively telling against the Descriptivist theory (at least as he has formulated it), there nevertheless appears to be something right about what we might call, following Kripke's practice, the Descriptivist *picture*. For it turned out that precisely the *descriptive contents* of the statements expressed by those sentences containing the names 'Moritz Schlick' and 'Otto Neurath' which Helmut actually endorsed *could* make a difference to our intuitive verdicts regarding Helmut's proper name references.

Although there is perhaps *something* right about each story, in short, what I conclude that *neither* classical Descriptivism, as Kripke has formulated it, *nor* his own alternative causal-historical picture, neither as he has presented it nor as it has been theoretically elaborated by Devitt, provides an account of proper name reference that satisfactorily accords with all of our commonsense convictions, our "pre-theoretical intuitions". What we evidently need is yet another account of proper name reference, one that does justice to the strengths and insights of both the Descriptivist and the causal-historical pictures while avoiding the failings and excesses of each. In the next chapter, consequently, I turn to the project of beginning to develop such a *tertium quid*.

4
Theoretical Desiderata for Nominal Reference

THE MAIN business of this chapter will be to collect a set of general constraints on any acceptable account of proper names, that is, some criteria of adequacy for a philosophical theory of nominal reference. Several of these desiderata emerge directly from our discussions up to this point; others will come to light as we proceed.

We can begin with Kripke's own non-circularity condition (C). For our purposes, we will want to reformulate it in more general terms:

> (CA1) An adequate explication of the reference of a proper name must not itself ineliminably employ or presuppose the notion of reference.

Both Descriptivism and Kripke's own causal-historical picture *proposed* to satisfy this condition. Descriptivism offered an account of proper name reference in terms of the notion of an object's (uniquely) satisfying a description, and Kripke suggested an account in terms of causal relations and communicative transactions between persons. In each case, however, we have found reasons to call into question whether the respective account could be *completed* without lapsing into a vitiating circularity of just the sort that (CA1) is intended to rule out.

Second, Kripke has stressed the point that truth-values are not preserved across substitution of *de facto* co-referential expressions

Theoretical Desiderata 87

in all subjunctive or counterfactual contexts. For example, since Socrates and Socrates alone was Plato's chief philosophical mentor, the proper name 'Socrates' and the uniquely individuating description 'Plato's chief philosophical mentor' (henceforth abbreviated as 'Plato's mentor') are *de facto* co-referential expressions. But whereas, for example, the (counterfactual) subjunctive conditional

> If Socrates had been hook-nosed, then Plato's mentor would have been hook-nosed

is intuitively true, the subjunctive conditional

> If Socrates had been born two years after Plato's death, then Plato's mentor would have been born two years after Plato's death

is not only false but indeed necessarily so, since it is true that

> If Socrates had been born two years after Plato's death, Socrates could not have been Plato's mentor.

The significance of these observations for our present purposes is that they imply that it is at best a contingent truth that the referent of a given proper name satisfies any particular contentive description. It follows that indefinitely many of the descriptive beliefs that any particular speaker *de facto* associates with a given proper name might prove to be false, a conclusion evidently confirmed by Kripke's observation that one can sensibly entertain the hypothesis that, for example, Moses actually did none of what is attributed to him in the Scriptures. One can, in short, refer with a proper name to an individual even if most of one's *explicit* beliefs about that individual are false,[1] and an adequate theory of proper name reference, in turn, must acknowledge this possibility:

> (CA2) An adequate explication of the reference of proper names must allow for the possibility that a speaker can

use a proper name to refer to an individual (item) while entertaining arbitrarily many false beliefs regarding that individual (item).

Kripke's own causal-historical account was explicitly intended, *inter alia*, to satisfy this condition, whereas Descriptivism, as Kripke formulated it, demonstrably did not.

Kripke's causal-historical picture was also explicitly intended to satisfy a further condition, which we might call "the possibility of descriptive ignorance". The point here, epitomized by Kripke's 'Cicero' and 'Feynman' examples, is that one can successfully refer with a proper name to an individual (item) while knowing, or even believing, very little indeed *about* that individual (item).[2] One can evidently refer with the name 'Cicero' to the Roman orator Cicero while knowing about Cicero only that he was a Roman orator, and one can refer with the name 'Feynman' to the eminent physicist Richard Feynman while believing of Feynman only that he was some sort of scientist.[3] We may conclude, in other words, that

(CA3) An adequate explication of the reference of proper names must allow for the possibility that a speaker can use a proper name to refer to an individual (item) while being largely ignorant regarding the contentive descriptions in fact satisfied by that individual (item).

Again, the causal-historical account was designed to satisfy (CA3), whereas Descriptivism, in Kripke's formulation, was in essence based precisely on its rejection.

At this point, however, we part company with Kripke's exposition. Our exploration of the example of Helmut, Heidi, and the early Logical Positivists uncovered a datum that the causal-historical picture inevitably leaves relatively mysterious: one person's conversational proper name references appear to be preserved over descriptively equivalent retellings by a second person to a third, independently of the intermediary speaker's semantic intentions. Even more significantly, when, in such a communicative transmission, proper names and descriptive contents so to speak "come apart", speaker's reference *can* track with the content rather than with the name. (This is the modest moral of the example of Helmut's confusion regarding Schlick and Neurath.) A satisfactory theory of proper names should account for these phenomena as well. That is,

> (CA4) An adequate explication of the reference of proper names should explain how a speaker's reference in the case of content-preserving communicative transactions can track with the descriptive content of the statements actually made rather than with the proper names actually used.

The Descriptivist *picture* is obviously better suited to satisfy (CA4) than is any purely causal-historical story.

Finally, we need to confront a question that has so far hovered implicitly in the background of our discussions. One way of bringing it into the foreground is by recalling Kripke's remark that "[t]here may be a causal chain from our use of the term 'Santa Claus' to a certain historical saint, but still the children, when they use this, by this time probably do not refer to that saint" (93). What we need to ask, of course, is whether such children, supposing that they do not refer to a historical saint, nevertheless refer to *someone*, and, if they do, then to whom. Kripke himself remains essentially noncommittal on the question, but it seems contrary to the spirit of his causal-historical picture to suppose that one could refer to a fictional character.[4]

This, however, would seem to be an excellent occasion to turn for guidance to our pre-theoretical linguistic intuitions, and, at least when I consult *my* intuitions, what I discover is the unqualified conviction that one can *of course* refer to fictional characters, and that we in fact do so all the time. We use the proper name 'Santa Claus' to refer to Santa Claus, 'Sherlock Holmes' to refer to Sherlock Holmes, 'Katarina Blum' to refer to Katarina Blum,[5] and so on.

More precisely, what I discover is that one can of course *talk about* fictional characters, and that we in fact do so all the time. When the chips are down, however, I don't believe that we actually have any commonsense convictions or pre-theoretical intuitions about *reference*. In these discussions, 'reference' is a term of art, a term of philosophical semantics that arrives trailing a colorful dialectical history and carrying a heavy load of connotations. We do, however, have commonsense convictions regarding what or whom someone is, on this or that occasion, *talking about*, and it is in fact these untutored opinions that we transpose into the philosophical semantic idiom of 'reference' when we debate such matters.[6]

The intuitive datum I have most recently been canvassing, then, suggests that we should also adopt

(CA5) An adequate explication of the reference of proper names should be consistent with the possibility of proper name reference to fictional, mythical, legendary, and other non-existent entities.

We will shortly need to spend some time exploring the very notion of reference to fictional characters, but it is worth noting first that there is another way, *independent* of our convictions about (CA5), in which considerations regarding fictional, mythical, and legendary discourses puts pressure on the causal-historical picture of reference.

Consider, for example, Robin Hood.[7] According to the well-known accounts, at some time during the twelfth century, there lived in Sherwood Forest, in Nottinghamshire, England, an outlaw named Robin Hood, who, together with a small band of followers, robbed from the rich and powerful, including both crown and clergy, and shared the spoils with the poor and needy.

His exploits are memorialized in early ballads, many of which were collected as *A lytell geste of Robin Hode*,[8] and he receives an explicit mention in *Piers Plowman*. Later elaborations of the story describe him as a dispossessed nobleman—perhaps the Earl of Huntingdon[9]—and date his activities to the reign of Richard the Lion-Hearted (1189–1199) or, even more narrowly, to the regency of his brother, John, while Richard was absent on the Crusades. Robin Hood subsequently appears in a vast number of literary works, including Sir Walter Scott's *Ivanhoe* (where he is the Earl of Locksley), Alexandre Dumas' *Robin Hood, Prince of Outlaws*, and Alfred Lord Tennyson's *The Foresters, Robin Hood and Maid Marian*, and he is the title character of at least two memorable films, one starring Erroll Flynn and another starring Kevin Costner.

The current state of *historical* scholarship is perhaps best summed up in the title of a recent popular article: "The real Robin Hood was a medieval Englishman named Robert Hood. Or Robyn Hode. Or Robert Fitzooth, Earl of Huntingdon. Or maybe there was no real Robin Hood, after all".[10] But let us in fact suppose, in good Kripkean fashion, that there indeed lived in twelfth-century England an overweight, sedentary, law-abiding peasant, actually named Ruben Houde, whose conspicuous timidity and particularly wretched skills at archery inspired his drinking companions at the local pub to cast him as the subject of an increasingly elaborate series of satirical tales of derring-do which, in the course of time, evolved into the Robin Hood stories, old and new, that we know today. Ruben Houde, in short, was the actual, historical person about whom what became the legend of Robin Hood *originally* took form. Were this (presumed) fact to come to his attention, the author of the popular article mentioned above would doubtless report it by writing "The real Robin Hood was a medieval Englishman named Ruben Houde".

The example is analogous to the case of Jonah mentioned by Kripke (67–68) and elaborated upon by Devitt. Devitt formulates it so:

> It is unlikely that the biblical story of Jonah *as a whole* is true of any actual man or even that *substantial parts of it* ... are true of anyone. Does it then follow that 'Jonah' is an empty name? It does not, *because Jonah may have been a real person about whom a legend has grown.* Imagine we discover that the facts were as follows: There was an ordinary man called 'Jonah' who lived out his life in an ordinary way. The only unusual thing about him was that he was regarded in a superstitious way by his associates; they tended to tell peculiar stories about him. After his death these stories blossomed into what we now know as the story of Jonah; *all* the truths about this man, except the trivial ones ... were quickly forgotten. ...
>
> In the situation imagined, our uses of 'Jonah' designate the man described: earlier predications using the name, such as those in the Bible, are mostly false because that man lacks the required properties; on the other hand, present predications, reflecting this discovery, are true because the man has the required properties. (D, 18–19)

Given his remarks in this last paragraph, we may fairly suppose that, in our Robin Hood example, Devitt would analogously conclude that, in the situation I have imagined,

(1) our uses of 'Robin Hood' designate Ruben Houde;

(2) earlier predications using the name 'Robin Hood' were mostly false, because Ruben Houde lacked the required properties; and

(3) present predications using the name 'Robin Hood' reflecting the historical discovery are true because Ruben Houde had the required properties.

In contrast, I want to suggest that, although (3), on its most natural reading, is probably trivially true, (2) is plainly false, and (1), in consequence, turns out to be crucially ambiguous.

The reading of (3) on which it likely says something trivially true is one which stresses the restrictive phrase "reflecting the historical discovery". A predication using the name 'Robin Hood' will *fail* to "reflect the [presumed] historical discovery", I suggest, just in case what it predicates of Robin Hood was *not* actually true of Ruben Houde. An author who begins by writing "The real Robin Hood was a medieval Englishman named Ruben Houde" and proceeds to report that, consequently, *Robin Hood* was overweight, sedentary, law-abiding, timid, and an inferior archer is pretty clearly using the name 'Robin Hood' to talk about Ruben Houde. But it certainly does not follow from this that *everyone else* who ever used the name 'Robin Hood' was *also* talking about Ruben Houde—and that is precisely what (2), falsely, presupposes.

In particular, I would argue that Sir Walter Scott was not talking about Ruben Houde, and neither was Alexandre Dumas, nor Alfred Lord Tennyson, nor Erroll Flynn, nor Kevin Costner, and neither was *I*, when I earlier wrote that Robin Hood appears in a vast number of literary works and is the title character of several films. One way to come to appreciate this is to reflect on the results of substituting 'Ruben Houde' for 'Robin Hood' in the relevant contexts, for, to the best of my knowledge, Ruben Houde appears in neither literary works nor films. Another is once again to recall the truism that "one person's modus ponens is another's modus tollens". The Robin Hood that Scott, Dumas, Tennyson, Flynn, Costner, and I were talking about (thinking about, writing about) was both an outlaw and an outstanding archer, lived in Sherwood Forest with a band of Merry Men, harrassed the Sheriff of Nottingham, was enamored of the fair Maid Marian, and so on. Since, *ex hypothesi, none* of these things were true of Ruben Houde, what I conclude is that the Robin Hood whom *we* were talking about was *not* Ruben Houde. Ruben Houde may have been "the *historical* Robin Hood" or even "the *real* Robin Hood", but we were talking about the *legendary* Robin Hood, the one who split his opponent's arrow in the center of a distant target to win the golden prize. That is, each of us was engaging in a *different sort of discourse*, one to which the presumed historical findings are simply irrelevant.

What makes (2) false, in other words, is the same fact that makes (1) ambiguous: somewhere along the line, the Robin Hood stories took on a life of their own. That is, somewhere between the twelfth century and the present, 'Robin Hood' *became* the name of a legendary character (what Devitt would call an "empty name"). Today, subsequent to our (presumed) historical discoveries, 'Robin Hood' is an *ambiguous* proper name. We can still use it to talk about the legendary outlaw—and that, I think, is what we would still normally do. But we *can*, given the quite *special* discursive context of historical research, also adopt the usage of our hypothetical popularizer, saying such things as "Robin Hood was (actually, really) overweight, sedentary, law-abiding, timid, and an inferior archer", and then we will indeed be talking about Ruben Houde.

The tacit step in Devitt's reasoning to which I take exception, in other words, moves from a premiss of the form

(O) Stories using a name, N, were *originally* told about a particular historical figure, P

to a conclusion to the effect that

(S) *All* subsequent uses of the name N refer to P.

What I have been suggesting instead is that something might happen to the name along the way.[11] Surprisingly, Devitt acknowledges this possibility in passing—it is essentially Kripke's 'Santa Claus' case—but he is not appropriately sensitive to its implications regarding the *critical* intuitions that he, following Kripke, initially brought to bear on traditional Descriptivism. Here is Devitt, late in the game, remarking on Kripke's example from the standpoint of his own elaborated version of the causal-historical theory:

> Kripke suggests that it may be the case that our present use of 'Santa Claus' is causally linked to a certain historical saint. Even if this were so, it seems unlikely that 'Santa Claus' would designate that saint; it is unlikely that the causal network underlying the name would be grounded in the saint in the required way. Objects can be involved in the causal explanation of a name in various ways without being the object the name designates. (D, 177)

The notion of being grounded "in the required way" is, of course, utterly crucial here, but the present point is *prior* to such internal matters of theoretical detail. The present point is that the hypothetical case of Jonah bears critically against (all versions of) Descriptivism only if it is tacitly supposed that the name has *not*, so to speak, become "uncoupled" from its historical origins in the way that Kripke speculates 'Santa Claus' has and that I have just suggested 'Robin Hood' has as well. According to Devitt,

> A description theory must conclude that the imagined discovery shows that 'Jonah', in its earlier uses at least, is an empty name: none of the earlier predications, even the trivial ones we still think true, can be true. We have not replaced a false theory about a certain man, Jonah, with a true theory about him; until the "discovery" we had no theory *about him* at all. Note that it was *not possible,* according to description theory, for an earlier scholar to speculate, or to find evidence, that Jonah was a certain ordinary man that he, the scholar, has tracked down; that Jonah was the subject of superstitious stories; and so forth. Such speculations and evidence cannot be *about Jonah* because they deny the descriptions on which our use of the name depends. This is not a plausible claim. (D, 19)

But nothing prevents a description theorist from distinguishing the *biblical character* Jonah, who was swallowed by a great fish while traveling to preach in Nineveh, from a hypothetical historical figure about whom such fanciful stories were initially told, that is, from speculating that 'Jonah' might be or might have become an ambiguous name. Thus, prior to any discoveries, a scholar might speculate that *there was* a historical figure, perhaps (also) named 'Jonah' but otherwise quite unlike (the biblical) Jonah, about whom the relevant stories originally took shape, and subsequent to the envisioned discoveries, it becomes appropriate to speak, not just of "Jonah", but more precisely of "the historical Jonah" and "the biblical Jonah".

Although the observations I have just been making require that we distinguish among historical, fictional, legendary, and mythical *discourses*, they are so far noncommittal about fictional *reference*. That certain tokens of the name 'Robin Hood' or 'Jonah' are not being used to talk about a historical figure (e.g., Ruben Houde, the historical Jonah) does not by itself imply that they are being used to talk about someone or something else (e.g., the legendary Robin Hood, the biblical Jonah). Just that, however, is what (CA5) in essence proposes. Less paradoxically phrased, (CA5) expresses the proposition that a philosophical account of the semantic or referential functioning of proper names should be *univocal,* independent of the discursive context—whether matter-of-factual or fictional—within which those names occur. That is, (CA5) proposes that the difference *between* these modes of discourse not be treated as a *semantic* difference. This is plainly a substantial constraint, and it will consequently repay us to spend some time getting clear about its resonances and implications, and about our alternatives.

We might observe, to begin with, that, although (CA5) appears to be contrary to the spirit of Kripke's causal-historical picture, there is no special reason for an advocate of Descriptivism to balk at it. Proper names of fictional characters, legendary figures, mythical animals, and so on match up with descriptions (or families of descriptions) no worse and no better than do proper names of "actual characters, living or dead".

There is no *prima facie* compelling reason to deny, for example, that the description

> (DSC) the jolly, chubby, white-bearded, red-suited elf who lives at the North Pole and each year on Christmas Eve travels around the world in a sleigh pulled by flying reindeer to deliver toys to deserving children

is uniquely satisfied by Santa Claus in the same sense that the description

> (DKG) the person who first proved the incompleteness of any formal system adequate for elementary arithmetic

is uniquely satisfied by Kurt Gödel, or, to suggest another example that must inevitably prove awkward for a causal-historical account, that the description

> (DNT) the successor of the smallest positive integer which yields its square when added to itself

is uniquely satisfied by the number three.[12] Each of these descriptions is uniquely satisfied by the correlative item precisely in the sense that the description in question is *true of* the item in question, and true *only* of that item. That is,

> (TSC) Santa Claus (and only he) is a jolly, chubby, white-bearded, red-suited elf who lives at the North Pole and each year on Christmas Eve travels around the world in a sleigh pulled by flying reindeer to deliver toys to deserving children,

> (TKG) Kurt Gödel (and only he) first proved the incompleteness of any formal system adequate for elementary arithmetic, and

> (TNT) The successor of the smallest positive integer which yields its square when added to itself equals three

are all *true*.[13]

If the idea that "intuitions" embody the ultimate epistemological touchstone for philosophical stories about logic and language has any merit, then it is surely with such naive, pretheoretical convictions about *truth* that philosophical stories about reference and meaning will properly begin. Devitt initially appears to endorse this standpoint. He speaks of our intuitions regarding "what we would say" using this or that bit of semantic terminology as reflecting a "folk" theory, and argues that we cannot "uncritically rely" on our untutored answers to questions about reference and designation as such,

> for they will be laden with undeveloped folk semantics. However, in the absence of a semantic theory which is both radically inconsistent with folk theory and a better explanation of linguistic phenomena than folk theory, we have nothing else to test our theories against but our ordinary intuitions embodied in folk theory. . . . [We] can rely most confidently on our intuitions about the circumstances in which a statement would be *true*. For truth plays an important extrasemantic role in our lives. (D, 89)

Devitt, however, understands philosophy's task to be "not to study folk theory but to develop it into a *scientific* theory" (D, 88; my emphasis), and, correlatively, the picture of truth that he proceeds to sketch turns out to be a picture of *scientific* (matter-of-factual, empirical) truth:

> We have a great practical interest in establishing which of our neighbor's words are true. Why? Briefly, because true theories correspond to reality, a reality we are all interested in understanding. . . . We are bent on the good life in a hostile world, and the more we understand of that world the better our chances of achieving it. By locating the true statements we place ourselves in the best position to explain the past, manipulate the present, and predict the future. So the test for a semantic theory of (definite) singular terms is this: which object *would* we say, or *should* we say, taking account of the role of truth, makes a statement containing such a term true or false? (D, 89)

I have already flagged the issue of whether philosophical accounts of aspects of logic and language should pretend to, or even aspire to, the status of scientific theories as one of the leading questions of the present study, and, in due time, it will indeed occupy the center of our field of vision. At this point, however, what needs to be remarked is that, to the extent that I understand the notion of an object's "making a statement true" at all, what I would "intuitively" say is that, if Kurt Gödel is the object that makes (TKG) true, then Santa Claus and the number three are the objects that, respectively, make (TSC) and (TNT) true. One can, that is, accept Devitt's claim that true (empirical, scientific) *theories* "correspond to reality", while simultaneously rejecting the tacit assumption that the concept of truth *per se*—in particular, in its application to individual statements—is properly or even usefully explained or analyzed in terms of "correspondence". The dialectic centered about such notions is as complex as it is familiar, and this is not the occasion to review it.[14] The immediate point is simply that, correlative to the desideratum to which (CA5) gives expression—namely, that a philosophical account of the semantic or referential functioning of proper names should be univocal—will be a commitment to the idea that a philosophical account of *truth* should be univocal in the same way. The two desiderata stand or fall together. If there is a question about the acceptability of (CA5), in consequence, it is not settled—positively *or* negatively—simply by an appeal to the notion of truth.

Devitt's own account of the names of fictional characters—"fictitious names"—posits two "implicit operators":

> [Statements] *in* fiction are implicitly preceded by a storytelling operator, roughly paraphrasable by "let us pretend that." When we talk *about* fiction we are making reference to this pretence, to this imaginative act. So . . . a statement about fiction is (usually) implicitly preceded by a fiction operator roughly paraphrasable by "it is pretended that" or "in fiction". Let us use 'S' for

the storytelling operator and 'F' for the fiction operator. (D, 172)

On this view, the single sentence

(1) Tom Jones is illegitimate

can be used to make claims having at least three distinct "logical forms". If Fielding's novel itself includes the sentence (1), then

[that] token of (1) is paraphrasable by

(2) S (Tom Jones is illegitimate)

and is neither true nor false (because it is not a statement). On the other hand, suppose I assert (1), then my token is paraphrasable by

(3) F (Tom Jones is illegitimate)

and is true. (D, 172)

More precisely, I would suppose, my token of (1) will be paraphrasable by (3) just in case, when I assert (1), I am talking about Tom Jones, *the (fictional) character in Fielding's novel*. If, on the other hand, I am talking about Tom Jones, the popular contemporary Welsh entertainer, when I assert (1), my token will presumably wear its logical form on its face and (to the best of my knowledge) be used to say something false.

Now the idea that a sentence can have a "logical form" or a "deep structure" that is substantially and significantly different from its "syntactical form", "grammatical form", or "surface structure"—or, to put the point in less jargon-ridden terms, that the ways in which a sentence is properly and appropriately *used* or *understood* may be ill indicated by its syntactic structure—is nowadays not a paradoxical idea but a philosophical commonplace.[15] But it is a considerable journey from this commonplace to the view that *every* sentence will have *several* logical forms, each different from its syntactical form, as a function of its being tokened in this or that discursive context. Nothing short of this, however, is what Devitt is proposing, and, if so radical an interpretive step is to be warranted, the theoretical payoff will need to be substantial indeed. What might it be?

According to Devitt, it is this: introducing such tacit operators enables us to accommodate our intuitions about truth and falsehood *vis-à-vis* the statements that sentences are used to make in various (e.g., fictional) discursive contexts within a semantic theory committed to the principle—call it "Frege's principle"— that "the truth conditions of a sentence are a function of *the referential properties* of its parts" (D, 174). Devitt's own paradigmatic truth characterization for a (stylized, operator-free) "base language" (D, 71–72; cf. 164)—adapted from familiar ways of mapping formal systems (first-order predicate calculi) into set-theoretic model structures—is designed to satisfy Frege's principle, and the implication of introducing new (tacit) operators at this point is plainly that a commitment to the principle can be sustained *only* if the statements which sentences are used in fictional contexts to make are assigned logical forms *different* from any already accommodated in that truth characterization.

Devitt's own discussion of the *way* in which the singular terms occurring in sentences implicitly governed by the operator 'F' contribute to their truth or falsehood, however, proves curiously unsatisfying.

> Intuitively F-sentences are true if there are fictions "having the appropriate form" out of which they arise. Consider a designational fictitious name. According to the [causal] theory [of designation] this will have underlying it a causal network arising out of certain parts of a fictional work. Those are just the parts to which we would look to see if the fiction is of the appropriate form for an F-sentence containing the name to be true. Just how these truth conditions are to be worked out in detail is, of course, quite unclear. However, I claim that the parts of reality from which fictitious names arise are the parts to which the F-operator directs us to determine the truth of

F-sentences. The truth conditions of an F-sentence depend on the referential properties of its contained name. I shall not attempt to go into this more. (D,180–181)

Devitt's circumspect talk of "the appropriate form" here is necessitated by the fact that, in these cases, the only available causal network stretches back to original uses of a fictitious name in S-sentences which, on his view, do not themselves express statements having truth-values. Here is his picture:

> Suppose that we are gathered round a storyteller. In the course of his story he introduces a character by the name 'Jum Eli'. At the end of the story one of us says, 'Jum Eli is sinister.' My picture of this is as follows: The storyteller's imaginative act is in the form of a series of S-sentences. Among these are many that use the name 'Jum Eli'. These uses of the name are heard by the audience. On the basis of this causal link to the imaginative act . . ., one of the audience uses the name in the above statement, an F-sentence. This statement will be true or false as the case may be with the imaginative act that gave rise to it. (D, 175)

But how are we to understand this last remark? One possibility, of course, is that Devitt is supposing that his hypothetical storyteller actually utters the very sentence 'Jum Eli is sinister'. The listener's comment—*ex hypothesi* having the logical form 'F (Jum Eli is sinister)', in which an operator, F, is applied to the operator-free "base sentence", 'Jum Eli is sinister'—will then be true by virtue of its correspondence to a sentence used in telling the story whose logical form results from applying a *different* operator, S, to the *same* base sentence. If everything we wanted to say about a fictional character had this "echoic" character, something like this account would perhaps serve. But so, too, would a much simpler story, for in *this* account, the two "tacit operators", S and F, are entirely idle, as, for that matter, is the very idea of *any* term's "referential properties". Purely syntactic (structural) sentence-matching does all the work.

But, of course, as Devitt himself stresses, most of our talk about fictional entities does not merely echo sentences occurring in the original stories. "No sooner is a story spun than we are off, speculating about *a*'s moral growth, *b*'s courage, *c*'s villainy, and so forth" (D, 172). Assuming, then, that the hypothetical storyteller does not actually utter the *words* "Jum Eli is sinister", how are we to evaluate the listener's comment? In particular, how then are we to understand Devitt's remark that "this statement will be true or false as the case may be with the imaginative act that gave rise to it"?

The most forthright and plausible answer is surely that, when the storyteller does not actually *say* that Jum Eli is sinister, then the truth or falsehood of the listener's comment to that effect will depend upon whether it is *implied* by what the storyteller *does* say about Jum Eli. But Devitt cannot avail himself of this response, for, on his official account, what the storyteller utters is a series of *S-sentences*, none of which makes a statement having a truth-value. Accordingly, nothing that the storyteller says *can* stand in logical relations to the listener's comment. But even stipulating truth-values for the storyteller's sentences—for nothing significant is compromised by treating them all as (trivially) true "by default"—only postpones the problem, since we would still stand in need of an account of the *inferential* relationships obtaining between (the statements made by) S-sentences and (those made by) F-sentences, and it is difficult to see how Devitt could provide such an account while consistently maintaining his root conviction that, since they contain "empty names", the corresponding operator-free *base* sentences do not themselves have truth-values or stand in logical relationships.

What I conclude from these observations, *inter alia*, is that Devitt's posited "tacit operators" in fact make no contribution at all toward sustaining the Fregean principle that the truth conditions of a sentence are a function of the referential properties of its parts. On the contrary, the most straightforward way to preserve that principle is surely to hold that the storyteller's utterances be counted ("by default") as expressing a series of *true* statements about a fictional character named 'Jum Eli', that the listener is talking about that same character (namely, Jum Eli), and that the listener's comment "Jum Eli is sinister" is true just in case the predicate 'is sinister' is *true of* (applies to, is satisfied by) Jum Eli. The most straightforward way to preserve Frege's principle, that is, is to treat Devitt's combinatorial truth characterization as *itself* entirely univocal.

At this point, the objection may well be pressed that I am riding roughshod over a fundamental *ontological* criterion of adequacy upon which I myself repeatedly insisted in my earlier critical discussions of the notion of "intentions to refer":

(CA6) An adequate explication of the reference of proper names should be consistent with a naturalistic ontology.

Since reference is a relation between language and the world, the objection continues, if I wish to hold, for example, that 'Santa Claus' refers to Santa Claus, I am committed to believing *either* that Santa Claus, although he is not an ordinary empirically discoverable entity in the world, nevertheless somehow exists after all *or* that reference is a mysterious non-natural relation, somehow capable of obtaining between two relata despite the fact that one of them does not exist. If I proposed to take refuge in a Descriptivist account of reference and my earlier claim that Santa Claus uniquely satisfies the description (DSC), in turn, I could then continue to hold that Santa Claus does not exist in any literal sense only if I were prepared to treat *satisfaction* as a non-natural *sui generis* (semantic, intentional) relation. In any case, the objection concludes, I am forced to choose between positing different senses of 'exist' (in at least one of which fictional characters *do* exist) and positing some primitive intentional relation (be it "reference" or "satisfaction"). If I wish to retain (CA5), then reference must either be an ordinary natural relation whose range includes some ontologically extraordinary items or an ontologically extraordinary relation obtaining between existing and non-existing ordinary natural items—and either choice violates (CA6).

The objection is certainly well-taken, but I do not for a moment propose to abandon either (CA5) or (CA6) as a condition of acceptability for an account of proper-name reference. For while I agree that (CA6) would be violated by either of the choices envisaged by our hypothetical objector, I do not agree that these two possibilities exhaust the field of theoretical options. One can run between the horns of this particular dilemma, for example, by holding that reference is not a relation between language and the world *at all*, ordinary or extraordinary. On this conception, "philosophical semantics"—including accounts of reference and truth—would be ontologically *noncommittal*, and distinct from the theory of *representation*, that is, the more general enterprise of explaining how a language or other representational system sometimes can and does secure extralinguistic import.

Now, although the very idea that reference (or satisfaction) might not be any sort of word-world relation may initially strike one as too paradoxical even to consider, I nevertheless propose to take it seriously and to see where it leads us. Earlier, I remarked upon the philosophical commonplace captured by the remark that a sentence can have a "logical form" different from its "grammatical form", namely, that syntactic structure may prove a poor indicator of the ways in which some sentences are properly and appropriately used or understood. The relevant observation here is that there is no methodological rule which renders sentences containing semantic terminology—'refers', 'designates', 'satisfies', 'true', and so on—automatically, necessarily, and in principle exempt from being grist for the mill of "logical *vs.* grammatical form". Of course, there *are* relations which can be properly understood to obtain between words and (other) items in the world, and I do not intend my current suggestion to imply that this is not the case. The hypothesis which I propose to explore is not the absurd proposition that there are no word-world relations but only the more modest thesis that the "logical form" of semantic claims differs from their "syntactic form", that is, that such claims as

(r1) 'Socrates' refers to Plato's chief philosophical mentor,

(r2) 'Santa Claus' refers to the generous North Pole elf,

and

(r3) 'three' refers to the successor of the smallest positive integer which yields its square when added to itself

are not most fruitfully thought of as instances of the general scheme

(RR) *expression R entity*, [or: *word R world*].

How then should we understand such claims? This is doubtless an excellent question, but I do not think that the most promising course at this point is to tackle it directly. Instead, I want to ask first what we should expect a satisfactory philosophical account of nominal reference to enable us to *do*. If the job of "philosophical semantics" is not to describe "truth-making" word-world relations, then what *is* it? Which *questions*, for instance, should an acceptable account of proper-name reference tell us how to answer?

There are, I think, at least three. Let us suppose that 'N' is a variable for which we may substitute proper names (in a sense broad and theoretically noncommittal enough to include 'Santa Claus' and 'three' as well as 'Socrates' as proper names), and that S_1 and S_2 are speakers of the language to which the substituends for 'N' belong. Then an acceptable account of proper-name reference should surely tell us how to answer questions about *semantic* reference having the form:

(QN1) To what or whom does (the proper name) N refer?

and questions about *speaker's* reference, on the model of:

(QN2) To what or whom does (a speaker) S_1 refer by (using) N?

An acceptable account of proper name reference, that is, should explain what correct answers to (QN1) and (QN2) look like (what forms they can take), and it should explicate the conditions that a possible or suggested answer to either question must satisfy in order to qualify as a correct answer.

One lesson that we have learned from, for example, Helmut's confusion regarding Schlick and Neurath is that the answer to (QN2) need not coincide with the answer to (QN1). Just as one can, in appropriate circumstances, use a description to refer to an individual whom it does not fit (Donnellan's "referential use"), so, too, one can use a proper name (e.g., 'Otto Neurath') in certain circumstances to refer to an individual (e.g., Moritz Schlick) whom it does not (semantically) denote. Thus, given two speakers, S_1 and S_2, both of whom use a single proper name (type), N, it will also always make sense to ask,

(QN3) Are S_1 and S_2 referring to *the same* item by (their uses of) N?

This is the third form of question that an adequate account of proper names should tell us how to answer.

Of course, if we were able to answer questions of the form (QN2), regarding individual speakers' references, then we would automatically be equipped to answer questions of the form (QN3), regarding *co*-referentiality for pairs of speakers. One methodological strategy, therefore, would be to take (QN2) as fundamental and attempt to provide an account of proper-name reference that supplies answers to questions of the forms (QN1) and (QN3) *by way of* supplying answers to questions of the form

(QN2). Both classical Descriptivism and Kripke's causal-historical picture adopt essentially this strategy. Significantly, however, there is a methodological alternative.

It was Quine who reminded us[16] that, if we can give an account of what it is for an expression to be meaningful (to "*have* a meaning") and what it is for two expressions to be synonymous (to "have the *same* meaning"), then there is no need to hypostatize meanings, that is, to identify anything (any existing item) as "*the* meaning" of an expression. Suppose, now, that we were to adapt this methodological strategy to the present discussion. Something like "speaker co-referentiality" would then become our *fundamental* notion, and answers to questions of the forms (QN1) and (QN2) would be supplied by way of supplying answers to questions of the form (QN3). Roughly, to give the speaker's reference for a specific use of a proper name (type) would be to assign the name-token actually produced to a certain class of co-referential expressions, and to give the semantic reference of a proper name would be similarly to classify normal or standard (i.e., correct) tokenings of the name-type. Since statements regarding both speaker's reference and semantic reference would basically be *classificatory* rather than relational claims, the upshot would be that we would be well along toward an account of the very sort that just a short while ago seemed utterly paradoxical, a non-relational theory of proper name reference.

That, in outline, is the task to which I now turn. With three questions, (QN1)–(QN3), and a half-dozen criteria of adequacy, (CA1)–(CA6), in hand, in other words, I shall embark in the next chapter upon the *prima facie* counter-intuitive project of sketching a *non*-relational picture of nominal reference.

5
Idiolectic Sense, Confluence, and Isonymy

I CLOSED the last chapter with the unusual suggestion that reference might not be most usefully regarded as a relation between words and the world at all, i.e., that the "logical form" of sentences containing the word 'refers' is not most usefully viewed as that of a simple dyadic relational sentence. The aim of the present chapter is to begin sketching out an alternative story about nominal reference consonant with that suggestion.

Let us begin with an example suggested by a case mentioned elsewhere in passing by Kripke himself.[1] Suppose that Greta and Petra both have in their linguistic repertoires the proper name 'Jan Paderewski'. Greta and Petra, however, have quite different *beliefs* about the person they think of as bearing that name.

Greta, we shall suppose, is a talented classical cellist. Her "Jan Paderewski" was an acclaimed Polish pianist and composer. She believes that Paderewski studied in Warsaw and in Vienna in the late 1800s; that he was renowned during the first part of the twentieth century for his charismatic concert performances of a repertoire favoring pieces by Chopin, Bach, Beethoven, and Schumann; that his own compositions, apart from an opera, *Manru,* and the familiar *Minuet in G,* were largely undistinguished; and that late in life, in the 1930s, he edited an important edition of Chopin's works.

Petra, on the other hand, is a learned political scientist. Her

"Jan Paderewski" was an influential Polish patriot and statesman. She believes that, in 1910, Paderewski presented the city of Cracow with a monument commemorating the five-hundredth anniversary of the Battle of Grunwald; that, shortly after World War I, he persuaded Woodrow Wilson to include a paragraph in support of Polish independence as the thirteenth of his Fourteen Points; that he was the prime minister and foreign minister of the postwar Republic of Poland during 1919; and that, except for a brief period of service as president of the Parliament of the Polish government in exile during 1940, shortly before his death, he essentially retired from active political life in 1921.

Each of Greta and Petra, in other words, has a set of beliefs which are "about Jan Paderewski" in the ontologically (semantically) noncommittal sense that each speaker is disposed to assert and assent to a set of (indicative, purely descriptive) sentences,[2] each of which has the proper name 'Jan Paderewski' as its grammatical subject. I shall call these two sets of beliefs (respectively) Greta's and Petra's *idiolectic senses* for the name 'Jan Paderewski'. As it happens, everything that Greta believes about (her) "Jan Paderewski" and everything Petra believes about (her) "Jan Paderewski" is true of one person. How might Greta and Petra discover this?

Here's a natural suggestion. Correlative to one's idiolectic sense for the name 'Jan Paderewski' is an associated family of *procedures of inquiry* for "finding out more about Jan Paderewski", that is, for *revising* the beliefs constituting one's idiolectic sense for the name, and, in particular, for adding new beliefs to it. Call such a family of procedures of inquiry an *epistemics*. Since we may assume that each of Petra's and Greta's idiolectic senses for the name 'Jan Paderewski' includes, for example, a belief to the effect that Jan Paderewski was an actual historical figure of the late nineteenth and early twentieth centuries, it seems reasonable to conclude that both Petra and Greta will acknowledge the methods of *historical inquiry* as appropriate for revising those idiolectic senses. Although their idiolectic senses for the name differ, then, we can say that Petra and Greta *share* an epistemics for 'Jan Paderewski'.

Suppose now that Petra and Greta each undertook to "find out more about Jan Paderewski", that is, to revise and expand their respective idiolectic senses for the name 'Jan Paderewski', in accordance with this shared epistemics. Each could then discover that she was warranted in adding to her repertoire of "Jan Paderewski" beliefs the collection of beliefs constitutive of the other's idiolectic sense of the name. When fully *commensurated* according to their shared epistemics of historical inquiry, in other words, Petra's and Greta's initially different idiolectic senses for 'Jan Paderewski' would *converge*. In such a case, I shall say, Greta and Petra use the name 'Jan Paderewski' *confluently*. Their respective idiolectic senses "flow together". Convergence of idiolectic senses when commensurated under a shared epistemics is criterial for such confluence of use.

I propose to interpret

(QN3) Are S_1 and S_2 referring to *the same* item by (their uses of) N?

as the question

(QC) Do S_1 and S_2 use (the proper name) N confluently?

to which the answer will be "Yes" or "No" according to whether it is or is not the case that S_1's and S_2's respective idiolectic senses of the proper name N would converge if fully commensurated under an epistemics for the name that they in fact share. It is important to notice that, according to the account I am now developing, an assertion to the effect that two speakers, S_1 and S_2, use a proper name, N, confluently does *not* abbreviate a quantified conjunction of claims regarding "speaker's reference":

($\exists$x)(S_1 uses N to refer to x & S_2 uses N to refer to x) but will rather itself be used to *explicate* the notion of speaker's reference. It is equally important to see that the fact that two speakers use a given proper name confluently neither records nor presupposes the obtaining of any determinate natural relation (causal, historical, or otherwise) between that name and any object, item, or entity in the world (or out of it) by virtue of which the name refers to the object. The simplest way to establish this is to note that there are *many* epistemics, in consequence of which the notion of confluent use can be straightforwardly carried over to proper names that are *not* the names of empirical existents. Thus, for example, Jorg and Jutta might agree that Sherlock Holmes was a *literary character* and that Hercules was a *figure of Greek mythology*. Each of these predicates adverts to an epistemics, and each of these agreements signals a consilience or commonality of epistemics. Here, again, it is reasonable to suppose that if Jorg and Jutta were to expand their respective idiolectic senses for 'Sherlock Holmes' or 'Hercules' according to such shared epistemics, those idiolectic senses would converge. Jutta and Jorg, that is, use each of these names confluently.

Each of the predicates emphasized in the preceding paragraph adverts to a different species of *fictional* epistemics. In contrast, the epistemics that Petra and Greta both associate with the name 'Jan Paderewski' is an instance of what we might most generally describe as the *empirical epistemics,* that family of procedures of inquiry appropriate to discovering empirical matters-of-fact and confirming empirical hypotheses and theories. The empirical epistemics will obviously play an especially central role in the account of nominal reference I am presently engaged in sketching out.

The general form of a fictional epistemics is: *consult the canonical texts.* Its species, however, differ according to differences among sorts of texts and according to what qualifies a text as canonical. Thus, to find out more about a literary character, one consults the canonical *literary works*—novels, plays, short stories, poems, and so on. These are characteristically works by a particular author, and qualifying such a work as canonical thus frequently consists in establishing its authorship and authenticity. Similarly, to find out more about a figure of Greek mythology, one consults the canonical Greek myths. In contrast to literary works, however, myths typically have no known or discoverable author. They characteristically belong, rather, to the *oral tradition* of some determinate group of people. Qualifying the text of a myth as canonical, in consequence, will as a rule entail tracing its historical pedigree within such an oral tradition.

The unique and special status of the empirical epistemics is shown, in part, by the fact that the question of whether a given literary work or mythical account is canonical is itself a question to be answered by the methods of empirical inquiry, an inquiry, for example, into the authorship or authenticity or historical pedigree of a particular text. In this sense, fact is epistemically prior to fiction. But that Sherlock Holmes sometimes injected cocaine when bored and that Hercules cleaned the Augean stables by diverting the river Alpheus through them are not themselves empirical matters-of-fact, and, correlatively, the method of inquiry by which one becomes entitled to add such beliefs to one's idiolectic senses for the respective names is not the empirical epistemics *per se*.

Confluence of use is normally conversationally *presupposed*. It is the conversational "default condition". Normally, that is, when two people use the same proper name in conversation, they enter into a tacit contract, so to speak, to exchange idiolectic senses. Less metaphorically, each speaker is initially *prima facie* authorized to add to his or her idiolectic sense for the name those claims made by the conversational partner in which that name occurs, and each speaker's idiolectic sense for the name thus dynamically alters and evolves as the conversation proceeds.

If two speakers' idiolectic senses for a given name initially contain no contrary or contradictory claims, such a purely conversational commensuration will proceed smoothly. It is only if the families of beliefs constituting the original idiolectic senses are not collectively logically or nomologically coherent that the speakers' shared epistemics for the name comes *explicitly* into play. It is the methods of inquiry prescribed by that epistemics which are the final court of appeal for settling disagreements regarding which, if either, of two conflicting beliefs expressed by sentences containing the given name is ultimately justified or warranted.

The next point to note is that the notion of a shared epistemics necessarily presupposes that individual speakers belong to broader *communities* of language-users within which norms of inquiry and justification are constituted and sustained, in terms of which the epistemic credentials of individual claims can be assessed. *Pairwise* confluent uses of a proper name, then, occur within wider communal contexts of *mutually* shared epistemics that can, in principle, give rise to families of *mutually* confluent name-usings.

The processes of commensurating idiolectic senses in accordance with a shared epistemics—and the epistemics variously associated with particular names themselves—can plainly allow for "division of linguistic labor" and for differential *expertise* with regard to the correct use of a proper name. Just as a person can be an *authority* with regard to membership in a natural kind—for example, regarding such questions as whether a certain tree is a beech or an elm; a given animal, a shrew or a vole; or a piece of metal, a sample of molybdenum or titanium—so too, a person can be an authority on Jan Paderewski or Hercules or Sherlock Holmes—for example, regarding the answers to such questions as whether Paderewski ever performed in Prague, how Hercules killed the Hydra, or why Sherlock Holmes traveled to Reichenbach Falls.

Call the set of beliefs on which the revisions of S_1's and S_2's respective idiolectic senses for a name N converge when commensurated according to their shared epistemics (assuming that they do so converge) the *fusion* of those idiolectic senses. We can then straightforwardly define the fusion of *three* idiolectic senses for a name, in turn, as the fusion of any one with the fusion of the other two. Since the process is obviously symmetric and associative, it is plainly indifferent in what order we envisage such commensurations being carried out. Continuing this line of thought, we arrive at the notion of a *communal sense* for a proper name as the fusion of the idiolectic senses of that name across all the members of the relevant community, that is, the set of warranted beliefs expressible by purely descriptive indicative sentences containing the name that would result from successive pairwise commensurations of those manifold diverse idiolectic senses under the control of the appropriate shared epistemics. The notion of such a communal sense for a given proper name is, of course, not something that is or could be realized in any actual speakers' linguistic practices, but rather a sort of *regulative ideal*, reflecting the conviction that the resources of our shared epistemics are always in principle sufficient to resolve *de facto* inconsistencies among individual idiolectic senses.

On the view I am exploring here, the fundamental job of a proper name is in this way to collect descriptive propositions. A proper name is a sort of durable peg on which to hang descriptive predicates, an accumulation point for claims. A name, as it were, stays put, while commitments to claims (beliefs) expressible by sentences containing the name come and go according to the results of exercising the epistemics associated with it, that is, in consequence of diachronic and intersubjective processes of inquiry. Thus Paul Ziff: "A name is a fixed point in a turning world."[3]

It is useful in this connection to contrast proper names with demonstrative expressions. Russell notoriously thought of 'this' and 'that' as the only "logically proper names", but the function of such demonstrative elements is, in a sense, arguably logically derivative from that of genuine proper names. Roughly, a demonstrative 'this' or 'that' is a *temporary* proper name associated with the empirical epistemics. Unlike genuine proper names, such demonstratives do not represent *in absentia* and consequently have no durable diachronic role. Rather, they provide momentary and transient centers for the collection of (empirical) *entry claims*, paradigmatically perceptual judgments; descriptive content condenses around a given 'this' or 'that' only so long as that content includes the representation of this or that *as* then and there present to the representer.[4]

I have introduced the notion of two speakers' confluent use of a given proper name to describe the situation in which their respective idiolectic senses for the name would converge under a process of commensuration controlled by the shared epistemics associated with it. By analogy, we can form the notion of a single speaker's use of a proper name being confluent with that of a linguistic community just in case the speaker's idiolectic sense for that name would converge to the *communal* sense for that name (reckoned, so to speak, across the other members of the community) when systematically "expanded" according to the epistemics the speaker associates with the name.

Since communal senses were themselves explained in terms of a fusion of idiolectic senses across the relevant linguistic community, it will obviously *normally* be the case that a given speaker's name-uses are uniformly confluent with those of the speech community to which he or she belongs. (That this is normally the case, indeed, is surely part of what it *means* for the speaker to belong to that linguistic community.) When this presumption fails to obtain, however, questions regarding *speaker's reference* may arise, on the model of

(QN2) To what or whom does (a speaker) S_1 refer by (using) N?

Our second interpretation of the conclusion that Helmut had confused Schlick and Neurath, for example, was framed in terms that exemplify one style of *answer* to questions of this form:

(A2.1) When Helmut used the name 'Moritz Schlick', he was referring to Otto Neurath,

or, equivalently,

(A2.2) (Each of) Helmut's uses of the name 'Moritz Schlick' referred to Otto Neurath.

On the received traditional account, such remarks incorporate a commitment to a referential *relation* between words (Helmut's word-tokens) and an entity in the world (Otto Neurath). In analogous circumstances, however, Helmut's poor memory might just as easily have led him to confuse, for instance, Gawain and Lancelot, neither of whom is ontologically available to serve as a relatum. And this, in turn, suggests that it is worth trying to extend the current "non-relational" outlook to such remarks as well.

Our recent reflections on idiolectic and communal senses suggest a suitable strategy. Instead of understanding, for example, (A2.2) in terms of a relation between word and object, we can rather interpret it as aligning Helmut's individual uses of 'Moritz Schlick' with a specific communal sense. On this reading, in other words, (A2.2) is a claim to the effect that Helmut's uses of 'Moritz Schlick' are confluent with the communal sense of 'Otto Neurath' within *our own* linguistic community.

So interpreted, the occurrences of the name 'Otto Neurath' in (A2.1) and (A2.2) are not being straightforwardly used to say something about Otto Neurath. Rather, in a sense, they are being *exhibited*. Compare, for example, the occurrences of the word 'and' in such remarks as

(SM1) When Helmut uses the word 'und', he means *and*,

and

(SM2) Helmut's uses of the word 'und' mean *and*.

The tokens of 'and' occurring in these sentences are not performing the normal linguistic function of 'and's. They are not, that is, *conjoining* two sentences (or noun phrases). The claims (SM1) and (SM2) rather advert to that normal linguistic function itself and invite us to understand Helmut's uses of 'und' in terms of it, that is, by rehearsing the (conjunctive) role of 'and's in our own linguistic community. Analogously, the name 'Otto Neurath' in (A2.1) and (A2.2) is not performing its normal linguistic function as a single subject of diverse descriptive predications. These remarks instead similarly invite us to understand Helmut's *idiosyncratic* uses of 'Moritz Schlick' by rehearsing the *standard* (claim-collecting) role of 'Otto Neurath' in indicative, purely descriptive discourses within our own linguistic community.

Over a period of several decades, Wilfrid Sellars developed a sophisticated philosophical semantics, according to which the "meaning" idiom represents a specialized form of the copula in terms of which *structurally* distinct utterings or inscribings are classified in terms of their *roles* or *functions* in the organized behavioral economies of speaking organisms. To signal the distinct families of criteria, structural and functional, according to which lexical items can consequently be sorted and individuated, he introduced two separate styles of quotation marks—star-quotes and dot-quotes—as *illustrating*, and thus indexical, devices for forming common nouns. Star-quotes form a common noun that is true of empirical structures appropriately design-isomorphic to the token exhibited between them. In contrast, dot-quotes form a common noun that is true of items in any language that play the role or do the job performed in *our own* language by the token exhibited between them.[5] In terms of these notational conventions, for example, both (SM1) and (SM2) can be paraphrased by the *classificatory* remark that

> (SM) Helmut's *und*s (i.e., those he utters or inscribes) are ·and·s.

It would be useful to extend these Sellarsian notational devices to encompass proper names. But whereas the functional criteria for being an ·and· are specifiable in terms of the formal rules of inference governing conjunction and, on Sellars' view, those for being, say, a ·green· or a ·north·, in terms of *material* inference principles governing the cogency of reasonings in which such predicates essentially occur,[6] it is not yet clear how we should specify the role or job or function performed in our language by a given *proper name*, for example, 'Otto Neurath'. How, in other words, might we specify the functional criteria for being an ·Otto Neurath·?

Given what has gone before, the *general* strategy is clear enough. The role or function of *Otto Neurath*s in our language will be specified in terms of the confluence of their tokeners' idiolectic senses for the name with each other and, *a fortiori*, with a single communal sense. In first approximation, then, to be an ·Otto Neurath· is to be an item used confluently with the communal sense (in our own linguistic community) of the token exhibited between the dot-quotes. Extending the Sellarsian notational devices in this way enables us to recast claims about speaker's reference as explicitly classificatory. Thus, on this account, both (A2.1) and (A2.2) can be paraphrased by

(A2) Helmut's *Moritz Schlick*s (i.e., those he uttered while retelling Heidi's story) were ·Otto Neurath·s.

Such systematic confusions as Helmut's are rare, but, as we shall later have occasion to see, questions regarding a speaker's reference can also arise when there is no reason to suppose that the speaker is *confused* about anything at all. Before exploring such topics, however, it will prove useful first to consider the notion of *semantic* reference, that is, to examine answers to questions of the form

(QN1) To what or whom does (the proper name) N refer?

As in the case of speaker's reference, one characteristic form of answer to questions regarding semantic reference (of a given proper name) makes *prima facie* use of a (different) proper name, for example,

(A1.1) 'Hesperus' refers to Venus

and

(A1.2) 'Mark Twain' refers to Samuel Langhorn Clemens.

How are such claims to be understood?

The principal notions required here should be relatively straightforward extensions of the ideas we have already developed. To discover exactly what we need, however, it helps to begin by asking whether we want to conclude, for instance, that *Hesperus*s, as they are normally used in our language, *are* ·Venus·s. According to our provisional interpretation, to be a ·Venus· is to be an item used confluently with the communal sense (in our own linguistic community) of the token exhibited between the dot-quotes. Now, trivially, *Hesperus*s, as they are normally used in our language, are ·Hesperus·s. They are, that is, normally used confluently with the communal sense of the token exhibited between the last pair of dot-quotes. What we need to decide, then, is whether to regard the communal sense of 'Hesperus' as being the *same* communal sense as that of 'Venus'. Once the question is framed in this manner, one can in fact argue that there are at least good *methodological* reasons for treating these two communal senses as distinct.

A proper name's "communal sense", as I have been using the term, is a collection of beliefs or claims *identified via* a set of purely descriptive indicative *sentences* paradigmatically used to express them. Strictly speaking, then, the communal sense of 'Hesperus' will be identified by a set of sentences whose grammatical subject is 'Hesperus', while the communal sense of 'Venus', in contrast, will be identified by a distinct set of sentences whose grammatical subject is 'Venus'. It is arguably consistent with the conventions I have so far adopted to hold that, far from being identical, the two communal senses have no members in common at all.

On the other hand, it can surely be objected, although the beliefs or claims constituting a communal sense are identified *via* sentences, I have not (at least not yet) identified them *with* sentences, and there is surely a sense in which, for example, the sentences 'Hesperus is a planet' and 'Venus is a planet' make the *same* claim or express the *same* belief. What's more, since Hesperus *is* Venus, this will be true for every pair of purely descriptive indicative sentences which differ only in that the name 'Hesperus' occurs in one where 'Venus' occurs in the other. In light of these considerations, the objection continues, the communal sense of 'Hesperus' ought to be regarded as being the *same* as that of 'Venus'.

The issue of how closely to identify a claim or belief with its characteristic sentential expression(s) is indeed a vexing one. I shall indeed want to return to it later, but I do not think that I need to resolve it here. Rather I propose to adopt a sort of methodological minimalism. This implies, *inter alia*, that I shall consistently attempt to introduce my expository apparatus in a manner which prejudges the fewest substantive questions. Consonant with this minimalist posture, then, I shall treat communal senses in terms of what I shall call a name's *characteristic sentences*, those purely descriptive indicative sentences expressing beliefs upon which communal epistemic commensuration for a given proper name would converge which contain that name *per se*.

Let us say that the communal sense of one proper name, N_1, is *equivalent* to the communal sense for another, N_2, just in case the set of *characteristic sentences* associated with one of these names could be derived from the set associated with the other by substituting the one name for the other. And let us call two proper names *isonymous* if they are (respectively) normally used confluently with *equivalent* communal senses. Consistent with our commitment to methodological minimalism, the question of what, if anything, the equivalence of communal senses implies regarding the sameness or difference of any person's *beliefs* remains open. Nevertheless, we have now assembled enough apparatus to address the matter of semantic reference.

It should now, in fact, be reasonably clear how, consistently with the strategies adopted earlier, we need to interpret

(A1.1) 'Hesperus' refers to Venus

and

(A1.2) 'Mark Twain' refers to Samuel Langhorn Clemens.

As in the case of speaker's reference, I shall want to interpret such claims as *classifying* particular structural linguistic forms (token designs)—*Hesperus*s and *Mark Twain*s—in terms of specific communal senses. In this instance, however, the classification occurs, so to speak, at one remove. Like the name 'Otto Neurath' earlier, the proper names 'Venus' and 'Samuel Langhorn Clemens' here do not occur in their fundamental roles as the subject terms of indicative descriptive sentences, but are again, so to speak, being *exhibited* as a means of adverting to their corresponding communal senses.

Now my recent terminological decisions imply that I cannot straightforwardly interpret (A1.1) as a claim to the effect that the idiolectic senses associated with normally used *Hesperus*s are confluent with the communal sense of 'Venus', i.e., that *Hesperus*s *are* ·Venus·s. Rather, I shall understand (A1.1) as saying that *Hesperus*s are normally used confluently with a proper name whose communal sense is *equivalent* to the communal sense of 'Venus', i.e., that *Hesperus*s are normally used confluently with some proper name *isonymous* to 'Venus'. If we adopt 'N' as a variable for which dot-quoted proper names can be substituted, in other words, (A1.1) can be paraphrased[7] by

(A1.1*) (∃N)(*Hesperus*s are N's & N is isonymous to ·Venus·)

and (A1.2) by

(A1.2*) (∃N)(*Mark Twain*s are N's & N is isonymous to ·Samuel Langhorn Clemens·).

I have taken the trouble to introduce the contrived term 'isonymous' in this context, because it is important to remember that, like claims regarding confluent uses of names, such remarks as

(I.1) 'Hesperus' is isonymous to 'Venus'

and

(I.2) 'Mark Twain' is isonymous to 'Samuel Langhorn Clemens'

are fundamentally *epistemic* and, in consequence, ontologically noncommittal. (I.1), that is, does not abbreviate a quantified conjunction of claims of "semantic reference"

(∃x)('Hesperus' refers to x & 'Venus' refers to x).

Instead, just as the epistemic notion of confluence was used to explicate the notion of *speaker's* reference, I have used the related epistemic notion of isonymy to explicate the notion of *semantic* reference. Thus, as everyone who is familiar with the appropriate canonical texts knows, it is also true that

(I.3) 'Clark Kent' is isonymous to 'Superman'

and

(I.4) 'Batman' is isonymous to 'Bruce Wayne'.

These last remarks have brought us to a point in the dialectic where it is appropriate to pause and take stock. I ended the preceding chapter with the suggestion that we needed a new account of proper-name reference which would do justice to the strengths and insights of both the classical Descriptivist picture of proper names and Kripke's own causal-historical picture while avoiding their failings and excesses. We now have at least the rudiments of such an account in hand—what we might call the *epistemic picture* of proper names.[8] At this point, in fact, this epistemic picture has attained at least as articulate a formulation as Kripke offers of the Descriptivist and causal-historical alternatives to it. It is surely appropriate, then, to measure this account, at least provisionally, against the criteria of adequacy for a philosophical account of nominal reference, (CA1)–(CA6), collected in the preceding chapter.[9]

The epistemic picture of proper name reference resembles Descriptivism in being a picture drawn in terms of *senses*, the idiolectic senses entertained by individual speakers at particular times and the communal senses which (in principle) would result from the commensurations of many such idiolectic senses across time under the control of the relevant epistemics. It differs significantly from Descriptivism, however, precisely in being diachronic and dynamic where the former is synchronic and static, and it is primarily this difference that enables the epistemic picture to satisfy the criteria of adequacy on which Descriptivism principally founders:

(CA2) An adequate explication of the reference of proper names must allow for the possibility that a speaker can use a proper name to refer to an individual (item) while entertaining arbitrarily many false beliefs regarding that individual (item)

and

(CA3) An adequate explication of the reference of proper names must allow for the possibility that a speaker can use a proper name to refer to an individual (item) while being largely ignorant regarding the contentive descriptions in fact satisfied by that individual (item).

On the Descriptivist account, a speaker uses a name to refer to an object (entity) just in case the speaker's beliefs expressible by sentences containing that name are conjointly *then-and-there* uniquely true of that object. But (CA3) belies the uniqueness requirement—since, at any given time, the descriptive content of a speaker's idiolectic sense for a given name may be arbitrarily impoverished—and (CA2) belies the requirement of truth—since, at any given time, a speaker's idiolectic sense for a given name can include arbitrarily many false beliefs.

On the epistemic picture, in contrast, questions regarding a speaker's reference for particular usings of a given proper name are to be resolved, not in terms of the speaker's then-and-there beliefs expressible by sentences containing the name, but rather in terms of the *expansion and revision across time* of that synchronic idiolectic sense in accordance with the relevant epistemics. The possibility of diachronic expansion allows precisely for an initial poverty of descriptive content (CA3), and the possibility of diachronic revision, for an initial commitment to erroneous beliefs (CA2).

On the epistemic account, to say that a speaker uses a proper name to refer to a specified object is in essence to say that, when expanded and revised according to the relevant epistemics, the speaker's then-and-there idiolectic sense would converge across time to the communal sense (in our own linguistic community) of the expression used to specify the object. The epistemic picture thus resembles Kripke's causal-historical picture in recognizing that proper names *themselves* have histories of use, and that the concrete consequences of episodic speaker-hearer conversational transactions are directly relevant to questions of both speaker's and semantic reference. It differs from Kripke's picture, however, in understanding proper names *not,* in the first instance, as devices for empirically relating language users to objects, but as instruments for structuring and channeling the transmission and accumulation of *descriptive content,* issuing from *various* forms of inquiry, within a language community, and it is chiefly this difference that enables the epistemic picture to satisfy the criteria of adequacy on which we earlier found the causal-historical account wanting:

> (CA4) An adequate explication of the reference of proper names should explain how a speaker's reference in the case of content-preserving communicative transactions can track with the descriptive content of the statements actually made rather than with the proper names actually used.
>
> (CA5) An adequate explication of the reference of proper names should be consistent with the possibility of proper name reference to fictional, mythical, legendary, and other non-existent entities.

Kripke's causal-historical picture is retrospective and ontological. It understands two speakers' present name-usings to be co-referential, for example, just in case they lie at the proximate ends of causal chains of name-usings emerging (paradigmatically) from past encounters with a single object. As we have seen, in the context of an overarching commitment to naturalism, (CA6), the ontological character of this causal-historical picture immediately puts it at odds with (CA5). What prevents it from coming to terms with (CA4), on the other hand, is its commitment to the idea that the causally related events constituting the pertinent history of speaker-hearer transactions are theoretically identifiable in a manner completely independent of questions of descriptive content. The relevant episodes are rather picked out, in the first instance, simply by their instantiating tokenings of the proper name *per se*, and secondarily, perhaps, in terms of various speakers' "referential intentions", although precisely here, as we have noted, there emerges a further tension with the requirement of non-circularity,

> (CA1) An adequate explication of the reference of a proper name must not itself ineliminably employ or presuppose the notion of reference.

Our alternative picture, in contrast, is prospective and self-consciously epistemic. It understands two speakers' present uses of a single proper name to be confluent, for example, just in case they lie at the *beginnings* of commensurate *inquiries* converging (in principle) on a single set of beliefs. This forward-looking focus precisely on the (potential future) commensuration of descriptive content allows idiosyncratic and aberrant name-tokenings to be properly referentially classified in accordance with the intuitions underlying (CA4). Correlatively, precisely by treating discourse regarding reference *as* classificatory rather than relational, and by recognizing diverse modes of inquiry (including various fictional epistemics), the epistemic picture readily accommodates (CA5). Its acknowledgment of the central, unique, and ultimately privileged status of the *empirical* epistemics, however, simultaneously satisfies the cardinal ontological constraint

> (CA6) An adequate explication of the reference of proper names should be consistent with a naturalistic ontology.

With regard to the criterion of non-circularity, (CA1), the epistemic picture on the face of it appears to be at least as well situated as the two alternative accounts. We should recall that it has not been demonstrated that either Descriptivism or the causal-historical account of nominal reference *must* ultimately violate the non-circularity condition. In both cases, the considerations adduced in evidence of potentially vicious circularity proved more suggestive than conclusive. With regard to Descriptivism,

Kripke proposed that the uniquely individuating descriptions actually available to an individual speaker will characteristically fall into tight circles of mutual interdependence (e.g., Cicero = the Roman orator who denounced Catiline; Catiline = the Roman senator denounced by Cicero). With regard to Kripke's own causal-historical picture, in turn, I suggested that its implicit reliance on notions of *reference-fixing* (baptismal) events and *reference-preserving* causal transactions could well prove similarly problematic.

The epistemic picture which we have been sketching is, of course, not without its own notional presuppositions as well. In particular, I have repeatedly made essential use of the still-unexplicated notion of a "purely descriptive indicative sentence". One can obviously ask, then, whether, like the notion of a reference-fixing event or a reference-preserving causal transaction, this notion, too, might not be tacitly "contaminated" with the idea of reference *per se*.

There is clearly, for instance, *one* potential elucidation of "purely descriptive" sentential contexts which identifies them with "extensional" or "referentially transparent" contexts, that is, sentential contexts for which substitution of co-referential expressions is truth-preserving. *If* the epistemic picture were inescapably required to understand its notion of purely descriptive sentential contexts in such terms—for example, as contexts which are truth-preserving under substitution of *isonymous* expressions—then it would obviously be infected with a conceptual circularity no different from that which threatened to undermine the causal-historical picture. Correlatively, however, to the extent that it is *not* obvious that the epistemic picture is ultimately and inescapably committed to some such explication of "purely descriptive", we may conclude that it is at least no *worse* off with regard to the non-circularity condition (CA1) than Kripke's causal-historical alternative.

It may, moreover, actually be better off. For while it is utterly unclear where one might begin even to *look* for an elucidation of "reference-fixing" events and "reference-preserving" causal transactions that is independent of the notion of reference as such, the notion of a *description* is embedded in families of conceptual contrasts and affinities which, at least on the face of it, are not themselves semantic. Thus, for example, descriptive contexts can be contrasted with contexts that are "prescriptive" or "normative". More significantly for our purposes, however, descriptions are correlative to (empirical) *explanations,* in the sense that it is in virtue of their satisfying determinate (possibly theoretical) descriptions that empirical phenomena (events, states, etc.) fall within the scope of determinate explanatory laws.[10]

We can, in other words, think of the notion of a "descriptive context" as one which is itself to be elucidated in *epistemic* terms. On this understanding, descriptive contexts are fundamentally those which arise from the exercise of the methods of inquiry constituting the empirical epistemics. The threat of circularity along this path, in turn, is defused by noting that what makes an inquiry "empirical" is not a matter of semantic (referential) relations between linguistic items and objects or entities in the world, but rather of relationships between specific epistemic conducts (e.g., adopting or abandoning explanatory claims, laws, or theories) and the broader contexts of sensory perception and practical action.

The dynamic and diachronic aspects of the epistemic picture insulate it, as well, from circularities of the "Cicero–Catiline" sort. It is indeed true that, at any given time, an individual speaker may be able to express the beliefs constituting his then-and-there idiolectic sense for the name 'Cicero' only by sentences containing the name 'Catiline', and conversely. According to the epistemic account, however, a speaker's "referring to Cicero" is to be understood, not in terms of an object's uniquely satisfying the descriptive conditions implied by his synchronic beliefs, but rather in terms of his using the name 'Cicero' confluently with its *communal* sense (within our own linguistic community). Since there is plainly no reason to suppose that the beliefs constituting the communal sense for any name will be expressible *only* by sentences containing a second name whose communal sense is, in turn, expressible *only* by sentences containing the first name, there is no reason to fear that the epistemic account is infected with ineliminable circularities of the sort whose existence, Kripke hypothesized, vitiates traditional descriptivism.

In fact, the indexical character of the *empirical* epistemics supplies the basis for an argument in support of the conclusion that the set of beliefs constituting the communal sense of a proper name will always include a uniquely individuating purely descriptive proper subset expressible by sentences containing *no* proper names. The key insight is that the world whose story emerges from our inquiries in accordance with the empirical epistemics is a world which has us *in* it. The space and time of the empirical world are a space and time in which we ourselves are located—along with our conceptual activities, their objects, and their products. It is precisely at our transient subjective '*here*'s and '*now*'s within this unitary space and time that the world exercises its ontological contraints on our (conceptual, representational) epistemic activities, constraints reflected in the indexical form of the (empirical) *entry claims* expressing the perceptual judgments whose systematic explanatory accommodation is the ultimate *raison d'être* of the empirical epistemics as such.

The 'here's and 'now's of a representer's perceptual judgments, however, already carry a full *conceptual* commitment to the 'there's and 'then's of a unitary space and time occupied by both representers and representeds. An individual's explanatory accommodation of his perspectival (indexical) perceptual judgments thus entails, *inter alia,* his determinately and coherently relating their 'here's and 'now's to this comprehensive space and time. Correlatively, a speaker must consistently believe of each of the named entities that he represents as objectively spatio-temporally locatable[11]—and so, *a fortiori*, as falling within the scope of the empirical epistemics—that it is determinately and coherently related to his (then-and-there) perceptual 'here' and 'now'. It follows that every speaker has in principle *available* a uniquely individuating indexical or perspectival sense (a "perspectival limit-sense") for each of the proper names that he uses under the auspices of the empirical epistemics, descriptively isolating the named entity in terms of its spatio-temporal relationships to the 'here' and 'now' of his spatio-temporal present.

Furthermore, we may also conclude that any two such uniquely individuating perspectival limit-senses would in principle admit of a consistent pairwise fusion. For every potential *communicant* with whom a particular speaker might undertake to commensurate his idiolectic sense for a given proper name under the empirical epistemics will also in principle be a nameable (empirical) *object* for that speaker, and thus also in principle descriptively identifiable by him in terms of *her* determinate locatability within the comprehensive space and time "perspectivally coordinatized" with respect to the speaker's 'here' and 'now'. Indeed, since this state of affairs will obtain symmetrically with respect to both participants in any sense-commensurating empirical inquiry, what would emerge from such a process of fusion would be two *isomorphic* perspectival limit-senses, one for each speaker, each recoverable from the other through a mapping of its perspectival space onto that of the other by systematic transformations of 'here's and 'now's into appropriate 'there's and 'then's, and conversely. This is the reasoning that stands behind my claim above that the *communal* sense of a proper name will contain a uniquely individuating purely descriptive proper subset of beliefs expressible by name-free sentences.

We can now see that the notion of a communal sense is, so to speak, the product of two orthogonal idealizations. On the one hand, it sums over the diachronically evolving beliefs of individual speakers to arrive at the notion of multiple mutually isomorphic uniquely individuating perspectival limit-senses. On the other hand, it also sums socially over successive pairwise fusions of idiolectic senses to arrive at the notion of a family of *non*-perspectival beliefs, expressible by *non*-indexical sentences, which are indifferently *instantiable* to any of these indefinitely many perspectival limit-senses through mappings of its places, times, and descriptive contents onto the 'here's, 'now's, and 'this-suches' of perceptual judgments. Since a communal sense, while being itself wholly aperspectival, would in this way embody the consistent fusion of multiple uniquely individuating individual perspectival limit-senses, it would in turn be itself descriptively adequate for unique individuation.[12] As I have already remarked, then, the notion of a communal sense thus ultimately functions in these accounts as an epistemic regulative ideal, one whose "cash value", so to speak, is given by just such convergent procedures of commensuration.

I noted earlier that the traditional Descriptivist picture imposed indefensible requirements of uniqueness and correctness on the descriptive contents of a speaker's *de facto* idiolectic sense for a given proper name at a given time. The epistemic picture, we can now see, recovers the fundamental intuition lying behind these ultimately unacceptable Descriptivist requirements, namely, the intuition that nominal reference (indeed, all singular reference) must be understood in terms of *appropriately constrained* description.[13] By locating the appropriate constraints not in speakers' idiosyncratic descriptive beliefs but in a *shared epistemics* for revising and expanding upon such beliefs, the epistemic picture properly relocates the necessary uniqueness and correctness of descriptive content in the limit—that is, in the (commensurable) perspectival limit-senses of individual speakers for a given proper name and (the regulative ideal of) the aperspectival communal sense of a linguistic community for that name.

Despite the fact that this epistemic account treats the semantic *idioms* as fundamentally non-relational, there is a sense in which it arguably successfully recovers and properly relocates certain fundamental intuitions of the causal-historical picture as well. On the one hand, proper names of items in the world are characteristically *bestowed* on them at determinate places and times, and it is consequently reasonable to expect that a belief to that effect would characteristically sooner or later be added to the idiolectic sense of a name if it were expanded under the auspices of the *empirical* epistemics.[14] On the other hand, there are good reasons to believe that an adequate philosophical elucidation of that empirical epistemics must at several crucial junctures—for example, in its accounts of perception and memory—itself appeal to causal connections between the knower and the known. Correlatively, sense-communicative exchanges and sense-commensurating inquiries are *also* causal transactions, and so, again for empirical objects, although they will not play the reference-determining role he assigns to them, causal chains of the sorts Kripke envisions linking later name-using events to earlier name-bestowing events will characteristically *exist*.

What I want to contest, then, is not the idea that there are causal-historical communicative chains of the sort that Kripke describes, nor even the claim that they play *a* role in the genesis and transmission of proper names. What I want to contest is only the claim that such causal chains are related to the *semantic functioning* of proper names in the way Kripke suggests. Near the beginning of this study, I suggested that a fundamental failing of Kripke's philosophical framework is its inability to accommodate a humanly useable epistemology for its main concepts and contentions. The idea, which became increasingly visible during the course of this chapter, that a series of causally related events constituting a *reference-determining* history of speaker-hearer transactions can theoretically be identified in a manner altogether independent of questions of descriptive content, belongs to the story of these epistemological shortcomings. What I want to do next, in fact, is to engage the topic of Kripkean causal-historical chains precisely from an epistemological perspective. Perhaps not surprisingly, this exploration will also bring us around once again to the delicate business of the relationships between sentences and beliefs.

6
Reference and Belief in Epistemological Perspective

SUPPOSE THAT we happen to overhear Gracie using the name 'Barbara Cartwright'. How, on Kripke's picture, should we proceed to determine to whom Gracie is referring by the proper name 'Barbara Cartwright'?

According to the causal-historical account, what is directly relevant to this question is what lies at the origin of a causally linked series of communicative events terminating in Gracie's present name-usings. What it is therefore, in the first instance, presumably appropriate to investigate is not what Gracie says about whomever she is calling 'Barbara Cartwright', but rather the communicative transactions in the course of which Gracie *acquired* her present command of the name 'Barbara Cartwright'. More generally, the epistemological strategy appropriate to answering such questions regarding a speaker's proper-name references will be an inquiry into a history of particular *linguistic* events, in this case, the communicative transactions in the course of which the name 'Barbara Cartwright' was transmitted from speaker to speaker until it reached Gracie. The epistemological picture most straightforwardly corresponding to the causal-historical account, in other words, is of our beginning with Gracie's present discourses and, guided by signposts labeled 'Barbara Cartwright', conceptually traversing a historical communicative chain from link to link into the past until we, so to speak, *encounter* the object of reference in an "initial baptismal" setting, rather like traveling upstream from Alexandria in Egypt to locate the source of the Nile.

As it happens, however, Gracie has never heard or read or otherwise encountered the name 'Barbara Cartwright' in her life. As it happens, Gracie is referring to Barbara Cart*land*, the elderly British lady who is the world's most prolific author of romance novels. That is, following our notational conventions,

> Gracie's *Barbara Cartwright*s are ·Barbara Cartland·s.

This is immediately obvious once we discover what Gracie actually *says* about ''Barbara Cartwright'', namely, that

> ''She's that elderly British lady who wrote all those wonderful romance novels.''

But Gracie, as all her friends will tell you, has ''never been very good with names''.

Now Gracie obviously acquired her beliefs regarding the authorship of romance novels *somewhere*, presumably by hearing or reading something about Barbara Cartland, and so there will undoubtedly *exist* a historical chain of causally linked linguistic events connecting Gracie's present uses of the name 'Barbara Cartwright' with (let us suppose) initial baptismal usings of the name 'Barbara Cartland', and thereby with Barbara Cartland herself. Notice, however, that this is not a chain of communicative events in the course of which the name 'Barbara Cartwright' was transmitted from speaker to speaker until it reached Gracie. Gracie did not acquire the name 'Barbara Cartwright' in this way at all. How, then, did she acquire it?

This way: The American actress Barbara Stanwyck once played a strong, dignified matriarchal character named 'Victoria Barkley' in a television series entitled *The Big Valley*, the story of a powerful family living on a sprawling ranch in the old West. This series was thematically very closely modeled on *Bonanza*, the story of a different powerful family living on another sprawling ranch in the old West, in which the Canadian-American actor Lorne Greene played a strong, dignified *patriarchal* character named 'Ben Cartwright'. As it happens, it is from the resulting association of the names 'Barbara Stanwyck' and 'Ben Cartwright' that Gracie actually arrived at the name 'Barbara Cartwright', a name which she in fact had never read nor heard nor otherwise encountered. In short, there also exists a historical chain of causally linked linguistic events connecting Gracie's present usings of the name 'Barbara Cartwright' with the American actress Barbara Stanwyck.

Come to think of it, it follows that there also exists a causal chain of linguistic events linking Gracie's present usings of 'Barbara Cartwright' to the Canadian-American actor Lorne Greene. And, since I am taking the liberty of creative omniscience, I shall add one more interesting fact to our collection. The conversation in which Gracie actually first encountered the name 'Barbara Cart*land*', we will suppose, in fact concerned the remarkable literary successes of *two* elderly female British authors, Barbara Cartland and Agatha Christie. There exists, in consequence, yet another causal-historical chain of linguistic events, whose *first* link is the same as the first link of the chain connecting Gracie's present uses of the name 'Barbara Cartwright' with Barbara Cartland, but whose *subsequent* links lead (let us suppose) to initial baptismal usings of the name 'Agatha Christie', and thereby to Agatha Christie herself.

Now, on the face of it, a question of speaker's reference, for example,

> To whom did Gracie refer by (her use of) the proper name 'Barbara Cartwright'?

is itself an empirical, matter-of-factual question, and consequently the appropriate epistemological strategy for arriving at a correct or warranted answer to it is surely to initiate an empirical inquiry. Specifically, the causal-historical picture suggests that we should inquire into the *ancestry* of particular linguistic events, the communicative transactions in the course of which the *name used* was transmitted from link to link until it reached the present speaker. One point of the present imaginative exercise, then, is to show that the question of speaker's reference can have a correct and warranted answer even if there is *no such* historical chain to be discovered. Gracie's present use of the proper name 'Barbara Cartwright' is the *terminus ad quem* of indefinitely many chains of linguistic transactions, diversely originating in "reference-fixing events" that causally implicate countless persons, but *none* of them is a chain of transactions in the course of which the name *'Barbara Cartwright'* has been transmitted from certain "initial baptismal" users to Gracie.

A second moral of our current exercise, however, is that, even if we possessed a guarantee that an inquiry into the historical ancestry of an individual's present propensities to use a given proper name would always turn up sufficient evidence of the existence of *some* causal chain connecting the speaker to *some* object, this would not satisfactorily solve the problem of the epistemology of speaker's reference. Even in principle, such an inquiry could supply an acceptable answer to the question of speaker's reference only if we also had reason to believe that we had successfully discovered the *correct* such causal chain. But this observation simply relocates the epistemological question, for in virtue of *what* will this or that causal chain be the "correct" one?

In the case of Gracie's present propensities to use the proper name 'Barbara Cartwright', for example, the "correct" causal chain is presumably one connecting her with Barbara Cartland. Nevertheless, the discovery that Gracie's proper-name uses were causally-historically connected to Barbara Cartland would not *establish* that Gracie was referring to Barbara Cartland. On the contrary, it is the fact that Gracie is referring to Barbara Cartland which singles out *that* causal chain as the "correct" one here rather than one of the others I have sketched. For one could instead have discovered that Gracie's proper name uses were similarly, causally-historically, connected to Barbara Stanwyck, although Gracie was *not* referring to Barbara Stanwyck.[1]

Now hold everything else about the example fixed, but suppose that what Gracie actually said about "Barbara Cartwright" was

"She's that elderly British lady who wrote all those wonderful *detective stories*."

Then, I submit, our intuitive answer to the question of speaker's reference will also have changed. On *this* scenario, Gracie will be referring to Agatha Christie, that is, her *Barbara Cartwright*s will now be ·Agatha Christie·s. In addition to being, so to speak, *phonetically* confused about *Barbara Cartwright*s and *Barbara Cartland*s, Gracie, who was never very good about names, is now *also* making a mistake of the sort that Helmut made earlier regarding Schlick and Neurath. She is confusing Agatha Christie with Barbara Cartland. All the historical chains of causally linked communicative transactions which I originally sketched remain intact. They are all still there to discover. But now it is the one linking Gracie with Agatha Christie that is "correct".

The causal-historical picture gains a certain spurious plausibility from an exposition that, like Kripke's own, limits itself to examples in which speakers' references—that is, the answers to questions of the form

(QN2) To what or whom does (a speaker) S_1 refer by (using) N?

—are assumed to coincide with semantic reference—that is, the answer to the question

(QN1) To what or whom does (the proper name) N refer?

All one in principle needs to do, the story then goes, is to trace *the name*—'Feynman' or 'Gödel' or 'Cicero' or whatever—from link to

140   Chapter 6

link back to Feynman or Gödel or Cicero or whoever. The speaker's contentive descriptive beliefs will then indeed turn out to be irrelevant to the answer to (QN2)—but precisely because it is already being *presupposed* that, *whatever* the speaker believes, the answer to (QN2) is going to coincide with the answer to (QN1). Since "the name" used by the speaker coincides with "the name" that (semantically) denotes whomever the speaker refers to, it appears that there can be no question about *which* name to trace. As we have repeatedly seen, however, this irenic picture collapses as soon as speaker's reference is allowed to *diverge* from semantic reference.

For one is then explicitly confronted with an embarrassing *plurality* of historical chains of communicative transactions—or with none at all. One is plainly confronted with a plurality in a case like Helmut's, where a speaker is systematically confused about who's who. In such a case, there are *two* equally salient names—for example, 'Moritz Schlick' and 'Otto Neurath'—and nothing beyond the descriptive contents of the speaker's beliefs is available, even in principle, to tell a causal-historical investigator *which* name to trace. But an epistemic appeal to those descriptive beliefs can then consistently be regarded as settling the question of speaker's reference quite *independently* of Kripkean causal-historical communicative chains. As we have seen, one can assimilate the case of Gracie to this pattern as well. But there is also a strictly literal reading of the causal-historical picture's strategic epistemological proposal to trace the communicative ancestry of "the name" according to which, in this instance, no *such* chain is available to trace. For, in Gracie's case, the name 'Barbara Cartwright' has no communicative ancestry. It is a fresh coinage. In this case, the question of speaker's reference can be answered *only* by an (independent) appeal to the speaker's descriptive beliefs.

The closest Kripke himself comes to directly acknowledging and defending the operative presupposition—that a series of causally related events constituting a *reference-determining* history of speaker-hearer transactions can theoretically be identified in a manner altogether independent of questions of descriptive content—is in the extended footnote addressing Donnellan's distinction between "referential" and "attributive" uses of a definite description upon which we have already commented. To refresh our memories, here's what Kripke says:

> Donnellan's distinction seems applicable to names as well as to descriptions. Two men glimpse someone at a distance and think they recognize him as Jones. 'What is Jones doing?' 'Raking the leaves'. If the distant leaf-raker is actually Smith, then in some sense they are referring to Smith, even though they both use 'Jones' *as a name of* Jones. In the text, I speak of the 'referent' of a name to mean the thing named by the name—e.g., Jones, not Smith—even though a speaker may sometimes properly be said to use the name to refer to someone else. Perhaps it would have been less misleading to use a technical term, such as 'denote' rather than 'refer'. My use of 'refer' is such as to satisfy the schema, 'The referent of "X" is X', where 'X' is replaceable by any name or description. I am tentatively inclined to believe, in opposition to Donnellan, that his remarks about reference have little to do with semantics or truth-conditions, though they may be relevant to a theory of speech-acts. Space limitations do not permit me to explain what I mean by this, much less defend the view, except for a brief remark: Call the referent of a name or description in my sense the 'semantic referent'; for a name, this is the thing named, for a description, the thing uniquely satisfying the description.
>
> The speaker may *refer* to something other than the semantic referent if he has appropriate false beliefs. I think this is what happens in the naming (Smith-Jones) cases and also in the Donnellan 'champagne' case; the one requires no theory that names are ambiguous, and the other requires no modification of Russell's theory of descriptions. (25, n3)

We are now in a position to give a more extensive account of why this simply will not do as it stands. To begin with, as we noted earlier, the *Descriptivist* theory that Kripke presents and criticizes later in the text is clearly a theory of *speaker's* reference. Kripke's formulations of that theory begin with an individual speaker, A, whose beliefs are then treated as fixing a description (or cluster of descriptions) associated with a name or other designating expression, X. Satisfaction of *that* description (or of a weighted majority from the cluster), in turn, is *ex hypothesi* what the Descriptivist treats as criterial for determining "the reference" of X.

But this can only mean, "criterial for determining to whom or what *A* is referring by X", for it is no part of traditional Descriptivism to hold that the substantive descriptive beliefs of just any arbitrary, randomly selected individual must fix the *semantic* reference of a proper name. Indeed, it is not even clear to what extent classical Descriptivism engages the *Kripkean* notion of "semantic reference" at all, but *if* classical Descriptivism allows that each name has a referent which is independent of every individual speaker's idiosyncratic beliefs, then it must *also* envision a method for fixing, independently of every individual speaker's beliefs, the descriptive sense by which it supposes that referent to be determined.

One obvious strategy, for example, would be to characterize the semantic reference of a term as its speaker's reference for *most* speakers. But, just as there is no reason that a Descriptivist theory of speaker's reference must treat all properties alike, there is also no reason that a Descriptivist theory of semantic reference must treat all speakers alike. Such a theory could allow for Putnamian "linguistic division of labor" in the case of proper names as much as in the case of general terms. Just as there can be "experts" whose judgment is authoritative regarding what properties something must have or what tests it must pass to qualify as water or molybdenum or a beech tree, so, too, a sophisticated Descriptivism might, as our own epistemic picture does, allow for "experts" whose judgment is authoritative regarding what properties a person must have or what conditions a person must fulfill to qualify as Aristotle or Moses or Feynman. In this case, the semantic reference of a proper name might be characterized as the speaker's reference of the term for a *properly weighted* majority of speakers.

Correlatively, it is surely the *speaker-relativity* of the ostensibly reference-determining descriptions he explicitly envisions that gives many of Kripke's counterexamples their critical bite. For, although any or even all of the descriptive beliefs associated with a name by a given speaker at a given time may indeed be false or arbitrarily informationally impoverished, it does not follow that *every* method by which a Descriptivist might propose to affiliate a specific descriptive sense with a specific proper name as determining its *semantic* referent must issue in a family of beliefs that could be similarly flawed.

Second, Kripke's sanguine (if tentative) diagnosis of divergences between speaker's and semantic reference as uniformly a consequence of some speaker's *false beliefs* is not without its own problems and presuppositions. Helmut, for example, was obviously confused about *something*, but it is not clear that it is entirely correct to describe his confusion in terms of false beliefs. For the question of *what it is* that Helmut believes is, if not actually dependent on, then at least correlative to answers to questions regarding speaker's reference. If Helmut is referring to Moritz Schlick when he uses the name 'Otto Neurath'—if his *Otto Neurath*s are ·Moritz Schlick·s—then, although what Helmut *utters* may be an *Otto Neurath was shot on the steps of the university library*, what he thereby both says and *believes* may nevertheless be that *Schlick* was shot on the steps of the university library. The supposition that one can directly, so to speak, "read off" a speaker's beliefs from his sincere, candid, and spontaneous utterances, in other words, is here essentially equivalent to the presupposition that the speaker's reference of the name used will always coincide with its semantic reference. I shall shortly want to return to these themes in considerably more detail.

Third, however, it is a mistake to suppose that the contrast between speaker's reference and semantic reference necessarily derives from contexts of false belief. It is equally at home, for example, in contexts of referential *uncertainty*, for example,

> When she spoke of 'the most influential Hollywood gossip columnist of the 1940s and 50s', was she referring to Hedda Hopper or to Louella Parsons?

and in contexts of referential *ambiguity*, for example,

> By 'Alexandre Dumas', was he referring to Dumas *père* or Dumas *fils*?[2]

Since conversational and discursive contexts typically *dis*ambiguate, occasions for explicitly raising such questions of speaker's reference will in fact be comparatively rare. *What* is being said (its predicative descriptive content) usually leaves little room for indecision, for instance, regarding whether an acquaintance who uses the proper name 'Rod Stewart' in conversation is referring on that occasion to Rod Stewart, the internationally famous British rock singer, or to his *namesake* Rod Stewart, the talented young American philosopher.

But, finally, as the preceding example once again highlights, whether Kripke is happy about it or not, there is a clear sense in which proper names in a natural language frequently simply *are* ambiguous. Although it is a name of (at least) *two* numerically distinct people, since (as we saw in our earlier examination of the notion of rigid designation) Kripke evidently individuates proper names as such according to purely structural criteria, 'Rod Stewart' will by his lights be *one* proper name.[3]

Such sentences as

> (The name) 'Rod Stewart' refers to Rod Stewart

are on this account also multiply ambiguous. This may not be troublesome, since the sentence perhaps expresses a trivial truth on both (or, better, on all) of its readings. Kripke's claim that *his* use of 'refer' is such as to satisfy the schema 'The referent of "X" is X' in contrast, is *not* trivial. It assumes that the definite description 'The referent of "X" ' is itself well-defined, and therefore presupposes *inter alia* that the proper name embedded in that description is *not* referentially ambiguous. But, although the expression

the name 'Rod Stewart'

as Kripke evidently understands it, is well-defined, the expression

the referent of (the name) 'Rod Stewart'

is not. The (one) name 'Rod Stewart' has *many* referents.

Correlatively, the (one) name 'Rod Stewart' has reached me on various occasions by many *independent* causal-historical communicative routes. Rod Stewart, the young philosopher, introduced himself to me personally several years ago. In contrast, Rod Stewart, the rock singer, has always been known to me only through the mass media, but this was so long before I met his philosophical namesake. The causal-historical picture's strategic epistemological proposal to trace the communicational ancestry of the name 'Rod Stewart' in *my* idiolect will always in fact *ultimately* lead back to Rod Stewart, the rock singer, since it was as a name of the rock singer that I first acquired the name—and this will be true even when I am referring to (i.e., using the name as a name of) Rod Stewart, the philosopher.

For expository purposes, it has been customary to adopt the pretense that a natural language under philosophical study has been variously "tidied up" or *regimented*. In particular, it has been customary to pretend that ambiguous proper names have been *disambiguated* (e.g., with notational indices), so that each (regimented) proper name has one and only one semantic referent. When one is engaged in philosophical theorizing precisely about the semantics of proper names in a natural language, however, such expository conventions are at best infelicitous and most often simply disastrous. For they obscure, *inter alia*, the fact that ultimately it is *only* descriptive content that disambiguates nominal reference, and thereby function to mask the significant differences between genuine proper names and the individual constants of an interpreted logical calculus.

The tensions between Kripke's theoretical claims and the *de facto* semantic phenomenology of proper names in a natural language come properly into focus when Kripke's presuppositions are seen as deriving from the model of such individual constants. When a logical calculus is interpreted into, for example, a family of set-theoretic structures, its individual constants are normally assigned to elements of a domain *independently* of subsequent interpretative assignments covering predicative contexts and well-formed formulae. Analogously, Kripke proposes that a proper name can have a semantic referent independently of its occurrences in descriptive sentences expressing speakers' beliefs. Individual constants are mapped onto elements of a domain so that each constant receives one and only one interpretive assignment. Proper names, Kripke supposes, can be similarly treated, at least for purposes of philosophical theorizing, as referentially unambiguous. In interpreting a formal calculus, n-adic predicates are characteristically mapped onto sets of n-tuples of domain elements; truth-functions and quantifiers are treated recursively; and the resultant set-theoretic truth conditions for a well-formed formula can then be directly "read off" from its compositional syntax. Analogously, Kripke suggests that a speaker's (contentive, semantically classifiable) beliefs can be directly "read off" from (the structural surface forms of) his sincere, candid, and spontaneous utterances.

For a century now, the topics of reference and necessity have in fact been inextricably intertwined with such philosophical ideas regarding formal systems and their applications. It is therefore quite apposite to raise a number of methodological questions regarding the proper understanding of the relationships between natural languages and mathematical or quasi-mathematical formalisms (paradigmatically, logical calculi), and in the next chapter I shall indeed do so. Until we command an appropriate view of the powers and limitations of such conceptual tools, we can scarcely hope to make significant progress on more substantive fronts.

First, however, I must attend to some unfinished business. As promised, the subtle and complicated issue of the relationships between beliefs and sentences has once again become especially salient. Earlier I noted a certain reciprocity between questions regarding a speaker's reference and questions regarding that speaker's beliefs. Kripke characteristically assumes that speaker's reference and semantic reference coincide, and I suggested that this assumption also takes on the form of a supposition to the effect that one can "read off" a speaker's beliefs from his sincere, candid, and spontaneous utterances. As is well known, however, Kripke himself has explicitly explored the consequences of (a version of) this last principle and found it deeply, perhaps irredeemably, problematic.[4] A useful starting point, then, will be Kripke's own puzzle about belief.

The puzzle, we recall, concerns Pierre, "a normal French speaker who [to begin with] lives in France and speaks not a word of English or of any other language except French" (PB, 254). On various occasions, Pierre candidly utters and unreservedly assents to the French sentence '*Londres est jolie*', from which we (French-English bilinguals) naturally conclude:

(1) Pierre believes that London is pretty.

Later, Pierre comes to live in an unattractive part of London populated by fairly uneducated inhabitants who, like Pierre himself, rarely travel outside their shabby quarter. Since his neighbors know no French, Pierre is forced to learn English "directly", by mixing and talking with the people. In this way, he comes to know that the fellow residents of the city in which he now lives call it 'London'. Since his surroundings are markedly unattractive, after a time Pierre becomes inclined sincerely to utter and assent to the English sentence, 'London is not pretty', while having no inclination at all to utter or assent to "London is pretty". On the basis of these evidences, however, it appears that we are equally entitled to conclude:

(2) Pierre believes that London is not pretty,

and, *perhaps*, even:

(3) Pierre does not believe that London is pretty.

But (3), of course, directly contradicts our earlier conclusion from Pierre's behavior as a French speaker, (1).

What primarily shapes our reasoning in such cases is what Kripke calls the *disquotational principle:*

(DQ_E) If a normal English speaker, on reflection, sincerely assents to 'p', then he believes that p,

where 'p' is replaced, both inside and outside the single quotes, by any "appropriate standard English sentence" (PB, 248–249). Given Pierre's English linguistic behavior, (2) will be an immediate consequence of (DQ_E). We can arrive at (1) by a variety of more complicated routes. Kripke himself opts for a French language counterpart to the principle (DQ_E)—say, (DQ_F)—together with a *principle of translation*

(PT) If a sentence of one language expresses a truth in that language, then any translation of it into any other language also expresses a truth (in that other language) (PB, 250)

and a detour through the metalanguage. Thus, on Kripke's model, from Pierre's sincere and candid assent to the French sentence *'Londres est jolie'*, we bilinguals first infer, using (DQ_F):

(1f) *Pierre croit que Londres est jolie.*

With the help of tacit "Tarskian" disquotational principles,[5] from (1f) we can derive:

(vf) *'Pierre croit que Londres est jolie' est vrai (en Francais),*

which, translated into English, in turn becomes:

(tf) *'Pierre croit que Londres est jolie'* is true (in French).

Given then that the translation of the sentence *'Pierre croit que Londres est jolie'* itself into English is 'Pierre believes that London is pretty', the principle of translation (PT) will yield:

(te) 'Pierre believes that London is pretty' is true (in English),

from which, again with the help of Tarskian disquotation, (1) immediately follows.

Finally, to arrive at the most problematic (because explicitly contradictory) conclusion (3), Kripke suggests a strengthened 'biconditional' form of the disquotational principle (DQ_E):

(BDQ_E) A normal English speaker who is not reticent will be disposed to sincere reflective assent to 'p' if and only if he believes that p,

where again any suitable English sentence may replace 'p' in each of its occurrences. If we adopt (BDQ_E), (3) becomes a straightforward consequence of Pierre's failure (perhaps even better, his reluctance) to assent to the English sentence 'London is pretty'.

Let us first consider how the situation lies with respect to (1) and (2). Kripke argues persuasively that the linguistic evidence on the basis of which we conclude (2), that is, Pierre's English-language behavior during his later London days, does not warrant our withdrawing our initial acceptance of (1) on the basis of monolingual Pierre's original French-language conducts: "To allow such *ex post facto* legislation would, so long as the future is

150   Chapter 6

uncertain, endanger our attributions of belief to *all* monolingual Frenchmen" (PB, 256). Nor, given that his French-language behavior remains unchanged, is it plausible to suppose that, since coming to live in London, Pierre has changed his mind or abandoned his earlier belief.

Analogously, Kripke argues, our knowledge of Pierre's French past should not affect our acceptance of (2) on the basis of his English-language conducts.

> Suppose an electric shock wiped out all his memories of the French language, what he learned in France, and his French past. He would then be *exactly* like his neighbors in London. . . . We would then presumably be forced to say that Pierre believes that London is ugly if [as is indeed the case] we say it of his neighbors. But . . . no shock that *destroys* part of Pierre's memories and knowledge can *give* him a new belief. (PB, 257)

If it would be true of English-speaking Pierre after such a shock that he believes that London is not pretty, in other words, it must also be true that, despite his French background, he believed it before the shock. Thus, just as the facts regarding Pierre's English-language conducts do not impugn the truth of (1), the facts regarding his French-language conducts do not impugn that of (2).

The option of rejecting both (1) and (2), of course, simply combines the theoretical shortcomings of rejecting each separately. It therefore appears, Kripke concludes, "that we must respect both Pierre's French utterances and their English counterparts. So we must say that Pierre has contradictory beliefs, that he believes that London is pretty and he believes that London is not pretty" (PB, 257). "But", Kripke continues, "there seem to be insuperable difficulties with this alternative as well".

Since I have just endorsed Kripke's arguments in support of (1) and (2), this last alternative is plainly the only one still consistently open to me. It is crucial, therefore, that we properly appreciate and assess Kripke's "insuperable difficulties" here. His arguments in evidence of such difficulties flow from two modifications of the original case. In the first of these modifications, Pierre's circumstances and behavior remain the same, but he is granted, in addition, extraordinary logical acumen:

> We may suppose that Pierre . . . is a leading philosopher and logician. He would *never* let contradictory beliefs pass. And surely anyone, leading logician or no, is in principle in a position to notice and correct contradictory beliefs if he has them. Precisely for this reason, we regard individuals who contradict themselves as subject to greater censure than those who merely have false beliefs. But it is clear that Pierre, so long as he is unaware that the cities he calls 'London' and '*Londres*' are one and the same, is in no position to see, by logic alone, that at least one of his beliefs must be false. He lacks information, not logical acumen. He cannot be convicted of inconsistency: to do so is incorrect. (PB, 257)

Now Kripke is clearly correct in observing that Pierre is in no position to discover *by logic alone* that he holds inconsistent beliefs. But, whatever we posit regarding Pierre's logical acumen, it is hard to see why this should imply that he does not *in fact* hold inconsistent beliefs. Nor does the mediating principle to which Kripke explicitly appeals,

(PCB) Any (non-defective, sufficiently mature, reflective, etc.) person is in principle in a position to notice and correct contradictory beliefs if he has them,

lead to this conclusion. For we may agree that Pierre is *in principle* in a position to notice and correct his contradictory beliefs, and at the same time consistently deny that he is *in practice* in a position to do so. He is not in practice in such a position, in turn, precisely *because* he lacks the information that the cities he calls 'London' and '*Londres*' are one and the same. It is, indeed, precisely because he lacks this crucial information that Pierre's extraordinary logical acumen does not suffice to insulate him from holding contradictory beliefs about London. That is *why* Pierre cannot discover by logic alone that the totality of his beliefs about London forms an inconsistent set.

What we can legitimately expect from a "leading philosopher and logician", in other words, is only that he will never "let contradictory beliefs pass" *if he knows he has them*. What we cannot legitimately expect from any human being, however, is omniscience—not even limited omniscience with respect to the totality of his own beliefs. For a person can have false or fragmentary beliefs, not only about the world, but also about what it is that he believes about the world. That is why the question of whether Pierre should be regarded as "subject to greater censure than those who merely have false beliefs"—or whether he can be "convicted" of inconsistency—is not a straightforward matter-of-factual question. Certainly we may suppose that, if Pierre were *aware* that he believed both that London is pretty and that London is not pretty, he would promptly undertake to eliminate the inconsistency by revising one or another (or both) of his beliefs. But surely Pierre is epistemically at fault in this case only if, given his circumstances, he *ought to be* aware that he holds inconsistent beliefs, that is, if he ought to know that the cities he calls 'London' and '*Londres*' are one and the same. Since, however, the circumstances of Kripke's thought-experiment are originally explicitly designed to deny Pierre this crucial bit of knowledge, this normative claim cannot be sustained. Pierre's holding inconsistent beliefs in those circumstances consequently does not constitute an occasion for extraordinary epistemic censure. He is simply *non-culpably* ignorant of certain (linguistic) matters of fact.

From this point of view, Kripke's second modification fares no better.

Reference and Belief 153

> Suppose that, in France, Pierre, instead of affirming "*Londres est jolie,*" had affirmed, more cautiously, "*Si New York est jolie, Londres est jolie aussi,*" so that he believed that *if* New York is pretty, so is London. Later Pierre moves to London, learns English as before, and says (in English) "London is not pretty." So he now believes, further, that London is *not* pretty. Now from [these] two premises, . . . Pierre should be able to deduce . . . that New York is not pretty. But no matter how great Pierre's logical acumen may be, *he cannot in fact make any such deduction, as long as he supposes that 'Londres' and 'London' name two different cities.* If he *did* draw such a conclusion, he would be guilty of a fallacy. . . . Yet, if we follow our normal practice of reporting the beliefs of both French and English speakers, *Pierre has available to him (among his beliefs) both the premises of a modus tollens argument that New York is not pretty.* (PB, 257–258)

What we need to focus on here is Kripke's assertion that, from the two premises,

(4) If New York is pretty, London is pretty,

and

(5) London is not pretty,

both of which are among his beliefs, Pierre "should be able to deduce" that New York is not pretty. We can now see that these words can express two very different claims.

On the one hand, Kripke can be understood as claiming only that any person who believes both (4) and (5) is thereby *logically committed* to believing

(6) New York is not pretty

as well. This, of course, is true, for it is simply the *logical* claim that (4) and (5) together *imply* (6)—equivalently, that (6) follows from (4) and (5)—expressed, so to speak, in a different expository tone of voice. The fact that Pierre is thus (logically) committed to the conclusion expressed by (6), however, is entirely compatible with his in fact not being in an *epistemic* position actually to *draw* that conclusion.

On the other hand, Kripke's claim can be understood as belonging, not to logic, but to (normative) epistemology. Thus interpreted, the claim amounts to the assertion that Pierre *ought to be* in the epistemic position in fact to perform the appropriate inferential act, that is, actually to draw the relevant conclusion. Only on this reading will there be a tension between the fact, emphasized by Kripke, that Pierre "cannot in fact make any such deduction" and the claim that he "should be able to" do so. It will be the case that Pierre ought to be in a position actually to draw the conclusion (6), however, only if, in general, a person's having "available to him (among his beliefs)" the premises of a valid deductive argument for some conclusion and also commanding the appropriate levels of logical acumen ought to be jointly sufficient conditions for his actually drawing it. But that is simply not the case. For it is also necessary, at least, that the person *be (simultaneously) aware* that those premises are available to him.[6]

The premises (4) and (5) are "available" to Pierre precisely (and only) in the sense that it is true *of* Pierre both that he believes (4) and that he believes (5). Certainly we may again suppose that, if Pierre became simultaneously *aware* that he believed both that if New York is pretty, London is as well and that London is not pretty, he would straightaway conclude that New York is not pretty.[7] But, once again, what we cannot legitimately suppose is that Pierre must be omniscient, even about what he in fact believes. As the case has been constructed, Pierre's becoming simultaneously aware that he holds both these beliefs would require his coming to know that the cities he calls 'London' and '*Londres*' are one and the same, and, again, the circumstances of Kripke's thought-experiment are explicitly designed to deny him this crucial bit of knowledge. Pierre's *de facto* failure to draw the conclusion to which he is logically entitled (and, indeed, logically committed) consequently does not impugn his posited special logical acumen, nor is it an occasion for any other sort of epistemological fault-finding. It is simply another manifestation of his non-culpable matter-of-factual ignorance.

I conclude, then, that there is no reason not to grant both Pierre's French and his English linguistic behavior their full normal evidential weight and so to attribute to him inconsistent beliefs. Upon closer examination, we have found that the "insuperable difficulties" which ostensibly arise from our simultaneously endorsing both (1) and (2) instead turn on Kripke's failure properly to respect the difference between logical and epistemic norms. This theme, indeed, has already surfaced on various occasions during our investigations, and I shall want to return to it in some detail. First, however, we must address the matter of

(3) Pierre does not believe that London is pretty.

Having endorsed both (1) and (2), I can consistently be expected to reject (3), and so indeed I do. The truth of (1), indeed, *entails* the falsehood of (3). Since (3) itself was supported by an appeal to the strengthened "biconditional" disquotational principle

(BDQ_E) A normal English speaker who is not reticent will be disposed to sincere reflective assent to 'p' if and only if he believes that p,

(where each occurrence of 'p' is replaced by the same appropriate English sentence), it *should* follow that (BDQ_E) is false as well, and I am inclined simply to conclude that it is.

On the face of it, one could instead deny that Pierre is a normal English speaker. Certainly Pierre does not seem to be a *typical* English speaker. I venture to guess that a typical English speaker is *monolingual*. And surely even typical (English-French) *bilingual* English speakers will lack the peculiar history that, so to speak, "encapsulates" and "compartmentalizes" Pierre's earlier and later beliefs about London. But in fact being a normal English speaker in Kripke's sense has nothing directly to do with being a typical one. Kripke's sense of 'normal' is not statistical but normative. In this sense, Kripke tells us, a normal English speaker is one who "uses all words in a sentence in a standard way, combines them according to the appropriate syntax, etc.: in short, he uses the sentence to mean what a normal speaker should mean by it" (PB, 249).

I trust it is obvious that this "elucidation" of 'normal English speaker' as it stands is hopelessly circular, not just in terms of its explicit use of the very notion it proposes to elucidate (to refer to what a *normal speaker* should mean by a sentence), but in its appeal to such notions as "standard" word usages and "appropriate" syntax as well. For, on the most natural reading, these are themselves normative notions correlative to the notion of a normal speaker. A word is used "in a standard way", for example, if it is used in a way that normal speakers (normally) use it.[8]

In any event, whatever plausibility accrues to the problematic conditional,

> (QD_E) If a normal, non-reticent English speaker believes that p, then he will be disposed to sincere reflective assent to 'p'

—the other half of the biconditional (BDQ_E) being equivalent to the (at least provisionally) acceptable principle (DQ_E)—results from its tacit reliance on a limited first-person omniscience with respect to one's own beliefs. For otherwise the explanation of a given normal English speaker's failure to avow or assent to an English sentence, 'p', expressing a belief, that p, which he in fact holds might not be reticence but simply *ignorance*. That is, the suggestion, implicit in (QD_E), that the notion of a speaker's "reticence"—"shyness, a desire for secrecy, to avoid offence, etc." (PB, 249)—in principle encompasses *all* the reasons for such failure to assent is inconsistent with the idea that a normal English speaker might fail to assent to 'p' because he *does not know* that he believes that p.

I conclude, then, that the conditional (QD_E), and thus Kripke's own biconditional (BDQ_E), is indeed false. Nor does it alter the case if, as Kripke suggests in passing, we equip our hypothetical speaker (or Pierre) with an explicit sign to "indicate lack of belief—not necessarily disbelief—in the assertion propounded" (PB, 249). For what is wrong with (QD_E) and (BDQ_E) is not that the behavioral evidence on the basis of which they license us to draw conclusions about a speaker's lack of belief is too sparse or unacceptably ambiguous. What's wrong with (QD_E) and (BDQ_E) is that they presuppose a mistaken "Cartesian" principle of a speaker's "privileged first-person access" to his own beliefs. They presuppose, that is, that if Pierre himself sincerely and reflectively asserts, in English,

(7) I don't believe that London is pretty,

then what he says *must* be true.

We can conclude, too, that our normal epistemic practices of belief ascription, including our reliance on such principles as (DQ_E), are not irredeemably paradox-ridden. In normal circumstances, a person's beliefs track in an orderly fashion with the sentences to which he is inclined to assent. Consequently, we can normally legitimately "read off" a speaker's beliefs—and correlatively his references—from the sentences he is prepared candidly to utter and endorse.

What we learn from such cases as those of Helmut and Gracie and Pierre is, *inter alia*, that there are (indefinitely) many ways in which the circumstances of a person's linguistic conduct can fail to be normal. In Pierre's case, I have argued (*contra* Kripke), the envisioned circumstantial abnormalities do not in fact confound our normal epistemic practices with regard to belief ascription. The *point* of ascribing beliefs (and desires) to others, after all, is to enable us to explain and help us to anticipate various aspects of their conduct. In the case of Pierre, what we have at hand are various French and English *linguistic* conducts and, as Kripke himself argues, these are *severally* best explained by ascribing to Pierre a pair of inconsistent beliefs. What *is* frustrated by the circumstantial abnormalities of Pierre's case, in contrast, are the conventional *normative* consequences of such belief ascriptions, for example, the normal implication that Pierre is epistemically at fault and legitimately "subject to greater censure than those who merely have false beliefs" (PB, 257).

In contrast, as we have seen, the circumstantial abnormalities in the cases of Helmut and Gracie are sufficient to disrupt the normal relationships between speaker's reference and semantic reference, or, correlatively, a speaker's beliefs and their *de facto* linguistic expression. When viewed from an epistemological perspective, I have argued, such cases also challenge the customary expository fiction according to which the semantics of a natural language is to be understood on the model of the set-theoretic interpretation of a logical calculus and proper names on the model of individual constants. The theme of the relationships between natural languages and mathematical or quasi-mathematical formalisms has in fact been a persistent undercurrent throughout these investigations which, although it has occasionally surfaced, has not yet come fully into the light. It is high time, then, that we took a good look at it, and, in particular, at the key concept (or root metaphor) in terms of which such relationships have been characteristically construed, the notion of *logical form*. This then sets the agenda for my next chapter.

7
Logical Analysis in Epistemological Perspective

IT IS NOT clear who should be credited with introducing the notion of 'logical form' in its dominant contemporary sense. In the sense I intend—the sense in which, for example, Donald Davidson undertakes to explore[1] "the logical form of action sentences" or "the logical form of belief sentences"—'logical form' is a term of contrast. A story about logical form is thus typically a story about aspects of human language and language use which speaks of two forms, logical form and, for example, *grammatical* form. (There are, of course, various aliases for such notions, for example, 'logical grammar', 'depth grammar', or 'deep structure' on the one hand, 'syntactic form', 'surface grammar', or 'surface structure' on the other.) On this picture, elements of human languaging performances—phrases, sentences, arguments, conversations, discourses, or what have you—can be descriptively characterized in two distinct ways: in terms of features that can, as it were, be "read off" from the phenomenologically accessible linguistic "surface" and in terms of features that are epistemically accessible only by way of some sort of "deep" theoretical *analysis*.

Something along the lines of this two-level picture is frequently incorporated into the pedagogy of introductory instruction in formal, symbolic, or mathematical logic as part of an explanation of the relationships between the new formalisms and bits of reasoning conducted or expressed in a natural language.

Such natural language arguments or *NL-arguments,* as I shall speak of them, are described, in the first instance, as collections of (indicative, declarative) *sentences* among which certain *logical relationships* are supposed to obtain. In the simplest case, one sentence is represented as following from another sentence or group of sentences. Certain sentences are identified as premises, others as (mediate or ultimate) conclusions, and it is either explicitly claimed or implicitly indicated that specific collections of premises *imply* specific conclusions. Alternative terminological possibilities may be mobilized at this stage of the proceedings, for example: the conclusion "follows from" or "may be validly inferred from" the premises; the premises "entail" the conclusion; or the *denial* of the conclusion "is inconsistent with" or "contradicts" (the conjunction of) the premises.

I shall call such logical relationships, as they are ascribed to exemplary NL-arguments, *I-relations,* to remind us of 'inference', 'implication', and 'inconsistency'. (If we are also reminded of 'intuitions', so much the better—but more on that later.) I have begun by treating (indicative, declarative) *sentences* as the appropriate terms of such I-relations. Once again, there are other options, for example, the statements or assertions that such sentences are used to make; or the propositions or claims that they express. But whether and, if so, why we might instead want to talk in terms of such "abstract" relata are questions that in fact belong precisely to the problematic of "logical analysis" *per se,* and consequently ones that we should not implicitly prejudge by initial terminological decisions.

A goodly portion of the introductory pedagogy of formal, symbolic, or mathematical logic is devoted to the enterprise of "formalizing" or "symbolizing" such NL-arguments. Students are taught techniques for associating the individual premiss and conclusion sentences of such arguments with (well-formed) *formulae* of a logical *calculus,* that is, strings of symbols assembled in conformity with determinate structural rules. In addition to a symbolic vocabulary and a (typically recursive) structural-rule specification of well-formedness for strings drawn from that vocabulary, such a calculus also comes equipped with a sort of "operating manual" that specifies a set of *admissible transformations* of formulae into formulae. Like the structural formation rules governing well-formedness, the entitlement rules governing such inter-formulaic transformations are structure-responsive "effective procedures", which is roughly to say that they are meant to leave nothing to the imagination. Whether one formula is an admissible transform of one or more others must be something that can be determined, as one says, "purely mechanically".[2]

In terms of a calculus' formation and transformation rules, one can define various relationships among strings of its symbols. One string, for example, might contain specific other strings as proper parts or be transformable into another string by a series of admissible steps. Such relationships among formulae are often also called "implication", "entailment", or "contradiction", but this terminological custom, although historically explainable, at best blurs and at worst prejudges precisely the central issues regarding the relationships between natural language performances and formal (symbolic) systems that I am seeking to thematize here. I shall consequently speak here of *"S-transforms"* and *"S-derivations"*, to remind us that we are dealing with *s*eries of *s*teps involving only the *s*tructures of *s*trings *of s*ymbols, and *"D-relations"*, for the inter-formulaic relations *d*efinable in terms of such *d*erivations. (Perhaps we are reminded here of *d*eductive relations. No harm done—as long as we keep our NL and symbolic discourses straight.) When something more specific is needed, I shall speak of "D-consequence", "D-inconsistency", and the like.

What is of interest to us here is how NL-arguments and I-relations are supposed to fit together with S-derivations and D-relations. One story that is often told, at least in introductory pedagogical contexts, goes something like this: We can use such a

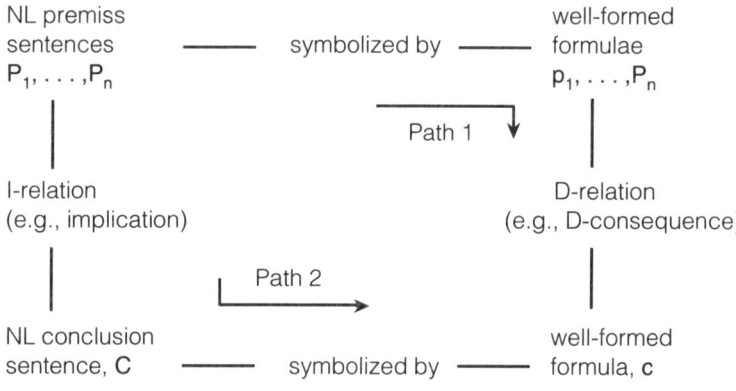

FIGURE 1

logical calculus to *evaluate* NL-arguments. Properly symbolized, a logically good (i.e., valid) NL-argument will correspond to an admissible S-derivation, whereas a logically bad (i.e., invalid) NL-argument will correspond to *no* admissible S-derivation. Otherwise put, a group of NL premiss sentences will imply an NL conclusion sentence just in case the formula which symbolizes that conclusion is a D-consequence of the formulae which symbolize those premisses (see Figure 1). If a path from the NL premiss sentences, through their proper symbolization, and over admissible S-transforms (Path 1) issues in the same formula as the path that runs from those premisses over the original inference of a conclusion sentence to its proper symbolization (Path 2), we declare the original inference to be logically acceptable; otherwise unacceptable.[3]

For a student encountering contemporary symbolic logic for the first time *in medias res*, however, it is unlikely that the central role played by the notion of *inference* in understanding logical form just sketched will be especially salient. The focus of logical theory seems rather to be on a special kind of *truth*—"logical truth"—and, correspondingly, a special class of S-derivations—

derivations of "theorems" (briefly, "demonstrations"), in the course of which all assumptions or hypotheses are "discharged". The road to metatheory is short and smooth. Logical calculi quickly take on lives of their own, as *objects* of study, and a great deal of time and effort is then devoted to exploring "interpretations" of such systems. Procedures are developed for modeling one formal system (a logical calculus) in another (typically, a set-theoretic system) with the aim of demonstrating within the latter that all and/or only the model-theoretic counterparts of demonstrable theorems of the calculus can or cannot be shown to have or to lack certain set-theoretic features. It is all too easy to lose track of the fact that logic, including formal logic, is first and foremost concerned with the proper canons of *cogent reasoning*.

The proper perspective can be partially restored by noticing how a *philosophical* practitioner of "logical analysis" proceeds about his business—say, investigating the logical form of action sentences in the Davidsonian style. Such an investigation typically begins by attending to a family of exemplary (NL-) *arguments* in which representative sentences of the relevant kind play an essential (premissory) role. Thus Davidson notes, for example, that from the premiss "John slowly buttered the toast at midnight in the kitchen with a knife" one can correctly infer that John buttered the toast, that John buttered the toast slowly, that John did something at midnight, that something happened in the kitchen, and so on. The analytical enterprise then becomes one of *symbolizing* these sentences in such a way that such intuitively obtaining I-relations among them are isomorphic to D-relations obtaining among the resultant corresponding formulae.

The practitioner of *Davidsonian* logical analysis has a determinate formal system, a logical calculus, ready at hand, namely, first-order predicate logic with identity. We can consequently think of him as beginning with two "grids", a vast (natural-linguistic) network of sentences interconnected by I-relations and a vast (symbolic) network of "uninterpreted" formulae interconnected by D-relations. The analytical enterprise consists in attempting to induce an isomorphism between the exemplary arguments and a region of the symbolic network, that is, to associate NL-sentences with symbolic formulae in such a way that every positive exemplar (logically good argument), but no negative exemplar (logically bad argument), corresponds to a *correct demonstration*, that is, a correct S-derivation of the conclusion formula from the premiss formulae.

If the effort succeeds, our logical analyst will conclude that he has "formalized" the arguments that he took as his exemplars. Each sentence in the original NL-arguments will be associated with a determinate formula of the calculus, its (proper) symbolization. The symbolization of a sentence, so the story concludes, then gives or specifies or exhibits or represents (the terminology varies) its "logical form".

I have so far been following one main channel of what in fact is a river with many branchings and confluences. A Davidsonian (or Quinean) logical analyst, for example, deliberately limits his formal toolbox to one sort of logical system—a first-order predicate calculus with identity. In contrast, other practitioners are prepared to supplement or enrich this (relatively austere) formal apparatus with additional notational and expressive resources—second- and higher-order predicates; adverbial predicate modifiers; alethic, deontic, and other styles of modal sentential operators; and even "topical", for example, tensed or semantic, connectives—and to modify their *transformational* resources to suit these alternative symbolizations. There thus exists a degree of "free play" between formational and transformational considerations in the construction of logical calculi, a fact which will turn out to be significant for a proper understanding of "logical analysis".

Again, tributaries branch off from the notions of logical form and logical analysis into diverse regions of the philosophical jungle. Some logical analysts advance from claims regarding "logical form" to claims regarding the "deep structure" of, for example, English sentences and thence, aided and abetted by certain sorts of theoretical linguistics, to provocative conclusions regarding "linguistic universals" and even the genetic endowments of human speakers. Others go on to draw conclusions about "the language of thought" or the way in which "information is stored in the brain". And still others invoke conclusions about logical form in support of metaphysical theses regarding "the ontological furniture of the world", for example, that "events" properly belong to our ultimate ontological inventory (since we must "quantify over them").[4] Like the "adjudicative" use of a logical calculus to evaluate NL-arguments, each of these philosophical applications of the results of "logical analysis" suggests that the symbolic forms and transforms of such a logical calculus possess a *verdictive authority* with respect to something else. Viewed "adjudicatively", a calculus is accorded verdictive authority with respect to the obtaining or non-obtaining of I-relations among NL-sentences; regarded in these more venturesome ways, with respect to the (genetic) preconditions of human natural-linguistic competences, or the "internal representation" of beliefs, memories, and desires, or even the ultimate ontological constitution of reality. Whether the symbolic forms and transforms of a logical calculus can *actually* possess such a verdictive authority—and, if so, from what (epistemic) source it derives—are central and difficult questions of the problematic of "logical analysis" I am in the midst of exploring.

With minor modifications, one could also broadly assimilate the earliest Fregean development of logical systems *as such* to the mainstream pattern exemplified by Davidsonian-style logical analysis (although other epistemic models will in due course also prove enlightening). Davidsonian studies of "the logical form of action sentences" pick out the sentences in question, and so collect an initial family of intuitively good exemplary arguments, by attending to a characteristic *vocabulary*—specifically, to verbs of conduct and their adverbial modifiers. Similarly, (alethic) modal logic is responsible to exemplary NL-arguments collected by attending to essential occurrences of 'necessary' and 'possible', and deontic logic to arguments collected by attending to 'ought' and 'may' (or 'obligatory', 'permitted', and 'forbidden'). In this spirit, one could think of Frege's constructions as also primarily responsible to a family of exemplary NL-arguments collected by attending to essential occurrences of a characteristic vocabulary—in this instance, the *logical particles*, for example, 'not', 'and', 'or', 'if . . . then . . .', 'all', 'some', and the like.

On this model, the chief difference between Frege's and Davidson's analytical projects is that, unlike Davidson, Frege did not already have a determinate symbolic system lying ready at hand. Frege had consequently to introduce his notations and their formation and transformation rules *ab initio*, simultaneously with their application as "symbolizing" the exemplary NL-arguments (e.g., the reasonings of mathematicians) which were the authentic original focus of his concern. This interpretation thereafter agrees with our mainstream model, however, in fixing the epistemic locus of *success* in the achievement of a partial isomorphism between correct and incorrect symbolic demonstrations and the "pre-analytically" logically good and bad NL-arguments corresponding to them under proper symbolization.

That this model of logical analysis here runs up against significant limits is suggested by the fact that we are left with the problem of elucidating the notion of a "logical particle", that is, of isolating in a principled manner those NL vocabulary items that are in fact determinative for the Fregean ur-project thus understood. The classical strategy of identifying them as "syncategoremata" nowadays founders on the absence of a suitable contemporary account of *categories*. At present the alternative most frequently invoked is likely to be an appeal to an intuitive distinction between *logical* and *descriptive* terms. This strategy appears to be more promising (especially in light of our earlier explorations of the conceptual connections between the notions of description and explanation), but it is clear that considerable elucidatory work remains to be done. Only in the next chapter, however, will we be in a position to engage this theme in appropriate detail.

Here our next step is to explore what can happen when the partial isomorphism induced between a limited group of exemplary NL-arguments and the fully determinate "grid" of a logical calculus successfully "calibrated" to them is *projected* over the entire network of NL-sentences together with their diverse presumptive I-relations. Crucially, logical analysts can here run up against "pre-analytic convictions" or "logical intuitions" which *conflict* with the verdicts regarding the goodness or badness of NL-arguments rendered by their symbolic results. Analogously, different groups of practitioners of logical analysis can "pre-analytically" disagree even about the logical goodness or badness of ostensible *exemplars*. Among modal and deontic logicians, indeed, such disagreement about exemplary NL-arguments is standard operating procedure, but the phenomenology extends to disagreements about "formalizations" of the logical particles *per se*. Thus "classicists" accept certain paradigms of *reductio ad absurdum* reasoning and non-constructive existence proofs which their "intuitionist" colleagues reject, and "relevance logicians" depart from the "truth-functional" mainstream in numerous convictions regarding implication and inconsistency.

Such disagreements are another locus at which the "free play" between formational and transformational considerations in the construction of logical calculi can become manifest. The closer the disagreement lies to the ur-project of "formalizing" the logical particles *per se*, however, the more likely we are to find a restriction of the set of admissible transforms over the corresponding core notations of a calculus rather than an enrichment of its notational and expressive resources to accommodate, for example, both "extensional" and "intentional" connectives. The upshot is a plurality of *logics*, that is, a multiplicity of *notationally* indistinguishable symbolic calculi roughly corresponding to the multiplicity of original "pre-analytic logical intuitions", in light of which the epistemic question of verdictive authority sketched earlier becomes particularly acute.

At this point in the dialectic, we can distinguish the "apostles of tolerance" from the "hard core". An apostle of tolerance begins by proposing a harmonious retreat to the relaxed pluralism of pure mathematics. Let a thousand systems bloom. And, indeed, such alternative calculi can certainly be developed and investigated for their own intrinsic interest as mathematical objects, quite apart from considerations of their relationships to NL-arguments. But this decision precisely severs the original constitutive connection between formal logic and *cogent reasoning*. Once the question of that connection is explicitly raised, what we find, curiously enough, is that the apostles of tolerance tend to adopt the same introductory *pedagogy* as their hard-core colleagues. That is, they teach the use of symbolizations and logical calculi to *evaluate* NL-arguments, and their initial congenial pluralistic resolve in fact tends to vary inversely with the extent that the question of the relationships between NL-reasonings and S-derivations is pressed. An ecumenical stance regarding I-relations is difficult to sustain in the face of, for example, fervent Thomistic urgings that the "pre-analytic", "intuitive" logical goodness of Aquinas' NL-arguments in support of the conclusion that God exists should properly constrain and be acknowledged by any adequate formalism (or, from a different initial perspective, anti-Thomistic urgings to the contrary).

Members of the hard core, in contrast (to which Kripke in essential respects belongs), stand by the verdictive authority of their chosen formalisms. While there is, of course, nothing wrong with studying a plurality of symbolic calculi from the purely mathematical point of view, one cannot coherently regard them *all* (indifferently) as systematically capturing the pre-analytic or intuitive notion of *logically correct reasoning*. Disagreement about the logical correctness of specific NL-arguments, then, can only be a reflection of *mistaken* intuitions. The disputed NL-arguments, that is, although they might *appear* to be logically good (or bad), are not *really* logically good (or bad).[5] Recourse to the idioms of reality and appearance (being and seeming) at this point is, in fact, a generally reliable sign of hard-core tendencies.

The introduction of these idioms here suggests one line of thought in terms of which a hard-core practitioner of logical analysis might undertake to legitimize and validate a symbolic formalism's claim to verdictive authority. According to this line of thought, a logical calculus has the epistemic status of a *theory*. Like, for example, kinetic thermodynamics, a logical calculus *qua* theory has a double subject matter. The subject matter of kinetic thermodynamics can be described both in *pre*-theoretical and in *intra*-theoretical terms. Pre-theoretically viewed, it is a theory of heat; intra-theoretically viewed, a theory of kinetic energy. Similarly, on the interpretation now before us, a symbolic system is *pre*-theoretically viewed as a theory of NL-arguments, that is, of natural language sentences and the I-relations obtaining among them. *Intra*-theoretically considered, however, a symbolic system is a theory of logical form. On this model, in other words, logical form is a *theoretical property* of NL-sentences themselves. Just as the kinetic energy of their constituent molecules is *the* (theoretical) property of gases by which their manifest (observable, phenomenological) thermodynamic behavior is actually determined, so logical form is understood on this interpretation as *the* (theoretical) property of natural language sentences by which their manifest (observable, phenomenological) *logical* behavior, that is, the obtaining or non-obtaining of I-relations among them, actually depends.[6]

A line of thought that assimilates symbolic calculi to theories and their verdictive authority to the epistemic authority of a natural science in this fashion will also tend to regard the pattern of relationships exhibited in Figure 1 as a determinate instance of

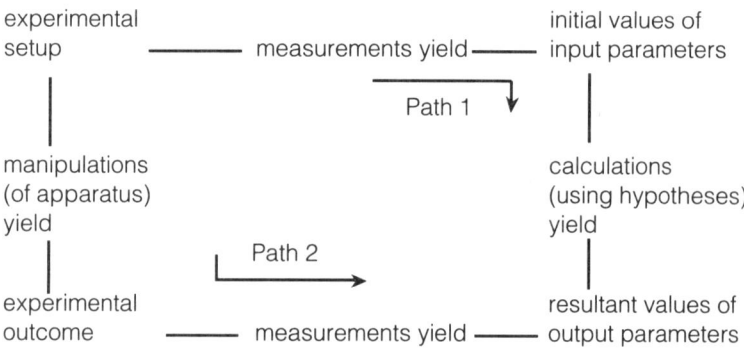

FIGURE 2

the more general pattern displayed in Figure 2. On one traditional understanding, Figure 2 exhibits the general epistemic structure of an experimental test of a theoretical empirical hypothesis. The experimental setup is, for example, some laboratory apparatus which one confirms by measurement has been adjusted to a certain set of initial (input) values for various parameters. The theoretical hypothesis in question is then used to derive, by calculation, a *prediction: if* the experimental setup is manipulated in such-and-such a fashion, *then* certain determinate resultant (output) values for specific parameters will be produced. The next step is actually to perform these experimental manipulations and determine, again by means of measurement, the actual resultant (output) values for the parameters at issue. According to the traditional interpretation, the theoretical hypothesis in question is thereby so far *confirmed* or *disconfirmed* according to whether the *observed* experimental outcome does or does not match the *predicted* experimental outcome. That is, the hypothesis is confirmed if the path from the experimental setup, through measurements of initial input values, and over the theoretical calculations (Path 1) leads to the same results as the path which runs from the experimental setup over the actual manipulations to their measured outcomes (Path 2). The hypothesis is disconfirmed if the two paths fail to issue in the same output parameter values.

On the line of thought we are presently exploring, the verdictive (epistemic) authority of logical analysis is taken to be the same as that of the natural sciences. Just as we can have mistaken views about the physical-chemical-biological world in which we find ourselves, we can also have mistaken views about the cogencies of the NL-arguments that we and others advance. *Inter alia*, it is the job of natural science to correct our "pre-scientific" beliefs about the world, to tell us what the world is *really* like. Similarly, it is the job of a "science of logical analysis" to correct our "pre-analytic" beliefs about our reasonings, to tell us which NL-arguments are *really* logically cogent. So, in any event, runs one sort of hard-core legitimization of the epistemic authority of logical analysis.

To claim the authority to distinguish in this way between *apparently* good (or bad) NL-arguments and *actually* good (or bad) NL-arguments is indeed to claim exactly the epistemic authority of a natural science, for natural science characteristically represents itself as exercising a method *par excellence* for discovering a "reality" which "underlies" and "gives rise to" empirical "appearances". What I want next to argue is that, however the case might stand with regard to "logical analysis", natural science itself is justified in these ontological pretensions. In particular, the epistemology of natural science is arguably best understood in terms of a systematic working out of the dialectic of appearance *vs.* reality as such.

This is not the occasion for a detailed exposition and defense of a ("convergent realist") normative epistemology for natural science developed along the indicated lines. I have attempted to carry through at least substantial parts of that enterprise elsewhere.[7] Here, I shall limit myself to a brief elucidation of the principal elements of such a picture. As it turns out, however, that will do for present purposes, for it will suffice to make it clear that it is, at the same time, the *wrong* picture to account for the (ostensible) epistemic authority of logical analysis.

What I want specifically to propose is that a proper understanding of the epistemology of natural science turns on appreciating the relationships between two motifs. The first is that the fundamental business of a natural science, its epistemic *raison d'être*, is to conceptually equip us to explain phenomena; the second, that what (conceptually) connects the ontological categories of "appearance" and "reality" is precisely an explanatory 'because'. If reality is something that "underlies" or "gives rise to" appearances, then *a fortiori* it is necessarily something that explains them as well: things will seem as they do *because* things are as they are.

One useful way to begin exploring the implications and interconnections of these two motifs is by noting that they both describe cognitive constraints at the interface of *two* (partial) "world-stories". In particular, both physical (empirical) phenomena and (speaking loosely) the circumstances or states of affairs invoked in aid of explaining them are *epistemically* present to inquiring subjects only as represented, that is, by way of judgments framed in sentences that draw on the vocabulary of one or another inferentially integrated system of descriptive predicates. An epistemological account of natural science must consequently undertake, *inter alia*, to devise and defend a principled story about the inferential (and perhaps other) relationships that will (or should) obtain *between* such descriptive systems when sentences formulated in their terms are (properly considered to be) related as explanadum and explanans.

The contentive concepts in terms of which a description of phenomena in need of explanation is drawn may already be elements of a quantitatively precise, theoretically articulated world-story. In our own epistemically mature scientific environment, phenomena are frequently themselves representable by assignments of numerical values to parametric properties which in turn are thought of both as observationally accessible to measurement and as confirmably subsumable under lawful mathematical relationships (after the manner schematized in Figure 2 above). A specification of phenomena in need of explanation may also, however, be drawn in terms of a purely qualitative, "pre-theoretical", and even quite crude and rudimentary descriptive phenomenology of nature. Thus the explananda falling within the scope of, for example, Newtonian astronomy encompass the Keplerian equations of planetary motion and the concomitant observational measurements (e.g., Tycho Brahe's) which they closely fit, but also the "pre-theoretical" qualitative phenomenology of "fixed" stars, a "rising" and "setting" sun, "wandering" planets, and a "waxing" and "waning" moon. Analogously, the explanatory reach of kinetic thermodynamics includes not only the quantitative relationships among the parametric properties temperature and pressure of a sample of gas and the volume of the container confining it that are mathematically codified in the equations of the classical theory of gases but also such rudimentary qualitative phenomenological observations as that, for example, inflated balloons expand when heated and contract when cooled.

Systematic reflection on such examples reminds us that, epistemologically considered, natural science is (or at least surely purports to be) a progressive enterprise and, at the level of explananda, in some sense also a cumulative enterprise. We learn, too, that the theoretical positing of micro-entities, of which macro-entities ontologically (mereologically or compositionally) *consist*, although itself clearly one mode of implementation of the fundamental explanatory strategy of scientific epistemology, does not belong to its essence. The basic epistemological moment of natural-scientific explanation is already exhibited in, for example, the transition from a geocentric (Ptolemaic) to a heliocentric (Copernican) cosmological world-story. In any event, however, natural science progresses by constructing new (partial) world-stories, that is, new theories, which not only *improve upon* their predecessors but also *supersede* them.

Natural science manages to pull off the trick of progressively cumulating over phenomena while at the same time methodically abandoning its successive commitments to the systems of contentive concepts in terms of which those phenomena are initially *described* precisely by adopting a "realist" self-understanding according to which the *fundamental* import of an explanatory theory is ontological. Phenomena are "saved" by being systematically relegated to the category of *appearance*, and their prior representations (phenomenological and theoretical alike) are correlatively recast in the language of "seeming". In short, the 'because' of theoretical explanation and the ontological 'because' of being and seeming are understood as one. *Sub specie* Ptolemaic astronomical theory, it is because the sun *actually* orbits a spherical earth that it *apparently* rises and sets. *Sub specie* kinetic thermodynamics, it is because a sample of gas *is* a swarm of tiny moving and colliding incompressible elastic (Newtonian) particles that it *appears* to be a continuous homogeneous compressible fluid whose behavior conforms to the equations of classical phenomenological gas theory.

Thus understood, the aim of theorizing is not simply, as philosophical positivism has traditionally characterized it, effectively to *précis* phenomena—that is, to model an ever-growing family of observations (measurements) over some conceptually privileged phenomenal domain by a series of equations successively yielding a steadily increasing accuracy of mathematical fit. The aim of theorizing is rather to explain observations and measurements by telling ontologically committed stories about *what it is* that is being observed or measured and thereby also, *inter alia*, about in what (physical interactions) its being observed or measured consequently consists. It follows that successive theories over a given phenomenal domain do not "meet" only in the original phenomena. Since the *nature* of the phenomena to be explained is ontologically reinterpreted under successive theoretical conceptualizations, a successor theory ultimately proposes to explain the phenomena ostensibly explained by its predecessor only *as appearances,* by making available resources for giving an account of the pragmatic meta-phenomena of the predecessor's actual explanatory failures and apparent explanatory successes. The predecessor's failures manifest themselves as *explanatory anomalies,* that is, breakdowns of *intra*-theoretical explanatory strategies, whose emergence (characteristically at extremes of measurement) intimates a need to pass beyond extant theory. The predecessor's apparent explanatory successes, on the other hand, correspond to the degree of purely mathematical (and, thus conceived, ontologically neutral) *descriptive fit* between measured and theoretically computed values exhibited by the predecessor's "observational base" of "inductive" confirmations (collected on the pattern schematized in Figure 2).

The first thing to notice now about logical analysis, in contrast, is that it lacks this sort of *double* explanatory accountability. Logical "theories" (that is, diverse logical calculi) in fact "meet", if they meet at all, *only* "in the phenomena". In particular, the epistemic vindication of a logical system characteristically disregards entirely even the very question of whether a proposed formalism empowers one to explain the degree to which its *predecessor(s)* descriptively fit the "intuitive" or "pre-theoretical" data. Unlike empirical theories, in fact, when logical systems are related as "predecessor" and "successor" at all, the relationship is without the slightest epistemic import. From the epistemological point of view, logical calculi do not progressively explanatorily cumulate, but rather present *mere alternatives:* alternative propositional and predicate calculi (classical systems *vs.* intuitionistic systems *vs.* "relevance logics"); alternative modal logics (S3 *vs.* S4 *vs.* B *vs.* S5); alternative deontic logics; and so on.

An experiential anomaly is a crisis of failed expectations. Our theoretical computations predict one outcome; what we measure, what we observe, is another. The more such anomalies arise, the more we feel the need of a new story, a better theory. The world, we are increasingly inclined to conclude, simply cannot actually be what our present theories *take* it to be. A new (successor) theory—when we are fortunate enough to have devised one—is a new story about how the world (really) is. It earns its epistemic credentials by simultaneously defusing the anomalies and saving the phenomena, that is, by empowering us to explain both why, in these instances, what we observed was not what our old theories led us to expect, and also why, *until* we explored these instances, we could interpret our measurements, and thus our world, through the conceptual (descriptive) medium of our predecessor theories *without* encountering such crises of failed expectations.

If we now proceed by strict analogy, a *logical* anomaly will be a crisis of failed expectations *in reasoning*. In our actual reasonings, we inevitably rely on our "logical intuitions", our implicit or explicit "pre-analytic" convictions about I-relations (about what implies what, what follows from what, and what contradicts what). If these intuitions are sound, reasoning from premises we endorse, we may expect to arrive regularly at conclusions we can also endorse—and this is normally the case. Usually we can accept what we conclude follows from what we believe. Sometimes, however, this is not so. Sometimes we find that we cannot accept the apparent consequences of some of our commitments. Sometimes, that is, such consequences are *prima facie* inconsistent with *others* of our commitments. If the commitments remain firm, our reasonings will then have lead us into paradoxes or absurdities. We will find ourselves committed to an antinomy, a pair of seemingly equally cogent reasonings, from premises that we continue to endorse, which issue in *prima facie* contradictory conclusions. An antinomy is an especially striking form of logical anomaly. It can make us feel the need of a new story about I-relations—about what *really* implies, follows from, or contradicts what. For in these circumstances, we may straightaway conclude that, "despite appearances", our original logical intuitions surely cannot *all* be sound.

These are attractive analogies, and consequently, although not always so explicitly articulated, they have in fact been widely influential in structuring hard-core views regarding the epistemology of logical analysis. I want to suggest, however, that they fail to stand up under sustained scrutiny. When the chips are down, "logical intuitions" are simply not epistemically analogous to observational data, and symbolization is not a special case of measurement.

The point about symbolization stands out clearly enough once we properly distinguish the (mathematical) *value* of a measurement from its (conceptual) *interpretation*. In the natural sciences, the *values* of our measurements are fixed independently of theory. They are determined by the world. What our theories are in charge of is the (conceptual, descriptive) *interpretation* of those values. Theory tells us what it is that we have been measuring, in what (physical interactions) our measurements consist, and thereby what to *make* of those (mathematical) values. But in logical analysis *nothing* is fixed "independently of theory". This is the epistemological significance of the "free play" between formational and transformational considerations in the construction of logical calculi that we noted earlier. We always have the choice *either* to commit ourselves to a determinate family of transformational resources and resolve to carry through our symbolizations within the Procrustean bed of the formational resources acknowledged by those (S-) transforms, *or* to elect instead to enrich our expressive (formational) resources and modify our transformational resources to suit our new symbolizations.

Another way of putting the same point is this: The observations in which our measurements consist are experiences with which we *find* ourselves. We may and we do, so to speak, choose when and where to look, but, once we have looked, what we then *see* is no longer optional. This is a point to be made with some care, for how we *take* what we see does indeed depend upon choices we have made. How we take what we see—what we see it *as*—is determined in part by the concepts we have available, and that, in turn, is a function of our creativity and success in constructing new, epistemically qualified stories (new theories). But at the heart of every observation also lies something which *admits of being taken* this way or that—for example, as an actual rising and setting of the sun or as a mere appearance engendered by a turning earth—and that is not something we choose.

When we encounter an empirical anomaly, an anomaly of experience, then, we are confronted with a phenomenon at the core of which lies something subsequently epistemically inescapable. This is the ultimate sense and ground of the metaphorical "hardness" of the "hard facts". Anomalous observations and measurements are consequently *data*. They are thrust upon us as constraints to which our conceptually contentive descriptive world-stories (our theories) are ultimately accountable. But to encounter a "logical anomaly", an anomaly of reasoning, is not to be confronted with such a *datum*. For not only is it (only) our "pre-analytic logical intuitions" which bring us to the point of inconsistency, absurdity, or antinomy, but our conviction that what we are brought to *is* a paradox or a contradiction is itself nothing but *another* such "pre-analytic logical intuition". We are referred from intuition to intuition, but never to anything outside the realm of intuition. We modify some of our logical convictions in the light of others, but it remains our choice which among our intuitions, if any, to alter or abandon.[8]

A logical anomaly is not a datum because, unlike the mathematical values of empirical measurements, logical intuitions are *labile*. In a standard truth-functional calculus, for example, every well-formed formula is admissibly S-derivable from any D-inconsistency. The corresponding claim about I-relations is that every sentence is implied by a contradiction. For "relevance logicians", this is an unacceptable paradox; for "classicists", in contrast, it is a *result*. Even contradictions are not "hard" data. "Don't you see that you've contradicted yourself?" we ask. But there is nothing here to see. "First you said X, right?" "Yes." "And then you said not-X?" "Yes, that too." "But don't you *see* . . . ?"

The elusive mistake here lies in the tacit supposition that "the contradiction" is something that somehow "inheres" in the spoken words, as the sensible content of our perceptual experiences inheres in those experiences. But, unlike the invariant core of an observation or measurement, a contradiction is not something epistemically inescapably thrust upon us. A contradiction is not something which is *there* independently of interpretation, something which admits of being "seen" whether anyone actually "sees" it or not, in the way in which a sensory content or the mathematical value of a measurement admits of being variously conceptually taken. For what does it mean for someone to "see the contradiction"? It is not for her to finally encounter something which stands in need of explanation. All that there is here to *encounter* are the words, and the words are there from the beginning. For someone to "see the contradiction" is rather for what has been said to become a *problem* for her, for the words to come to disturb her in the way that they disturb us.

Consider the idiom 'on pain of contradiction'. "You deny this only on pain of contradiction", we say—but what if "contradiction" *brings* no pain? Well, then that is the end of the matter. One cannot give another person reasons to attend to reasons—or rather, the enterprise is futile. This is one of the useful morals of the salutary tale of Achilles and the Tortoise, in the charming version of Lewis Carroll:[9] "Having granted those claims, you must grant these as well," says Achilles to the Tortoise. "Logic will *force* you to do so." To which the Tortoise replies, in essence, "Logic is welcome to try." For logic lacks *sanctions*. Logic (regrettably) can compel only those who embrace it.[10]

A contradiction, paradox, absurdity, or antinomy is more like an *obstacle* than a phenomenon. Nothing is an obstacle "in itself", but only relative to some project. A contradiction or a paradox also does not exist "in itself". The reason that there are no "*unproblematic* contradictions" is not that we somehow, fortuitously, happen to be constructed in such a way that we *find* contradictions problematic, as we happen to be constructed, for instance, in such a way that we find sugar sweet and tasty. The reason that there are no "unproblematic contradictions" is that a contradiction (or paradox, antinomy, or absurdity) *is* a problem. Its mode of being, so to speak, is not, as it is for data, "to be explained", but rather "to be resolved", as the mode of being of an obstacle is "to be overcome". A datum that has been successfully explained remains a datum for all that. An obstacle that has been successfully overcome, however, is an obstacle no longer, and a solved problem ceases to be a problem. So, too, like an obstacle overcome or a problem solved, a resolved contradiction ceases to be what it was.

What logical analysis can offer us in the face of logical anomaly, in consequence, is not theoretical explanations but only practical guidance. Logical analysis, that is, can at best articulate a strategy for abandoning or modifying *some* of our "logical intuitions" in order to get us past the point of paradox. The stories told by logical analysis earn their epistemic authority, then, if at all, not by empowering us to *explain* something but by enabling us to *avoid* something. When successful, they exhibit coherent strategies for adjusting our "pre-analytic" logical convictions in ways that eliminate the conflicts between our intuitions about particular inferential cases and our espousals of general inferential principles out of which such logical anomalies initially arise—and ideally, in terms of such revised intuitions and principles, we will no longer be able even coherently to *formulate* the absurdities and paradoxes, the antinomies and contradictions, which so disturbed us.

The epistemology of logical analysis, in short, is not the ontologically consequential explanatory epistemology of a natural science, but the method of "reflective equilibrium". A logical calculus is not an explanatory theory, but rather an instrument for bringing our various "pre-analytic" convictions about individual inferential cases and general inferential principles into stable and systematic harmony with one another. It is a tool for articulating techniques for systematically extending a group of intuitions from simple to more complex cases. We "establish" a logical calculus by first "fitting" a formalism to an initial set of dominant intuitions regarding a core family of simple paradigms of acceptable and unacceptable reasoning (NL-arguments) and then projecting the resultant formalism over more complex argumentation, where "intuitions" are less stable. In the face of emerging antinomy, paradox, or other "counter-intuitive" conclusions, we continuously modify *either* our developing formalisms *or* our "pre-analytic" logical sensibilities (or both) until our judgments about the cogencies of particular (NL) cases become stably and reliably consilient with our judgments regarding the cogencies of general (NL) principles as both are codified and represented within the formal system upon which we have, so to speak, converged.

A logical calculus thus neither is nor aims to be descriptively or explanatorily adequate to an antecedently "given" domain of inferential phenomena. It functions rather to *articulate a norm*, that is, to codify and make applicable a *standard of acceptability* (e.g., "validity") in terms of which (NL) inferential performances and the "logical intuitions" which are supposed to vindicate them can themselves be appraised and adjusted. The stories told by "logical analysis" earn whatever epistemic authority they have, in other words, not in theory—by proving themselves to be good explanations—but in practice—by proving themselves to be, as it were, good advice.

With these conclusions, we achieve a degree of closure on the question of the probative force of modal (and other) intuitions raised in the first chapter. I there cited Kripke's remark that "something's having intuitive content" is "very heavy evidence" in favor of it—in a way, the most conclusive evidence one ultimately *can* have. We can now see that there is both something right and something wrong about Kripke's claim.

What is wrong about it is its suggestion that intuitions are "evidence" in the sense that empirical observations and measurements can be evidence, i.e., that they can exercise "hard" constraints on the theoretical stories which they support. The explanatory epistemology characteristic of the natural sciences, I have argued, is the wrong model in terms of which to understand the probative force of "intuitive", "pre-analytic" logical convictions.

What is right about Kripke's remark, however, is its suggestion that there is no getting "behind" or "underneath" such original convictions. In the enterprise of "logical analysis", "logical intuitions" may not be *data*, but they are nevertheless always the last court of appeal. For the practical *point* of the enterprise—to articulate and stabilize norms of logical conduct—itself lies within the field of "intuitions".

In recognizing "logical analysis" ("logical theory") as fundamentally concerned with delineating and consolidating communal inferential norms, that is, as a department of an ethics rather than a science of reasoning, we have also arrived at the point where we can begin constructively to address the topic of the *subject matter* of logical analysis earlier left in abeyance. There I rejected the suggestion that "logical form" is properly understood as a theoretical property of natural language sentences, but I offered no interpretive alternative. It is time to lay one on the table. In the next chapter, therefore, I shall return to the question of the positive character and role of the notion of logical form and, not surprisingly, to the intimately related question, also earlier left on our agenda, of the identification of the "logical particles" as well.

8
Roots and Roles of Logical Form

WE ARE looking for a positive characterization of logical form. As is often the case in such quests, it will prove useful to begin by imagining, first, a sort of creature for whom, although it indeed engages in representational and (broadly conceived) inferential conducts, the notion of logical form fails of application. The sort of creature I have in mind is one, simpler than we, whose representational resources include no analogues to our own logical particles. For reasons that will become obvious, I shall speak of these creatures as *Humean* beings. Sophisticated "non-conversational" mammals—for example, dogs, cats, monkeys, dolphins, and anthropoid apes—are *perhaps* reasonably good *de facto* approximations to such creatures. In any event, they do provide useful illustrations of at least *some* of the points to be made about Humean beings, and, with proper cautionary commentaries, treating such animals as exemplary instances of Humean creatures will prove a helpful aid to the imagination.

Humean creatures, as I shall understand them here, can possess quite elaborate representational and behavioral repertoires. To simplify the exposition and sharpen the problematic focus, I shall suppose to begin with that, although they lack representational analogues to the logical particles, such creatures nevertheless regularly engage in representings that have *"propositional* form". Under the rubric "propositional form", I propose to understand the *functional* decomposability of a representing into two aspects answering approximately to the notions of "referring" and "characterizing" or "picking something out" and "classifying it". I shall suppose, in other words, that these creatures' representations are always representations *of* something *as* something. Compactly put, Humean creatures do more than simply register the presence of impinging stimuli ("surface irritations"); they represent (the obtaining of) *states of affairs*.

The paradigm of such a representing with propositional form is a *perceptual taking*. Perception, properly so called, is not the mere passive having of sensations but precisely the perception *of* something *as* something. In Aristotelian terms, it incorporates a representing of a *tode ti,* a this-such. The Aristotelian idiom is particularly apposite, for it reminds us that the "referential" aspect of a perceptual taking always has an "indexical" or "demonstrative" character. In perception, something is *literally* "picked-out" of a *presented* perceptual field, which is thereby functionally partitioned into "figure" and "ground", that is, a perceived *item* and its perceptual *environment*.

While an aspect of the representations of Humean creatures can in this way be a functional equivalent of our own indexical or demonstrative expressions, our "*temporary* proper names", it is less clear that Humean representations can functionally incorporate a complete analogue to our proper names *per se*. As we have seen the fundamental representational job of a genuine proper name is to provide for singular individuative reference both *in absentia,* in contrast to perceptual indexicals, and, in contrast to uniquely individuating descriptions, compatibly with an individual speaker's descriptive ignorance and mistaken beliefs. I have argued that a proper name fulfills the first of these functions by carrying an idiolectic sense for each speaker; the second, by falling within the scope of a shared epistemics, a family of mutually acknowledged norms and methods of inquiry, for commensurating such idiolectic senses. Whether Humean representations can incorporate a functional equivalent to proper names *per se,* then, will depend on the extent to which Humean creatures can satisfy these requirements of idiolectic sense and shared convergent epistemics.[1]

Humean creatures will, of course, (behaviorally) respond *differentially* to the items that they "referentially" represent or pick out. Their doing so, indeed, is part of what is meant by saying that such creatures represent states of affairs, i.e., that their representings also have a "characterizing" or "classificatory" dimension. To further simplify matters, we may suppose that they also respond *appropriately* (e.g., with flight or fight or feeding) to evolutionarily salient items (e.g., predators or conspecific rivals or edible plants). Crucially, however, Humean creatures can also *generalize* from their experiences, in the sense of acquiring propensities to respond consistently and appropriately to fresh instances of new stimulus kinds. Thus a Humean creature can learn to *associate,* for example, the smell of a predator with its threatening proximity, tracks and traces of conspecifics with the sorts of animals that make them, or the looks and tastes of certain plants with the consequences of ingesting them. Such a creature thereby comes to form *expectations* on the basis of its experience and to respond to proximate stimuli *conditionally,* on the basis of such expectations, with behavior or behavioral sets that are differentially appropriate to the expected states of affairs.

We make contact with our principal themes by noting that it has historically proved both easy and natural at this point to say that such Humean creatures (learn to) *infer* the obtaining of certain states of affairs from others. As Leibniz put it, in passing from one representation (e.g., of smoke as present) to another representation (e.g., of fire as nearby) in accordance with an acquired propensity to do so, a Humean creature at least manifests "a sort of consecutiveness which imitates reason".[2] Such a creature is consequently an ideal candidate for being characterized as (practically) *rational* in the sense of behaving in ways that are usefully described, understood, and predicted in terms of the categories (paradigmatically, beliefs and desires) of what Dennett calls "the intentional stance".[3]

The point of adopting the "intentional stance" with respect to some creature is to enable us to bring its behavior within the scope of rationalizing explanations, that is, to interpret that behavior *as if* it were the outcome of a course of practical reasoning (practical deliberation) which itself, in turn, is either sound or unsound. Whatever else beliefs and desires might turn out to be, then, they are at least (and essentially) intended to be items characterizable as having semantic values and consequently as capable of standing in *I-relations,* such inferential relationships as implication or inconsistency. In adopting the intentional stance with respect to an organism, therefore, we interpret the creature itself as, in some sense, committed to contentive inferential principles that serve to connect its representations of desired ends with representations of appropriate means for realizing them in the context of the states of affairs (it represents as) then-and-there obtaining.

We must be careful to handle such rationalizing idioms in this context with appropriate caution. In comparison to the rich conceptual load that these idioms carry in application to the likes of you and me, their literal content here is severely impoverished. The notion of an organism's engaging in practical, means-ends, reasoning *normally* carries with it the suggestion that the organism is capable of formulating complex plans, including alternative courses of action conditional on diverse contingencies, and undertaking temporally extended multi-phase projects, calling for periodic reevaluation and adjustment in the face of the partial or total misfires in the execution of intermediate steps or realization of intermediate stages. Such more elaborate reasoning activities *prima facie* lie outside the competences of the sorts of creatures we are presently engaged in imagining.

On the other hand, Humean creatures will surely be capable of, so to speak, "chaining" learned means-ends relationships into complex behavioral programs. And, while the explicit *representation* of alternative courses of action as such would require resources beyond those commanded by a Humean being, anyone who has seen, for example, a well-trained sheep dog maintain control of an unruly herd will know that the actual *behavior* of such a being need not on that account be in the least "stylized" or "mechanical", but can be exquisitely flexible and situationally adaptable.

In characterizing (some of) the conducts of our hypothetical Humean creatures as (broadly) inferential, we avail ourselves, in the converse, of the maxim that "Espousal of principles is reflected in uniformities of performance".[4] That is, we treat manifestations of acquired conduct uniformities as grounds for ascribing to the performing creature a commitment to the cogency of a "corresponding" general conditional inferential principle. Since the representational resources of Humean creatures *ex hypothesi* do not include functional analogues to the logical particles, however, any performance regularities *actually* enacted by such creatures will in this way necessarily reflect only (non-enthymematic, "immediate") *contentive* or "material" principles of inference, that is, principles licensing a transition from the representing of one state of affairs *directly* (without the mediation of supplementary premisses) to the representing of another.

As a Humean creature moves through the world, its material inferential commitments (so conceived) will undergo continuous modification—broadening or narrowing, strengthening or weakening—as its correlative expectations are or are not borne out by subsequent experience. In this connection, it important to recognize that such a creature, lacking logical particles, also cannot explicitly represent the (mere) failure of an expected state of affairs to materialize, that is, its *not* obtaining. Such creatures do not traffic in negations (negative representations) but only in *incompatibilities*, constituted by the differential effects of some, but not other, (positive) representations on acquired "inferential" behavioral propensities. Represented states of affairs come to be partitioned into families of *mutual contraries* according as to whether the represented obtaining of one state of affairs *de facto* weakens, strengthens, or proves irrelevant to an acquired general conditional propensity to (expectationally) represent the obtaining of another.

What I am calling an ascribed Humean material inferential principle is a relative of what Quine calls a (primitive) "observation categorical":

> A generality that is compounded of observables in this way—'Whenever this, that'—is what I call an *observation categorical.* It is compounded of observation sentences. The 'Whenever' is not intended to reify times and quantify over them. What is intended is an irreducible generality prior to any objective reference. It is a generality to the effect that the circumstances described in the one observation sentence are invariably accompanied by those described in the other.[5]

The critical difference between Quine's standpoint and our own is that, by stipulation, such a primitive observation categorical is not an implicitly espoused associative (conduct-regulating) *principle* but rather an explicitly articulated, compound (standing) *sentence.* As such, it presupposes a command of representational resources well beyond those we have attributed to our Humean creatures. For, although they indeed acquire propensities to pass "inferentially" from representing one state of affairs to representing another in patterns that generalize their *de facto* experiences, Humean beings are not equipped to form compound representations of relationships between distinct states of affairs nor, therefore, to represent the corresponding generalities as such.

The point of nevertheless marking the analogies between a Humean creature's implicit inferential principles and Quinean observation categoricals is to emphasize the epistemological import of such acquired representational propensities. A Humean creature, we might say, *enacts* an epistemics, in particular (by virtue of its relation to perception), a rudimentary form of the *empirical* epistemics. The creature's implicit commitments to general conditional inference principles and representational contrarieties embody its (implicit) *theory* of the world—its (implicit) partitioning of states of affairs into "natural" kinds and its (implicit) convictions regarding the "causal" relations obtaining among them. Each new stimulus is, so to speak, *automatically* appropriated by the organism as "evidence" with respect to this (implicit) global theory, modifying its contents to a greater or lesser extent in one or another fashion according to the resultant reshaping of the creature's representational behavioral propensities.[6]

A philosopher who is sensitive to the *normative* dimensions of logical, intentional, and epistemic discourses will take these three interlocking characterizations of our hypothetical Humean creatures—as inferentially active, practically rational, and epistemologically engaged—*cum grano salis*. Characterizing a state or transaction or condition or episode in logical, intentional, or epistemic terms, he will stress, is not providing an empirical, matter-of-factual, description of it, but rather locating it with a "logical space" of reasons and justification.[7] A creature properly in this "logical space" is one capable of having, giving, and responding to reasons *as reasons,* and that means, *inter alia,* capable of recognizing or acknowledging the superior (normative) authority of some representings *vis-à-vis* others. Such a creature responds to normative authority, for example, by adopting or endorsing some (implied) representations *because* (for the *reason* that) they are consequences of others and by abandoning or modifying some (contrary) representations *because* they conflict with others to which it is committed.

There is, to be sure, *a* sense in which our hypothetical Humean creatures can coherently be described as satisfying these last two conditions. When, for example, such a creature, in accordance with an acquired general propensity to do so, forms a determinate expectation in response to a represented state of affairs, we *can* say that the creature has come to entertain that expectation because it is a consequence of others to which it is committed. The fact that the acquired representational propensity "echoes", so to speak, a *de facto* regularity in the creature's experience can be treated as a non-arbitrary ground for characterizing the eliciting representing, not as a *mere* cause of the elicited expectation, but also as a reason for entertaining or adopting it. In this sense, a Humean creature can indeed "*have* a reason" for forming this or that expectation, and, analogously, such a creature can "have reasons" (of the sort discussed above under the rubric "incompatibilities") for abandoning one or another of its previously (implicitly espoused) inferential principles as well.

There is a crucial sense, however, in which Humean creatures necessarily fall short of genuinely satisfying the conditions for being in the normative "logical space" of reasons and justification, and this is the import of Leibniz's insistence that the "consecutiveness" of such creatures' behavior only "*imitates* reason". For, although such creatures can (in the sense just discussed) "have" and respond to reasons for adopting or abandoning both individual representations and general conditional representational propensities, they are nevertheless not equipped to acknowledge and respond to the reasons that they in this way "have" as reasons, for they are not suitably equipped to *represent* the reasons that they "have" in their role as reasons. What they are missing are precisely resources for representing the inferential (I-) relationships among representings by virtue of which they, so to speak, normatively qualify to function *as* reasons. An organism that can acknowledge and respond to reasons as reasons, that is, must not merely exhibit associative propensities, for example, to represent that fire is nearby whenever it represents that smoke is present—a propensity it might share with a simple domestic smoke-detector—but must also be equipped in *some* way to explicitly represent the (evidential) inferential and incompatibility relationships implicit in such propensities, for example, the fact that the presence of smoke *is* (generally) a reason for concluding that fire is nearby.

One way that an organism might satisfy this condition, of course, is the way *we* satisfy it, by being outfitted with resources for representing full-fledged generic semantic, logical, or epistemic concepts as such—for example, explicit concepts of correct and incorrect representings, sufficient and insufficient reasons, or good and poor evidence. Although any creature commanding such rich normative representational resources would obviously be able to represent the reasons it has *as* reasons, I want to suggest that there is also a more modest way in which an individual could pass beyond mere Humean "consecutiveness" to an explicit representation of the inferential and incompatibility relationships to which it is (behaviorally) committed.

A being who, so to speak, has mastered a comprehensive normative semantic, logical, or epistemic vocabulary thereby commands sufficient representational resources to *report* the obtaining of (normative) logical, intentional, or epistemic relationships among its contentive (world-) representings. But the condition that it be able somehow explicitly to *represent* the obtaining of such rational relationships is also satisfied by a creature whose representational resources, although inadequate for such reporting, are nevertheless sufficient for it to *express* their obtaining.[8] That, I want to propose, is the job of "logical" words. In particular, the logical particles are just such representational resources.

On this interpretation, the fundamental role of the logical particles is *expressive*. What the command of a logical vocabulary enables a creature to do is to make explicit in *representings* the principles that are otherwise only implicit in its (broadly) inferential *conducts*. In contrast to a (merely) Humean creature, whose behavioral responses (can be interpreted to) *exhibit* differential commitments to general conditional principles, what I shall call a *ratiocinative* creature can *represent* differences, generality, and conditional dependence. A ratiocinative creature, that is, is equipped with representational resources adequate for it to form negative, general, and conditional *judgments*—for example, that whatever is F is G; that (consequently) if x is F, then x is G; and that (although x is F) x is *not* G.⁹

Unlike the conduct propensities to which they correspond, such explicitly general, conditional, and negative representations are "transportable" and "freely repeatable", that is, thoroughly detachable from the contexts in which (and only in which) the implicit inferential principles that they express would become behaviorally manifest. Ratiocinative creatures are consequently representationally equipped to reason *about* the sorts of contentive (inferential) principles and material incompatibilities that a merely Humean creature only reasons *with* and, as it were, *because of*. A ratiocinative creature, in short, is not merely a *practically* rational being who theorizes, so to speak, "automatically" (as a Humean creature, even viewed from the intentional stance, proved to be a sort of "epistemological automaton"), but is a being in principle capable of exhibiting genuine *theoretical* rationality, a being for whom (as the saying goes) "its hypotheses can die in its stead". This is what Robert Brandom has in mind when he writes:

> [P]otentially controversial material inferential commitments [are] made explicit as claims, exposing them both as vulnerable to reasoned challenge and as in need of reasoned defense.
> It is in this process that formal logical vocabulary such as the conditional plays its explicating role. It permits the formulation, as explicit claims, of the inferential commitments that otherwise remain implicit and unexamined in the contents of material concepts. Logical locutions make it possible to display the relevant grounds and consequences and to assert their inferential relation. Formulating as an explicit claim the inferential commitment implicit in the content brings it out into the open

as liable to challenges and demands for justification, just as with any assertion. In this way explicit expression plays an elucidating role, functioning to groom and improve our inferential commitments, and so our conceptual contents—a role, in short, in the practices of reflective rationality that Sellars talks about under the heading of "Socratic method".[10]

I shall return to Brandom's notion of the "elucidating role" of logical expressions shortly. For the moment, however, it will repay us to continue to focus specifically on epistemological themes. The key observation here is that only a creature who is able explicitly to form such negative, general, and conditional judgments can representationally thematize the epistemics which it otherwise merely enacts. Making explicit experiential incompatibilities in the form of an inconsistent triad of judgments on the model sketched above—that whatever is F is G; that (consequently) if x is F, then x is G; and that (although x is F) x is *not* G—allows critical epistemic attention to be differentially focused. In particular, a creature who is able explicitly to represent both generalities and singular negations can not only elect to abandon or modify an espoused generality in the face of a *prima facie* counterinstance (the only option, in essence, "behaviorally open" to a merely Humean being), but can *also* elect to preserve the generality in its original form and reject one or both of the singular judgments, that x is F or that x is not G, instead. Since each singular judgment has experientially *arisen* (that is, so to speak, been thrust upon one), however, epistemically rejecting it in this way is tantamount to relegating it to the category of appearance—x only *seems* to be F and/or not to be G. The expressive resources embodied in the logical particles, in short, lie at the roots of an explicit command of the being-seeming distinction and so, correlatively, enable the transition from rudimentary Humean forms of empiricist epistemics to the mature ontologically-committed *explanatory* empiricist epistemics of natural science sketched in the preceding chapter.

The "transportability" and "free repeatability" of the negative, general, and conditional representations expressive of the inferential commitments embodied in Humean conducts (there not similarly detachable from their stimulus contexts) fits them, too, for their indispensable roles in communication and, crucially, in communal commensurations of beliefs under a shared epistemics. Since the very existence of a distinction between *correct* and *incorrect* (representational) practices arguably presupposes a social framework of consilient communal practices, the emergence of such explicit expressive resources is, at the same time, the satisfaction of an essential precondition for the emergence of authentic representational and inferential *norms* as well.[11]

We can see, too, that the expressive resources provided by the logical particles are the essential enabling conditions for the occurrence of genuine proper names, that is, singular individuative representings useable *in absentia* compatibly with an individual representer's descriptive ignorance and mistaken beliefs. For in making possible both the mature convergent explanatory empiricist epistemics and its specific application in the intersubjective commensuration of beliefs, the logical particles *a fortiori* allow for the commensurations of idiolectic sense which are a necessary precondition of such authentic names. *Inter alia*, representational resources adequate for negative, general, and conditional judgments can both expressively realize implicit commitments to uniqueness and explicitly articulate the sorts of individual differences that are required for the successful interpersonal disambiguation of multiply ambiguous name tokens. The appearance-reality distinction, already applicable in contexts of predicative classification, thus comes to be extended, on the basis of an explicitly expressible contrast between "the same individual again" and "another individual phenomenally indistinguishable from it", to contexts of singular identification as well.[12]

Mention of "name-tokens" reminds us that, unlike merely Humean creatures, ratiocinative beings arguably must be *symbol-*

manipulators. The notion of a Humean being's "propositional" representings and, correlatively, the distinction between the "referential" and "attributive" aspects of such representings, admits of a purely functional interpretation, as adverting, so to speak, to rational-explanatory "parsings" of what can *descriptively* be treated as structurally homogeneous conducts (e.g., trajectories of conditional approach or avoidance). The logical particles perform their expressive function, however, precisely by enabling the representational detachment of espoused inferential principles from Humean behavioral inferential practices. The representings which occur functionally as the arguments of connectives and quantifiers are therefore necessarily also "objectified", that is, from the descriptive point of view, empirically distinguishable component elements of complex structural wholes.

It follows, however, that the introduction of an explicit logical vocabulary which constitutes the transition from merely Humean creatures to authentically ratiocinative beings simultaneously creates the "syntactic" linguistic milieu in which "semantic" (e.g. referential) ambiguities, the divergence of speaker's meaning or reference from semantic meaning or reference, and, significantly, an individual's *de facto* commitment to mutually inconsistent families of beliefs first become possible. Once we understand these potential consequences of the "exteriorization" of representation in the manipulation of public symbols, it ceases to be at all surprising to discover that, as we saw in the case of Pierre, a ratiocinative individual's *epistemic access* to some of his own inferential commitments can be restricted to a determinate family of expressive symbolic resources.

Earlier I cited Robert Brandom's claim that the expressive capacities empowered by the vocabulary of logical particles play an "elucidating role" intimately related to the "Socratic method". But the "Socratic method", in turn, is surely nothing other than "logical analysis", informally pursued. In the last chapter, I argued that "logical analysis" or "logical theory" is properly understood as a department of the ethics, rather than as a science, of reasoning. Its function is to facilitate the articulation and stabilizing of communal norms of inferential conduct, and it does this, *inter alia*, by explicitly formulating and bringing together "pre-analytic (pre-theoretical) intuitions" about general inferential principles and particular inferential cases in an ongoing process of "reflective equilibrium". But I have just been arguing, first, that the *raison d'être* for introducing the expressive (representational) resources embodied in the logical particles is precisely to *make possible* the explicit articulation and, correlatively, the self-consciously critical evaluation of implicit inferential commitments embodied in thought (expectations) and practice (actions), and, second, that such critically attentive expressive articulation of tacit principles is in turn *necessary* because, in a "symbol-processing" linguistic milieu, our own implicit cognitive commitments can in fact be epistemically inaccessible to us by any "more direct" means. The point of our having a logical vocabulary in the first place, then, is to enable us to engage in a practice of "logical analysis" which the very existence of that vocabulary renders especially necessary. That this sounds paradoxical is only a reflection of the insidiously persistent picture of Cartesian first-person omniscience according to which an individual necessarily has "privileged" epistemic access to *his own* semantic, doxastic, and inferential commitments, independently of the descriptive or expressive representational resources that such commitments presuppose or that he himself happens to command.

Logical form is simply what is expressed by means of the logical vocabulary. The logical form of a (NL-) sentence, in other words, is a matter of its (inferential) conditions and connections, of the circumstances in which one becomes normatively entitled or committed to endorse it and the practical and theoretical consequences of one's having done so. To specify the logical form of a sentence is thus to produce a more or less explicit representation of its place in the rational inferential economy of the organisms who employ it in reasoning and communication—in their "logical space" of grounds and consequences, generalities and contrarieties, challenges and justifications—and to do this is primarily and essentially to inferentially locate *that* sentence with respect to *other* sentences.

A logical calculus is clearly one useful *expository medium* with which a person might undertake to represent such inferential interconnections among (NL-) sentences, that is, to represent I-relations. The formation and transformation rules of such a calculus induce a family of syntactic (D-) relations over its formulae that, by virtue of their purely structural basis and "mechanical" effectivity, are systematically and publicly *surveyable*. Mapping NL-sentences and their supposed I-relations onto such formulae and their tidy D-relations *a fortiori* renders a determinate proposal regarding the logical form of those sentences (i.e., their roles in the rational inferential economy of a community of thinkers and speakers) similarly surveyable. Treating the D-relations of such a calculus *as if* they were endowed with verdictive (epistemic) authority *vis-à-vis* I-relations among NL-sentences is thus often a felicitous technique for both vividly and explicitly expressing and systematically projectively extending a family of convictions regarding (normative) inferential relationships, that is, convictions about some of the conditions and connections of some of the things we say. It is important to be clear, however, that such an "as if" verdictive authority in the end is *only* an expressive and expository technique, and that, even as a technique, it remains useful only so long as and to the extent that the correlative strategies for mapping sentences onto formulae (i.e., for "symbolizing" NL-sentences) are themselves taken for granted.

Logical calculi, that is, are not theories, and they are not trumps. Such verdictive epistemic authority as they are, from occasion to occasion, treated as having is neither indigenous nor final but rather provisionally bestowed in aid of articulating and projectively extending a determinate set of initial convictions regarding inferential relations. It is consequently not surprising to notice that, like a philosophical framework, each logical calculus that is put to work representing logical form is supported (roughly equally well) by *its* intuitions.

Logical calculi and, more generally, the correlative methods of "logical analysis" are thus, in the end, just one more instrumentality of the "Socratic method". They are one family of techniques *among others*—"linguistic analysis", "conceptual analysis", studies of "ordinary language", "phenomenological reduction", "thought experiments", descriptions of "language games", and even "assembling reminders for a purpose"—for making explicit and exploring the normative constraints and commitments of our representations and reasonings in diverse contentive domains. And the structural automatism and clean-edged determinateness of such calculi that are surely their main strengths relative to a project of establishing a "reflective equilibrium" among inferential intuitions (both general and particular) are also, at the same time, their chief limitations. For, to adapt a Wittgensteinian metaphor,[13] the comparatively tidy inferential lines of our conceptual "suburbs", for example, mathematics and the sciences, are unlikely to be echoed by similar orderlinesses, however implicit, in the narrow and twisted streets of the "old town" that consists, first and foremost, of our ancient and complex contentive conceptions of *ourselves* as knowers and doers in a world not of our making.

NOTES

Preface

1. Much the same thing that had happened to Grice's "intentionalist" story of "non-natural meaning" a decade earlier.

2. Namely, an exploration of the Kantian thesis that the experiencing apperceptive self and the experienced objective world are correlatives, each being a condition of the possibility of the other. This project eventually issued in three books: *Linguistic Representation* (LR); *One World and Our Knowledge of It* (OW); and *The Thinking Self* (TS).

3. Besides, I had been trained and educated by philosophers who drew their methods and paradigms from intellectual activities very different from those shaping Kripke's convictions. Although they certainly regarded "formal semantics"—the modeling of one formal system (a logical calculus) in another (set theory)—as a nice enough bit of mathematics, when one could get it, they nevertheless also clearly understood that *logic* ultimately has to do with the distinction between good and bad *reasoning*, and that such tidy set theoretic models have little or nothing to do with the ways in which *natural languages* function as systems of representation and media of communication and understanding.

4. At the time, it was still *West* Germany. The first trickle of East German refugees across the newly permeable Hungarian piece of the old Iron Curtain occurred shortly after our arrival in Bielefeld. In the summer of 1989, however, what was to happen in Eastern Europe during the following months was well beyond anyone's most extravagant imaginings.

5. (Added in December, 1992:) Intimations of mortality on all hands. Since I originally drafted this Preface, another year has somehow slipped by, and we've lost dear old Torquata, too. He passed on peacefully in November, at nineteen years and eight months.

6. I have put the qualifier 'perhaps' just where it belongs. It is surprisingly hard to keep this simple fact conscientiously in view.

7. The party line is that this is the only alternative to "essentialism" and "foundationalism", both of which have been thoroughly and effectively "deconstructed", but one can't help thinking that an awful lot of babies are being tossed out alone with that used bathwater.

Dialectical Preliminaries

1. Originally published in G. Harman and D. Davidson, eds, *Semantics of Natural Language,* reprinted, with additions and modifications, as Saul A. Kripke, *Naming and Necessity.* Henceforth all citations of Kripke's work by page number alone will be to the latter, canonical, appearance.

2. The strictures are perhaps most explicitly set out in Quine's similarly influential essays "Reference and Modality" and "Three Grades of Modal Involvement".

Chapter 1

1. See, for example, "Synonymy and the Epistemology of Linguistics"; "Translation and Theories", chap. 4, pp. 49–71, of (LR); and "The Dispute on the Indeterminacy of Translation".

2. I don't mean to imply that Kripke thinks that (1), if true, is necessary. Quite the contrary. Assuming that gold is in fact yellow (in the actual world), nothing could be simpler than to stipulate a (different) possible world in which it isn't. The point is simply that, on Kripke's view, the thought-experiment which establishes that (1) is known *a posteriori* does not supply *that* stipulation and so does not yet settle the question of the modal status of (1).

3. See footnotes 56 and 57 on pp. 114–115 of *Naming and Necessity.*

4. Did it really? Well, it at least gave *some* philosophers that illusion. I think it still does, but that is perhaps nothing more than an idiosyncratic reading of the philosophical scene. (But why else would someone think

that shifting to the "possible worlds" idiom *clarifies* or *explains* anything?) Kripke himself, however, it must be conceded, never claimed this particular advantage for his apparatus.

5. It is surely this distinction that Kripke is attempting to articulate, for example, in the following passage: "Notice this question, whether Nixon could not have been a human being, is a clear case where the question asked is not epistemological. Suppose Nixon actually turned out to be an automaton. That might happen. We might need evidence whether Nixon is a human being or an automaton. But that is a question about our knowledge. The question of whether Nixon might have not been a human being, given that he is one, is not a question about knowledge, *a posteriori* or *a priori*. It's a question about, even though such and such things are the case, what might have been the case otherwise" (47). My colleague, Keith Simmons, deserves considerable credit for helping me to get clearer about and to formulate the intended distinction—although the E *vs.* M terminology is my own, and Keith, I believe, still thinks the distinction itself is much clearer than I find it actually to be.

6. Surprisingly many of Kripke's "intuition mobilizing" remarks have this trivial character and are consequently strictly irrelevant to the claims in support of which he makes them. I have earlier passed over one important example without mentioning it: "We could conceivably discover that, contrary to what we now think, this table is indeed made of ice from the river. But suppose that it is not. Then, though we can imagine making a table out of *another* [my emphasis] block of wood or even from ice, identical in appearance with this one, and though we could have put it in this very position in the room, it seems to me that this is *not* to imagine *this* table as made of wood or ice, but rather it is to imagine another table, *resembling* this one in all external details, made of another block of wood, or even of ice" (113–114). Notice the highlighted occurrence of 'another'. What is the block of wood from which we're to imagine making a table *other than*? Presumably, it is other than the block of wood from which *this* table is made. So both blocks of wood are, so to speak, in this picture simultaneously, and each has been made into a table: this block into this table, the other block into another table. Now, of course, it is *trivially* true that *coexisting* tables made from distinct blocks of wood are distinct tables, i.e., that another table is not this table. But

this trivial truth simply does not entail that this table couldn't *have been* made from a block of wood other than the block of wood from which it in fact *was* made—an hypothesis which brings only one block of wood (this one in the actual world; another one in the possible world) and one table (this one, in *either* world) into the picture at a time.

7. Hilary Putnam, "The Meaning of 'Meaning' ", (MM).

8. Putnam himself offers an example of such a case, the case of *jade*. "Although the Chinese do not recognize a difference, the term 'jade' applies to two minerals: jadeite and nephrite. Chemically, there is a marked difference. Jadeite is a combination of sodium and aluminum. Nephrite is made of calcium, magnesium, and iron. These two quite different microstructures produce the same unique textural qualities!" (MM, 241).

9. Following the actual discovery of an appropriate "Twin Earth", of course, we would not, on this account, continue to say that water is H_2O, *simpliciter*, but rather that *Earth water* is H_2O, whereas *Twin Earth water* is XYZ.

10. As is yet another: That Putnam's thought-experiment does not describe a *possible* world at all, i.e., that the supposition that the same phenomenal natural kind station *could* be occupied by structurally distinct substances is fundamentally incoherent. For some considerations in aid of eliciting this intuition, see my "Phenomenal Ontology Revisited: A Bergmannian Retrospective".

Chapter 2

1. It is, parenthetically, unclear whether *only* items belonging to a natural language can properly be classified as rigid designators, or whether the category 'rigid designator' is intended to bridge the distinction between natural languages and formal systems and be properly applicable to, for example, the individual constants of some specific quantified modal logics with identity as well.

2. One thing we should have learned from our exploration of Kripke's discussions of essential and accidental properties is that we need to attend rather carefully to occurrences of 'other' in his reasonings.

3. More precisely, a rigid designator is an expression that designates the same object in every possible world *in which that object exists*. In the interests of expository felicity—and in order to bracket a variety of

problems regarding the possible nonexistence of specific objects—I shall normally adopt the usual shortcut of simply supposing that all the objects under discussion exist in all the possible worlds under consideration.

4. I adopt the usual lazy but convenient expository device of pretending that natural language is *written* language. In the case of spoken language, 'inscription' gives way to 'utterance' and 'strings of marks' to 'sequences of sounds'.

5. Another citation: "[There] might have been a situation in which the planet seen in this position in the evening was not the planet seen in this position in the morning; but that is not a situation in which Hesperus is not Phosphorus. It might also, if people gave the names 'Hesperus' and 'Phosphorus' to these planets, be a situation in which some planet other than Hesperus was called 'Hesperus'. But even so, it would not be a situation in which Hesperus itself was not Phosphorus" (109). Here again Kripke acknowledges the possibility of a situation in which "some planet other than Hesperus was called 'Hesperus' ", that is, in which (b1) is false.

6. Prose such as this, by the way, is what comes of doing philosophy à la Kripke orally, into a tape recorder, instead of carefully, onto paper. It should be a lesson to all of us.

7. That is, something along the lines of: "For any possible world, W, if the object designated by ⌜E_1⌝ in W is identical to the object designated by ⌜E_2⌝ in W, then ⌜$E_1=E_2$⌝ is true in W."

8. For example: "Someone goes by and he calls two *different* stars 'Hesperus' and 'Phosphorus'. . . . He can't have pointed to Venus twice, and in the one case called it 'Hesperus' and in the other 'Phosphorus', as we did. . . . He pointed maybe neither time to the planet Venus—at least one time he didn't point to the planet Venus, let's say when he pointed to the body he called 'Phosphorus'. Then in that case we can certainly say that the name 'Phosphorus' might not have referred to Phosphorus" (102).

9. My colleague Bill Lycan suggests 'scenario': The stipulation of a possible world is simply the description of a possible scenario. "Expression 'N' designates object X at world W" would thus amount to "On the scenario where . . . , the expression 'N' will designate (object) X." This certainly seems a useful interpretive proposal, but I still have qualms. The everyday term 'scenario' can doubtless do much of the work that has been delegated to the technical expression 'possible world'. What is not clear is

Notes to Chapter 2

whether it can be made to do the relevant work *vis-à-vis the modalities* without first being transformed into the *technical term* 'scenario'.

Michael Devitt essentially agrees with my assessment of the situation. After reviewing Kripke's account of the behavior of proper names and descriptions in modal contexts, Devitt concludes: "In my view [Kripke's standard] explanation in terms of rigid designation of the differing roles of singular terms is either spurious or false. The problem with it is that the notion of rigid designation is explained by the metaphor of "possible worlds." This metaphor typically gives an illusion of explanatory power and understanding where none exists (*pace* David Lewis). We must remove the metaphor. When we do, interest in rigid designation disappears" (D, 212–213).

10. The citation is from "About Proper Names", p. 217.

11. Devitt is similarly unenthusiastic about the usefulness of Kripke's "intuitive test": "If we look to Kripke for guidance here, we get the following account of rigidity: a term is rigid if it does not give rise to ambiguities of scope in modal contexts and nonrigid if it does. That is why names are rigid and descriptions are not. But, of course, this makes [Kripke's] explanation [of the variant behavior of names and descriptions in modal contexts] completely spurious: the distinction between rigid and nonrigid designators simply labels the differing roles of names and descriptions in modal contexts" (D, 213).

12. The Apologist is, in fact, my brilliant young colleague Keith Simmons. In the contemporary world of photocopiers, laser printers, and networked computers, early drafts of a philosophical manuscript will typically circulate as *samizdat* long before it becomes codified and transformed into some traditional genre of publication. The present explorations are no exception—and no part of them has met with more resistance and, indeed, incredulity during that period than the reflections of this chapter. Kripke's admirers are legion, and I have found, in consequence, that I am swimming against what is a very broad, deep, and fast-moving current of consensus. (Reason enough, parenthetically, to slow down, step back, and cast a quizzical eye on the proceedings. Philosophy can be as much hostage to fad and fashion as any other discipline.) Keith is among those admirers, and the discussion which follows reflects a number of actual pleasant and spirited philosophical exchanges between us.

I adopt the fictive persona of "the Apologist" primarily to avoid saddling Keith personally with all the claims he articulates in support of Kripke's views and theses. This is in accord with his own understanding of things: "I've tried to respond as far as possible on Kripke's behalf, figuring that that will be most helpful to you. So if what I say seems overly contentious, blame Kripke, not me!" Also, while my Apologist will indeed mostly literally echo passages from Keith's correspondence, this expository strategy eliminates the need for quotation marks, thereby allowing me to take some small liberties with his text—relabelings of numbered sentences, interpolations to make explicit what is plainly tacit, and minor clarificatory paraphrases—without giving official scholarly notice on each such occasion.

13. On the other hand, (k7) *is* our old friend (E) about whose pedigree I earlier raised a question. So does this Apologist's argument, then, at least lay to rest my earlier worries about Kripke's entitlement to (E)? Well, it *would*, if analogous worries didn't arise about Kripke's entitlement to some of the steps in *this* argument—but, of course, they do.

14. Oddly enough, my worrying the question of single quotes *at all* once moved Bill Lycan to expostulate (in contrast to the present Apologist) that *of course* Kripke individuates expressions as sign-designs—and that I should stop wasting my readers' time belaboring the obvious.

15. Thus restricted, the proposal is, I think, in fact equivalent to my own earlier "three-termed" suggestion, where the outermost truth predicate was consistently relativized to the actual world.

16. "Direct reference" is not Kripke's idiom but, in the first instance, David Kaplan's. My colleague Bill Lycan points out that Kripke's considered *official* line is to reject a full-blooded UCLA-style "direct reference" theory on the grounds, *inter alia*, that it is refuted by his own "Pierre" example in (PB). Bill cheerfully concedes, however, that Kripke is certainly a direct reference theorist at heart—"intuitive Millianism" is originally Bill's expression—and, as we shall see in Chapter 6, Kripke's ostensible puzzle never manages to get off the ground in the first place. In any event, as an interpretive proposal, the Apologist's suggestion is very well-taken, and tracing the "direct referential" elements in Kripke's thinking over the next several chapters will correlatively prove to be a substantially rewarding enterprise.

Chapter 3

1. Here's how Kripke puts it: "Obviously A could be wrong about some things about X. You could take some sort of a vote. . . . Let's say democracy doesn't necessarily rule. If there is any property that's completely irrelevant to the reference we can disenfranchise it altogether by giving it weight 0. The properties can be regarded as members of a corporation. Some have more stock than others; some may even have only non-voting stock" (65).
2. Keith Donnellan's (RDD) is the *locus classicus*.
3. We will return to this quotation in Chapter 6, where it will receive a more focused and extended discussion.
4. Explored, for example, in Grice's "Utterer's Meaning, Sentence-Meaning, and Word-Meaning" and "Utterer's Meaning and Intentions".
5. Devitt, in contrast, follows Donnellan in acknowledging two different *conventional* uses of definite descriptions (and, ultimately, of other nonindexical referring expressions as well)—corresponding to "a distinction between designational and attributive tokens" (D, 42)—and he regards this as "a fact of considerable semantic significance" (D, 37). "The object that bears on the truth value of a statement containing a designational token is the object it designates. On the other hand, the object that bears on the truth value of a statement containing an attributive token is the object it denotes [e.g., for a non-empty definite description, 'the F', the one and only object to which 'F' applies]" (D, 53; cf. D, 42). The *details* of this reconstruction and extension of Donnellan's original referential-attributive distinction in fact presuppose a good deal of the specific machinery of Devitt's theoretical elaboration of Kripke's causal-historical picture of reference, at which we have not yet arrived, but its *root intuition* tracks with both Donnellan's and Kripke's: a designational referring expression used by a speaker designates the object that the speaker *"has in mind"*. (cf. D, 11 and passim). Very shortly we shall find ourselves engaged in an intensive examination of just this notion.
6. For a more detailed and extensive exploration of the perceptual case, see especially "Perceptual Experience and Conceptual Awareness", chap. 4 of (TS).
7. Devitt explicitly subscribes to this program—"I explain speaker meanings in terms of thought meanings" (D,82)—although with complexities which will later require some additional, independent attention.

An earlier treatment of the themes under consideration here can be found in my (LR), especially chap. 2, "A Mentalistic Theory".

8. Given Kripke's rejection of the mind-body identity theory (on at least one of the more popular of its many interpretations) and his consequent endorsement of a *kind* of dualism—although he explicitly denies (155n) that he endorses Cartesian substantial dualism—it is not clear to what extent he would be troubled by ontological mysteries of the sorts I have been noting. I take it, though, that an account of reference that is compatible with a naturalistic ontology is, *ceteris paribus*, preferable to one that is not, and that no-one has ever even suggested that Scholastic-Cartesian "modes of being", much less primitive intentional relations, can be reconciled with such naturalistic ontological constraints.

9. A further consequence of this line of thought, it may be worth pointing out, is that a speaker will not have "privileged access" to or "incorrigible knowledge" of what or whom he has in mind, but nowadays this is hardly a radical claim. Devitt, indeed, adopts what in essence is precisely that conclusion as a *constraint* on an adequate theoretical account of "having in mind" (D, 11–12).

10. There is a sense in which Devitt disagrees with this claim. For although "[public linguistic] conventions are explained in terms of speaker meanings" and "speaker meanings are explained in terms of thought meanings", on Devitt's account, "thought meanings are partly explained in terms of conventions" (D, 85). Devitt's strategy for coping with the evident circularity here is to suggest that "what we really have is more like a spiral, a spiral that starts from crude thought meanings" (D, 85). "We had thoughts before we were able to say anything and before we learned any linguistic conventions. This is true of us as a species and true of us individually. It is also true of the higher animals. These preconvention thoughts, primeval, babyish, or nonhuman, are very primitive, *so* primitive as to be quite unlike the thoughts of modern language-speaking adults. . . . To say that these thoughts are primitive is not to say that they have no structure. One supposes that they have structures, albeit very crude ones" (D, 83). Something like this picture is surely correct, but the question of whether it suffices to defuse the circularity threatening Devitt's account of singular reference will have to be postponed until Kripke's critique of Descriptivism and his constructive alternative, which forms the point of departure for Devitt's own ac-

counts, have been placed on the dialectical table. Indeed, we will not have assembled all the resources we need to deal with the question until the final chapter of this study.

11. We have not, however, seen the last of this issue. I shall return to it in some detail in Chapter 6.

12. This is clearly a mistake. Thesis [T3] makes no claims about to whom a person *means to* refer, and, indeed, the very notion of "meaning (or intending) to refer to X" is extraordinarily puzzling and much in need of investigation. Thesis [T3] does, however, assert that, in the envisioned circumstances, an ordinary man who uses the name 'Gödel' *is*, willy-nilly, referring to Schmidt, and Kripke is surely right to point out that this at least *seems* implausible.

There is a similar expository infelicity later in the selection. Kripke writes: "we, when we talk about 'Gödel', are always in fact referring to Schmidt"—but, of course, when we talk about 'Gödel', we are referring to a name, not a person. The context 'talk about ——' is a delicate one, which does not fit comfortably with counterfactual discourses of this sort. In this instance, for example, *both* 'talk about 'Gödel' ' and 'talk about Gödel' are problematic.

13. Although neither Kripke nor Devitt explicitly notes the fact, the fundamental ideas of the causal-historical picture were first formulated and developed by Ruth Barcan Marcus as early as the 1950s. Perhaps for some of the socio-dialectical reasons surveyed in my opening remarks, however, it was only with Kripke's discussion that the view caught on.

14. By one of those cosmic coincidences, Helmut, like Kripke, also has a pet aardvark in need of a name.

15. I am, of course, here reporting on how it seems *to me*, that is, on *my* intuitions—and tacitly inviting the reader to compare his or hers. I have already remarked that it is unclear what probative or epistemic force such appeals to intuition have, but, even if they are purely rhetorical devices, I also see no reason to deny myself these expository tools of which Kripke has so richly availed himself.

16. To me, I confess, it seems patently obvious that, on this scenario, when Helmut uses the name 'Moritz Schlick', he is in fact talking about Otto Neurath, i.e., that the second view is correct. *My own* intuitions about the matter, in other words, are entirely determinate. My argument does not, in fact, require that we actually reach a verdict on the

issue—but consider a parallel case in which, in consequence of his poor memory, Helmut winds up ascribing Moritz Schlick's views, accomplishments, and experiences to someone he calls 'Moritz Neurath' and Otto Neurath's views, accomplishments, and experiences to someone he calls 'Otto Schlick'. Here the verdict seems truly inescapable that, when he uses the name 'Moritz Neurath', Helmut is talking about Moritz Schlick and, when he uses the name 'Otto Schlick', about Otto Neurath. But all the significant differences between this scenario and the original one lie *outside* Helmut's competences and beliefs. On *either* scenario, what Helmut has is *two new names* (i.e., names previously entirely absent from his linguistic repertoire), together with two sets of descriptions that he believes to be true of their (respective) referents.

17. More precisely, Devitt adapts to this end some techniques pioneered by Hartry Field in "Theory Change and the Indeterminacy of Reference".

18. This is probably the best that we can do with some of Devitt's "Leibknecht" cases (D, 140–143). Regarding the example of 'mass' in Newtonian and relativistic mechanics which originally led Hartry Field to introduce notions of "partial designation" and "truth relative to a structure", see my "Coupling, Retheoretization, and the Correspondence Principle".

19. But suppose that, when Jemima was still present, Cato had answered the question "What cat are you talking about?" by saying "Michael Devitt's cat Nana; that cat over there." Wouldn't he then in some sense have been using 'Nana' to refer *both* to Nana *and* to Jemima when he originally said "Nana is black"? If we stick to questions of speaker's reference, I think not. For surely it makes more sense to say that, just as Cato's first utterance expresses a true belief about Jemima (that cat over there), namely that she is black, his second utterance expresses a *false* belief *also* about Jemima (that cat over there), namely that she is Michael Devitt's cat Nana. Indeed, even if Cato had answered *only* "Michael Devitt's cat Nana", we would *still* have the option of interpreting his original utterance "Nana is black" to be the expression of a true thought about Jemima and his answer to the question "What cat are you talking about?" as the expression of his *false* (semantic) belief that the cat he is talking about (*viz.* Jemima, that cat over there) is Devitt's cat Nana. If intuitive plausibility is supposed to be what is moving us,

210 Notes to Chapter 3

these strategies seem plainly preferable to *any* story which appeals to "degrees of designation" and "degrees of truth".

Chapter 4

1. The qualifier 'explicit' is meant to rule out such beliefs as that Moses was a human being, that Moses was a man, that Moses lived over fifty years ago, that Moses lived over sixty years ago, that Moses wore clothing, that Moses spoke at least one language, that Moses had two feet, and so on, perhaps even *ad infinitum*. One also, in any event, typically has indefinitely many *tacit* beliefs about Moses, and it is much less clear that all or most (or even many) of these tacit beliefs could also be false.

2. Whether it is possible to refer with a proper name to an individual (item) while knowing or believing *nothing at all* about that individual (item) remains to be seen. An acceptable account of proper name reference should perhaps set a rough lower bound here, including at least, say, an item's ontological category. A similar qualification applies with respect to (CA2). It seems implausible, that is, to hold that *all* of a speaker's descriptive beliefs regarding, say, Socrates—for example, the belief that Socrates occupied space—could be false. Devitt's proposal in this connection is that "we insist only that the object be in the same *very general* category as it is taken to be", while recognizing that there is "an element of arbitrariness in our determination of these categories" (D, 63).

3. Indeed, consonant with (CA2), we can even imagine circumstances in which we would conclude that someone was in fact referring to the notable physicist Richard Feynman even though she explicitly believed of Feynman only that he was a *chemist*. It is, however, not as clear that this claim remains true if we substitute for 'chemist', say, 'historian' or 'pilot' or 'automobile mechanic', while the (sole) belief that Feynman was a *physician*, on the other hand, returns us to the earlier intuitions.

The principle guiding my intuitions about such matters seems to be that we should be able to produce a plausible explanation of how it might come about that a person entertained just *that* false belief *about Feynman*. Thus we can easily suppose that someone has come away from a discussion of notable contemporary natural scientists somewhat confused about which were the physicists and which the chemists, and we can easily imagine someone's *mishearing* 'physicist' as 'physician', but it is much harder—although certainly not impossible—to sketch out a plausible scenario for someone's acquiring the belief that Feynman was a historian, pilot, or automobile mechanic.

4. This perhaps explains Kripke's curious reluctance in this passage even to call "Santa Claus" a *name*. (For one would surely have expected the wording: ". . . the children, when they use this *name*, . . .") On the other hand, in an addendum to the main text (p. 163), we find Kripke speaking both of "reference shifts . . . from a real entity to a fictional one"—which suggests that reference to fictional entities is possible—and of "real reference" *vs.* "fictional reference"—which suggests that it is not, i.e., that ostensible "reference" to fictional entities is not (really) a species of *reference* at all. (On p. 158, Kripke similarly adverts to "fictional names".) I think it would be a mistake to suppose that we can, or should be able to, extract any articulate account of fictional discourse from such passing remarks.

5. Katarina Blum is doubtless less well known to many Anglo-American readers than either Santa Claus or Sherlock Holmes. She is the protagonist of Heinrich Böll's superb novel, *Die verlorene Ehre der Katarina Blum.*

6. Curiously, Devitt agrees: "This term ['refer'] in philosophy is largely *a term of art*, gaining its meanings from its use in semantic theories" (D, 48).

7. The example of Robin Hood was urged upon me by Ruth Barcan Marcus in the course of a spirited discussion at the National Humanities Center in which George Bealer and Al Mele also energetically participated.

8. John Mathew Gutch (1776–1861), *A lytell geste of Robin Hode, with other ancient & modern ballads and songs relating to this celebrated yeoman to which is prefixed his history and character (London: Longman, Brown, Green, & Longmans, 1847).*

9. For example, in *The Downfall of Robert, Earle of Huntington, Afterward Called Robin Hood of merrie Sherwodde: with his loue to chaste Matilda, the Lord Fitzwaters daughter, afterwardes his faire Maide Marian,* a play by Anthony Munday (1553–1633).

10. *People Weekly,* July 8, 1991, p. 47.

212 Notes to Chapter 4

11. Once we are sensitized to the possibility of this sort of "reference shift", we can see that the causal-historical picture arguably gives the wrong answer in a variety of other cases as well, including some in which the distinction of fact from fiction plays no role.

Ruth Marcus, for instance, offers the hypothetical example of a sixteenth-century explorer who ventures across a previously uncharted uninhabited island and proceeds to christen it 'Glyph', dutifully recording the entire business in his logbooks. Some years later, a second explorer attempts to retrace the first explorer's voyage using those logbooks and, believing himself to have succeeded, arrives at an uninhabited island which he consequently proceeds to think of and talk about by using the name 'Glyph'. The second explorer, however, is mistaken. The island at which he has arrived is *another* uncharted uninhabited island, not the one christened 'Glyph' by the first explorer.

Be that as it may, the second explorer's descriptions of the beautiful regions he has visited prove enticing, and boatloads of settlers and colonists immediately set out for the island called 'Glyph' in those accounts. Given the second explorer's superior navigational charts and records, they have no trouble reaching it. (In contrast, no-one revisits the island reached by the *first* explorer for many, many years.) Of course, they also call it 'Glyph', and so do their children and their children's children, and so on—even unto the present day, when some of us, too, now book vacation flights to the beautiful tropical island of Glyph. (The case has substantial similarities with Gareth Evans' "Madagascar" example, cited by Kripke [163].)

Since, to use Devitt's terminology, *every* token of 'Glyph' belongs to a d-chain grounded in the island discovered by the first explorer, a causal theorist is apparently committed to the conclusion that, when they use the name 'Glyph', the original settlers and their children and their children's children and our own travel agents are all talking about (or at least "partially designating") the first explorer's island. Correlatively, what they say when they use the term is typically false (or at least "partially false"). On the contrary, however, it seems intuitively perfectly plain that—although the second explorer was doubtless talking about the first explorer's island when he triumphantly (but mistakenly) recorded in his logbook "At last, I have reached Glyph!"—by the time the settlers got down to making their plans, *they* were already talking about the *second* explorer's island—the one whose beauties he *in fact* described. 'Glyph', that is, had already become an ambiguous name, and the colonists' triumphant cry upon landing, "At last, we have reached Glyph!", consequently said something entirely true.

12. It is perhaps worth noting at this point that Kripke himself evidently regards numerals as (proper) *names of numbers*. Thus he argues that, unlike the descriptive phrase 'the number of planets', the numeral '9' rigidly designates (the number) nine. And he writes of the Greek letter 'π' that it "is not being used as *short for* the phrase 'the ratio of the circumference of a circle to its diameter' nor is it even used as short for a cluster of alternative definitions of π, whatever that might mean. It is being used as a *name* of a real number which in this case is necessarily the ratio of the circumference of a circle to its diameter" (60). Although Devitt, for instance, provides an extended treatment of fictional discourse ("empty terms"), the question of how such a view of mathematical terms might be reconciled with the causal-historical picture of nominal reference unfortunately remains undiscussed.

13. This is not to say, of course, that we cannot imagine someone rejecting (TSC), and hence denying that Santa Claus uniquely satisfies the description (DSC). A typical German child, for instance, might insist that no-one satisfies (DSC), i.e., that the description is true of *no-one*. She's never heard of anyone living at the North Pole, and, anyway, it's the Infant Christ who brings deserving children toys on Christmas Eve. But what follows from this, surely, is only that Santa Claus is not part of German children's *repertoire* of fictional, legendary, and mythological characters. Their closest traditional counterpart is probably St. Nikolaus—a tall, gaunt, bearded, peripatetic cleric, who puts sweets and small gifts into the shoes of deserving children, and coal and bundles of switches into the shoes of *un*deserving children, on 6 December (*Nikolaustag*). The German repertoire in some sense also includes *der Weihnachtsmann*—literally "the Christmas man", that is, (near enough) "Father Christmas"—but it's not clear whether Father Christmas and St. Nikolaus should be thought of as one and the same character. The sort of cross-cultural identification questions that arise in the case of Santa Claus and St. Nikolaus are characteristic for legendary and mythical figures (cf., for example, the question of the identity or non-identity of Zeus and Jupiter, Aphrodite and Venus, etc.). Characters who are strictly speaking

fictional, that is, characters introduced in determinate literary works of fiction, typically exhibit no such cross-cultural ambiguities.

14. For an extended discussion, see my (OW), especially chaps. 3–5.

15. This notion of "two forms", or, to put it differently, the idea that there can be appearance and reality with respect to language, is *the* distinctive methodological posit of analytic philosophy. The leading idea of Frege's *Begriffsschrift*, it received its definitive initial articulation in Russell's "On Denoting". Much more to these themes later.

16. In "Two Dogmas of Empiricism".

Chapter 5

1. In (PB), pp. 265–266.

2. What a "purely descriptive indicative sentence" is I will at this point prudently not attempt to say, except to note that the notion is clearly designed to exclude modal contexts and contexts generated by the so-called "propositional attitudes". The notion of a "purely descriptive indicative sentence" is thus approximately equivalent to the notion of an "extensional" context or of a "referentially transparent" context. The significant difference is that the latter notions are characteristically explained or defined *in terms of* the notion of reference (e.g., as contexts which are truth-preserving under substitution of *coreferential* expressions), whereas the notion of a purely descriptive indicative sentence in contrast belongs to the raw materials in terms of which the present account of nominal reference is to be constructed.

I might add that the notion of a purely descriptive indicative sentence is *not* intended to exclude fictional contexts. Thus, for example, I take 'Sherlock Holmes wrote the definitive nineteenth-century British monograph on the identification of brands of cigars and cigarettes from their ashes' to be a perfectly good example of such a sentence.

3. Paul Ziff, *Semantic Analysis*, p. 104.

4. Perceptual encounters consequently *can* play something quite like the "grounding" role that Devitt assigns them: "In a grounding a person perceives an object, preferably face to face, correctly believing it to be an object of a certain very general category. *The grounding consists in the person coming to have ''grounding thoughts'' about that object as a result of the act of perceiving the object.* A grounding thought about an object includes a mental

representation of that object brought about by an act of perception. The thought is one which a speaker of a public language would express using *a demonstrative* from that language. . . . However, I see no reason to deny that beings which do not speak public languages could have grounding thoughts. If they do have them, then they must have appropriate mental representations" (D, 133). The fundamental difference between Devitt's account and the one being offered here concerns the (semantic) import of the specific causal element that, uncontroversially, *epistemologically* distinguishes perceptual acts from, for example, hallucinating, dreaming, imagining, or remembering. Our disagreement will emerge most clearly in the case of non-linguistic creatures who, I shall argue, lack precisely the resources needed to move from perceptual representations to *singular* representations *in absentia* capable of functioning as (proper) names. A complete discussion, however, must await considerations appropriately developed only in the final chapters of this study.

5. See, for example, Sellars' "Abstract Entities", "Language as Thought and Communication", and "Meaning as Functional Classification".

6. For more regarding material inference principles see, *inter alia*, my (LR) and further references there cited.

7. Since dot-quoted expressions are strictly speaking common nouns, I have in fact taken some modest grammatical liberties here. A full dress paraphrase would need to introduce quantification over individual tokenings (inscriptions), for example:

$(\exists N)[*Hesperus*s$ are N's & $(t)(t')(t$ is an N & t' is a ·Venus·.$\to$. t is isonymous to $t')]$

It is perhaps also worth noting that, on the present account, such "echoic" claims as

'Hesperus' refers to Hesperus

have the *same* structure, for example,

$(\exists N)[*Hesperus*s$ are N's & $(t)(t')(t$ is an N & t' is a ·Hesperus·.$\to$. t is isonymous to $t')]$.

8. Not accidentally, the picture of nominal reference I am in the process of developing here bears significant analogies to an "epistemic" account advanced by Charles Chastain in his excellent, but surprisingly unappreciated, essay "Reference and Context". The specific relationship is explored in an early precursor of the present work, "Linguistic Roles and Proper Names".

9. This is not to say that other philosophers, for instance, Devitt—and, indeed, Kripke himself elsewhere—haven't developed and refined the causal-historical picture originally sketched in *Naming and Necessity*. Although I have taken the time to comment on some of these refinements, my chief interest remains the *leading ideas* of these competing accounts, not the details of various salvage operations that have from time to time been mounted to save one or another from specific counterexamples. If geocentric astronomy is fundamentally flawed, adding enough epicycles to fit it to a given set of data points does nothing to improve matters. My six criteria of adequacy, (CA1)–(CA6), thus provide only a coarse evaluative sieve, but one at the appropriate level of generality to feed into the broader dialectics encompassing such accounts.

10. In this connection, compare Wilfrid Sellars: "What is it to describe? In my opinion, the key to the answer is the realization that *describing* is internally related to *explaining*, in that sense of "explanation" which comes to full flower in scientific explanation—in short *causal* explanation. A descriptive term is one which, *in its basic use*, properly replaces one of the variables in the dialogue schema

What brought it about that x is φ?

The fact that y is Ψ.

where what is requested is a causal explanation." ("Empiricism and Abstract Entities", p. 265.)

11. Being spatio-temporally *locatable* should not be confused with being spatio-temporally *localized*. Locatability is a wider notion, intended to encompass, for example, the representation of empirical properties by way of exemplary spatio-temporally localized *instances* of those properties.

12. In this exposition, I have been sanguine about the matter, but the question of whether *all* the indexicality can be washed out of our world-stories, even in principle, is actually a deep metaphysical issue. At the time of writing the *Tractatus*, for example, Wittgenstein evidently thought so.

> 5.526 We can describe the world completely by means of fully generalized propositions, i.e., without first correlating any name with a particular object.

Then, in order to arrive at the customary mode of expression, we simply need to add, after an expression like, 'There is one and only one x such that . . .', the words, 'and this x is a'.

In contrast, Anton Koch has recently argued the opposing view at considerable length in his excellent and challenging book *Subjektivität in Raum und Zeit* (Frankfurt, Germany: Verlag Vittorio Klostermann, 1991).

A scientific realist should side with Wittgenstein on the issue, and since I have long been convinced that only such a realism is ultimately compatible with a thoroughgoing philosophical *naturalism*, I am, at least, consistent on the matter. Because this is obviously not the occasion for a more extended discussion, for the moment, alas, such consistency will have to serve in lieu of argument.

13. We have, however, by no means exhausted the problematic centered on this root conviction. We shall have occasion to return to it later.

14. There is no reason to suppose, however, that the communal sense of the proper name of an empirical object will include descriptions, not only of that object's subsequent history but of *the name's* subsequent history as well.

Chapter 6

1. Compare Simon Blackburn: "[We] have a multiplicity of causal relationships to things. When I refer to Napoleon, I may be prompted to do so by a text containing words; the words were written via a printing system, via an author himself relying on other authors, and so on. But it is Napoleon I am referring to, not any of the intermediate elements of the causal chain. Two questions arise. First of all, is there any prospect of a purely natural description of just the relations to things I have when I refer to them? Secondly, even if there is, what is it that makes just *that* causal or natural relationship the relationship of *reference*?" (*Spreading the Word*, p. 279).

2. Compare Devitt's 'Leibknecht' example (D, 140 ff.).

3. What it means for two persons (e.g., Rod Stewart, the rock singer, and Rod Stewart, the philosopher) to be *namesakes* is surely that they share one and the same name.

4. In his "A Puzzle About Belief" (PB).

5. "For each (French or English) replacement for 'p,' infer " 'p' is true" from "p," and conversely." (PB, 277, n26)

6. I suspect that Kripke himself knows this quite well, but, curiously, his only explicit acknowledgment of this epistemic requirement comes in a footnote: "If we wish to use the simple disquotational principle as a test for disbelief, it suffices that this be true of some individuals, after reflection, *who are simultaneously aware of both beliefs*, and have sufficient logical acumen and respect for logic. Such individuals, if they have contradictory beliefs, will be shaken in one or both beliefs *after they note the contradiction*" (PB, 276–277, n24, my emphases).

7. More accurately, Pierre would *either* straightaway conclude that New York is not pretty *or*, if he also already believed, for example, that New York *is* pretty (and was aware of that fact), would undertake to resolve the inconsistencies among his beliefs. In the remaining discussion, I shall generally ignore such nuances.

8. The alternative, of course, is to treat these elucidating terms themselves statistically, the "appropriate" syntax, for example, being the syntax employed by a *typical* speaker. That is why I earlier cautiously said that being a normal English speaker in Kripke's sense has nothing *directly* to do with being a typical one. From the epistemological point of view, however, it might turn out, for example, that statistical typicality is the best (or even the only) evidence for normative normality.

Chapter 7

1. For action sentences, see "The Logical Form of Action Sentences"; for belief sentences, "On Saying That".

2. Making these notions suitably precise turns out to be a nontrivial business. Thereby hang a variety of tales, but this is fortunately not an occasion on which we need to attempt to tell any of them in detail.

3. The closet that contains the skeletons in this formulation, of course, is the notion of a *proper* symbolization. Trying to figure out just what that might mean is a significant part of what the problematic of logical analysis is all about.

4. Davidson himself, it should be said, conscientiously avoids such striking extravagances. But Davidson, too, takes the conclusions of such

"logical analysis", of his investigations into logical form, to have wider philosophical import—in particular, to be contributions to an account of the *truth-conditions* of various sentences which, in turn, is a decisive element of the general philosophical theory of *interpretation, meaning,* and *understanding*.

5. Some "hard-core" Kripke: "[The views represented in *Naming and Necessity*] grew out of earlier formal work in the model theory of modal logic. Already . . . it had seemed to me . . . that the Leibnizian principle of the indiscernibility of identicals [i.e., $(x)(y)(x=y \ \&\ Fx .\rightarrow. Fy)$] was as self-evident as the law of contradiction. That some philosophers could have doubted it always seemed to me bizarre. The model theoretic study of modal logic ('possible worlds' semantics) could only confirm this conviction—the alleged counterexamples involving modal properties always turned out to turn on some confusion. . . . The model theory made this completely clear, though it should have been clear enough on the intuitive level. Waiving fussy considerations . . . , it was clear from $(x)\square(x=x)$ and Leibniz's law that identity is an 'internal' relation: $(x)(y)(x=y \rightarrow \square\ x=y)$. . . . If '*a*' and '*b*' are rigid designators, it follows that '*a*=*b*', if true, is a necessary truth. If '*a*' and '*b*' are *not* rigid designators, no such conclusion follows about the *statement* '*a*=*b*' "(3).

6. The parallelism can be made even more exact by coupling "logical theory" to "linguistic theory" in Chomsky's style and identifying the former's "logical forms" with the "abstract structures" posited by the latter. Such "deep" structures, in turn, are supposed to have "psychological reality" (and consequently "biological reality" as well), that is, to "reflect principles of mental operation that form part of the human language faculty", whose "fixed principles" are an innate part of the "biological endowment" of human organisms as such (Chomsky, LPK, pp. 25, 27). Such structures constitute the basis (raw materials) upon which "the computational principles of the mind . . . carry out a series of operations to yield the actual [spoken] sentence" (LPK, 84). Here we have a strict analogy to the kinetic properties of the "ontologically underlying" molecular structure of a substance which are manifested at the observational "surface" as a sensible and measurable phenomenology of heat.

7. See, for example, "Coupling, Retheoretization, and the Correspondence Principle" and "Comparing the Incommensurable: Another Look at Convergent Realism".

8. The paradigm to keep in mind here is Russell's analysis of (definite) descriptive phrases, according to which such *apparently* contradictory pairs as "The present king of France is bald" and "The present king of France is not bald", which *prima facie* exhausted a certain logical space, were mapped onto symbolic formulae that were *not* D-contradictories but merely D-contraries.

9. Lewis Carroll, "What the Tortoise Said to Achilles", *Mind* 4, n.s. no. 14 (1895): 278–280, and variously reprinted.

10. Somewhat surprisingly, although his own inclinations are pretty clearly "hard-core", Kripke occasionally appears to recognize this as well. The most salient evidence is in a footnote to "A Puzzle About Belief" that we have already encountered in another context: "If we wish to use the simple disquotational principle as a test for disbelief, it suffices that this be true of some individuals, after reflection, who are simultaneously aware of both beliefs, and have sufficient logical acumen and *respect for logic*. Such individuals, if they have contradictory beliefs, will be shaken in one or both beliefs after they note the contradiction" (PB, 276–277, n24, my emphasis).

Chapter 8

1. The proper answer, to anticipate, is arguably "No". In particular, although they are *ex hypothesi* capable of singular *indexical* reference, purely Humean creatures arguably lack sufficient representational resources to provide for singular reference *in absentia*.

2. *Monadology*, no. 26, cited by Wilfrid Sellars in "Mental Events". The present discussion is, and will continue to be, deeply indebted to this essay.

3. Daniel Dennett, "Intentional Systems". In this connection, see also Dennett's "True Believers: The Intentional Strategy and Why it Works".

4. See Wilfrid Sellars, "Language as Thought and Communication".

5. W. V. Quine, "Three Indeterminacies", p. 8.

6. In this sense, we can endorse Devitt's remark that "mental representations of the world come with theorizing about it" (D, 84).

7. Compare Sellars: "[The] idea that epistemic facts can be analyzed without remainder—even "in principle"—into non-epistemic facts, whether phenomenal or behavioral, public or private, with no matter how lavish a sprinkling of subjunctives and hypotheticals is . . . a radical mistake—a mistake of a piece with the so-called "naturalistic fallacy" in ethics" ("Empiricism and the Philosophy of Mind", p. 257).

8. The contrast between reporting and expressing the obtaining of rational relationships at issue here is analogous to the contrast between reporting and expressing such "propositional attitudes" as intention, belief, and desire. Compare, for example, the representational resources needed to *report* your intention, for example, to rent the *Batman* videotape—"I intend to rent *Batman* this weekend"—with those needed to *express* it—"I'm going to rent *Batman* this weekend". The former, but not the latter, requires that you be equipped with the *concept* of an intention (as such), including the ability explicitly to distinguish, for instance, between what you intend to do and what you (only) predict you will do.

In general, to report one's intentions requires a command of the "propositional attitude" verbs of the "intentional stance". To merely express one's intentions, however, a command of the first-person pronoun 'I' and the future tense suffices. Similarly, to express your belief that Gorbachev is a great statesman, you need only to be able to talk about Gorbachev ("Gorbachev is a great statesman"); to report it, you need to be able to talk about yourself and your beliefs as well ("I believe that Gorbachev is a great statesman"). One reports one's desire for a pepperoni pizza by "I want a pepperoni pizza"; one can express it by driving to the local Pizza Pit and ordering one. (G. E. M. Anscombe: "The primitive sign of wanting is trying to get.")

9. Such ratiocinative creatures are close cousins of—but not, I think, identical to—the sort of creatures that Jonathan Bennett describes as "rational" in his provocative little book, *Rationality*. In particular, I suspect that being, in my sense, ratiocinative is a necessary but not yet a sufficient condition for being, in Bennett's sense, "rational".

10. Robert Brandom, "Inference, Expression, and Induction", p. 276. Brandom's reference to Sellars here adverts to one of his early remarks regarding empirical reasoning: "In dealing with . . . [attempts to justify acceptance of a natural law by means of an argument from instances], philosophers usually speak of inductive arguments, of estab-

lishing laws by induction from instances. . . . I am highly dubious of this conception. I should be inclined to say that the use [a natural-scientific theorizer] will make of instances is rather in the nature of Socratic method. For Socratic method serves the purpose of making explicit the rules we have adopted for thought and action, and I shall be interpreting our judgments to the effect that A causally necessitates B as the expression of a rule governing our use of the terms 'A' and 'B' " ("Language, Rules, and Behavior", 136, n2). In this connection, see also Brandom's "Varieties of Understanding," which addresses, among other things, the question of how one might go about initially *introducing* logical particles and, correlatively, formal inferential principles, as a conservative extension of an original contentive (material) representational system.

11. See in this connection "The Concept of Linguistic Correctness" and chap. 4, "Correctness and Community", of (OW).

12. With these observations, we are finally in a position to say something about Devitt's explanatory "spiral", mentioned in Chapter 3. In order to explain how it can simultaneously be the case that (1) "[public linguistic] conventions are explained in terms of speaker meanings" *and* that (2) "speaker meanings are explained in terms of thought meanings" *and* that (3) "thought meanings are partly explained in terms of conventions", Devitt proposes that we begin with "crude thought meanings" (D, 85). He sketches out a sophisticated picture of "a language of thought expanding with the introduction into it of a public language" (D, 84). In consequence, on his view, in the case of a mature, linguistically competent *person,* the language of thought will in large part simply *be* "the spoken and/or written ("public") language of the thinker" (D, 75). In such a case, words in the language of thought "are mostly brought about by sound and inscription conventions, and the explanation of their meanings involves reference to those conventions. Thus my mental representation 'Socrates' means what it does because it was causally brought about by sounds and inscriptions conventionally related to that meaning" (D, 85–86). It follows that, when the claims are relativized to language-using animals, there is no problem in regarding (1), (2), and (3) as consistent. "Crude thought meanings" will be relevant to the *explanatory* story, then, only to the extent that they help us to understand the emergence of public language *per se* (or, analogously, the acquisition of a first natural language by an initially non-linguistic infant). For what our

investigation of purely Humean creatures has revealed is that the representational systems implicit in pre-linguistic "crude thought meanings" are too impoverished to yield the representational resources of a public language simply by being, as it were, *scaled up*. There is something of the nature of a "quantum leap" in the transition from merely Humean to ratiocinative beings, and, correlatively, something of the nature of a "quantum leap" in the transition from beings capable only of "crude thought meanings" to beings commanding sufficient representational resources for genuinely singular representation *in absentia*.

I have deliberately refrained from attempting to tell any story at all about such "quantum leaps". My aims at this point are phenomenological rather than genetic and, besides, I haven't really any plausible ideas about how such a story might go. Neither, I think, does anyone else, but Devitt dutifully gives it a lick and a promise: "The drive for understanding and control led our early ancestors, in time, to express a primitive thought or two. They grunted and gestured, *meaning something by* such actions: there was speaker meaning in the absence of conventional meaning. In time the grunts and gestures caught on and we had our first linguistic conventions" (D, 84). Devitt goes on a bit longer in the same vein, but we've seen enough to know that we're not going to get a story about the really interesting bit, the sort of "catching on" that produces the "first linguistic conventions".

But we've also seen enough to grant that Devitt is entitled to be sanguine about the *prima facie* circularity of the claims (1)–(3). For he is no worse off with regard to accounting for the transition from a pre- to a post-linguistic state, by either an individual organism or an entire species, than any other philosophical naturalist. Subject to the cautionary remark that we should not suppose that "crude thought meanings", although indeed *somehow* structured, must already contain, as it were, "crude proper names"—a point which I am *not* entirely confident Devitt fully grasps—there is no reason not to concede Devitt his claims, properly qualified, about "the primacy of thought meaning and speaker meaning over conventional meaning" (D, 86).

13. Compare *Philosophical Investigations*, §18: "Our language can be seen as an ancient city: a maze of little streets and squares, of old and new houses, and of houses with additions from various periods, and this surrounded by a multitude of new boroughs, with straight regular streets and uniform houses."

WORKS CITED

Blackburn, Simon. *Spreading the Word*. London and New York: Oxford University Press, 1984.

Brandom, Robert. "Inference, Expression, and Induction." *Philosophical Studies* 54 (1988): 257–285.

———. "Varieties of Understanding." In Nicholas Rescher (ed.), *Reason and Rationality in Natural Science* (New York: University Press of America, 1985), pp. 27–51.

Chastain, Charles. "Reference and Context." In Keith Gunderson (ed.), *Language, Mind, and Knowledge*, Minnesota Studies in the Philosophy of Science, vol. 7 (Minneapolis: University of Minnesota Press, 1975), pp. 194–269.

Chomsky, Noam. *Language and Problems of Knowledge* (LPK). Cambridge, Mass.: MIT Press, 1988.

Davidson, Donald. "The Logical Form of Action Sentences." In Donald Davidson, *Essays on Actions and Events* (Oxford: Clarendon Press, 1981).

———. "On Saying That." In Donald Davidson, *Inquiries into Truth and Interpretation* (Oxford: Clarendon Press, 1984).

Dennett, Daniel. "Intentional Systems." *Journal of Philosophy* 68 (1971): 87–106. Reprinted in *Brainstorms* (Montgomery, Vt.: Bradford Books, 1978).

———. "True Believers: The Intentional Strategy and Why It Works." In A. F. Heath (ed.), *Scientific Explanation* (Oxford: Oxford University Press, 1981).

Devitt, Michael. *Designation* (D). New York: Columbia University Press, 1981.

Donnellan, Keith. "Reference and Definite Descriptions" (RDD). *Philosophical Review* 75 (1966): 281–304.

Field, Hartry. "Theory Change and the Indeterminacy of Reference." *Journal of Philosophy* 70 (1973): 462–481.

Grice, H. Paul. "Utterer's Meaning and Intentions." *Philosophical Review* 78 (1969): 147–177.

———. "Utterer's Meaning, Sentence-Meaning, and Word-Meaning." *Foundations of Language* 4 (1968): 225–242.

Kripke, Saul A. "Naming and Necessity." In Gilbert Harman and Donald Davidson (eds.), *Semantics of Natural Language* (Dordrecht, Holland: D. Reidel, 1972).

———. *Naming and Necessity*. Cambridge, Mass.: Harvard University Press, 1980.

———. "A Puzzle About Belief" (PB). In Avishai Margalit (ed.), *Meaning and Use* (Dordrecht, Holland: D. Reidel, 1979), pp. 239–283.

———. "Speaker's Reference and Semantic Reference" (SRSR). In Peter A. French, Theodore E. Uehling, Jr., and Howard K. Wettstein (eds.), *Studies in the Philosophy of Language*, Midwest Studies in Philosophy, vol. 2 (Minneapolis: University of Minnesota Press, 1977), pp. 255–276. Revised and enlarged as *Contemporary Perspectives in the Philosophy of Language* (1979).

Putnam, Hilary. "The Meaning of 'Meaning' " (MM). In *Mind, Language, and Reality* (Cambridge, England: Cambridge University Press, 1975), pp. 223 ff.

Quine, W.V.O. "Reference and Modality." In *From a Logical Point of View* (New York: Harper Torchbooks, 1963), pp. 139–159.

———. "Three Grades of Modal Involvement." In *The Ways of Paradox* (New York: Random House, 1966), pp. 156–174.

———. "Three Indeterminacies." In Robert B. Barrett and Roger F. Gibson (eds.), *Perspectives on Quine* (Oxford and Cambridge, England: Basil Blackwell, 1990), pp. 1–16.

———. "Two Dogmas of Empiricism." In *From a Logical Point of View* (New York: Harper Torchbooks, 1963), pp. 20–46.

Rosenberg, Jay F. "Comparing the Incommensurable: Another Look at Convergent Realism." *Philosophical Studies* 54 (1988): 163–193.

———. "The Concept of Linguistic Correctness." *Philosophical Studies* 30 (1976): 171–184.

———. "Coupling, Retheoretization, and the Correspondence Principle." *Synthese* 45 (1980): 351–385.

———. "The Dispute on the Indeterminacy of Translation." In Marcelo Dascal et al. (eds.), *Handbuch der Sprachphilosophie* (Berlin: W. de Gruyter, 1993).

———. *Linguistic Representation* (LR). Dordrecht, Holland: D. Reidel, 1974.

———. "Linguistic Roles and Proper Names." In Joseph C. Pitt (ed.), *The Philosophy of Wilfrid Sellars: Queries and Extensions* (Dordrecht, Holland: D. Reidel, 1978), pp. 189–216.

———. *One World and Our Knowledge of It* (OW). Dordrecht, Holland: D. Reidel, 1980.

———. "Phenomenal Ontology Revisited: A Bergmannian Retrospective." In James E. Tomberlin (ed.), *Philosophical Perspectives*, vol. 1, *Metaphysics* (Atascadero, Calif.: Ridgeview, 1987), pp. 387–404.

———. "Synonymy and the Epistemology of Linguistics." *Inquiry* 10 (1966): 405–420.

———. *The Thinking Self* (TS). Philadelphia: Temple University Press, 1986.

Sellars, Wilfrid. "Abstract Entities." *Review of Metaphysics* 16 (1963): 627–671.

———. "Empiricism and Abstract Entities." In Wilfrid Sellars, *Essays in Philosophy and Its History* (Dordrecht, Holland: D. Reidel, 1974), pp. 245–286.

———. "Empiricism and the Philosophy of Mind." In Wilfrid Sellars, *Science, Perception and Reality* (Atascadero, Calif.: Ridgeview, 1991), pp. 127–196. Originally published by Routledge & Kegan Paul and Humanities Press (London and New York), 1963.

———. "Language as Thought and Communication." *Philosophy and Phenomenological Research* 29 (1969). Reprinted in *Essays in Philosophy and Its History*, pp. 93–117.

———. "Language, Rules, and Behavior." In Jeffrey Sicha (ed.), *Pure Pragmatics and Possible Worlds* (Atascadero, Calif.: Ridgeview, 1980), pp. 129–155.

———. "Meaning as Functional Classification." *Synthese* 27 (1974): 417–437.

———. "Mental Events." *Philosophical Studies* 39 (1981): 325–345.

Ziff, Paul. "About Proper Names." In D. L. Boyer et al. (eds.), *The Philosopher's Annual* (Totowa, N.J.: Rowman & Littlefield, 1978), pp. 209–223. Originally published in *Mind* 86 (1977).
———. *Semantic Analysis*. Ithaca, N.Y.: Cornell University Press, 1960.

GENERAL INDEX

aardvark, 73, 76, 208
abilities, 81–82
aboutness, 64–65
absentia, 73, 116, 184, 194, 215, 220, 223
absurdities, 176, 178–181
accumulation: of content, 126; point, 115
adverbial modifiers, 164, 166
alethic modal operators, 164, 166
alternative: logics, 175; symbolizations, 164
ambiguity, 47–48
ambiguous: designation, 52–53; proper names, 94, 96, 141, 144–145, 194–195, 213
analysis, 159–160, 163–167, 169, 175, 177, 180–182,191–192, 195–196, 198, 214, 221
analyticity, 2, 9
anomalies, 175–176, 178, 180
antinomies, 176, 178–181
aperspectival, 132
apes, 183
Apologist, 49–55, 204–205
a posteriori, 10, 22, 200–201
apostles of tolerance, 168

appearance: vs. reality, 169, 171–172, 174–175, 177–178, 214
aprioricity, 2, 6–7
archer, 91, 93–94
argument: Kripke's, 30–54
arguments. *See* NL-arguments
arithmetic, 70–71, 97
astronomy, 173, 216
atmospheric conditions, 6–7, 10
atomic number, 19–22
atomism, 3
attributive use, 59–60, 141, 195, 206
Au. *See* gold
authenticity, 113
authorship, 113
automaton, 192, 201

baby, 17, 72
ballads, 91, 211
balloons, 173
baptismal events, 73–74, 80, 128, 135–138
Bartender, 59
base language, 101–102
bears, 63
beech, 114, 142

229

General Index

behavior, 185–187, 189, 193
belaboring, 56, 205
belief: and conduct, 147–158; expressing, 221; mistaken, 58–60, 71, 79–80, 84, 87–89, 125, 143–145, 152, 184, 194, 209–210; sentences 59, 210
beliefs: and sense, 109–111, 113–115, 120–122, 127, 129–134, 140, 142–143, 186, 210
bilinguals, 147–148, 155
bush, 63

calculation, 170
calculi. *See* logical calculi
canononical text, 112–123, 123
categories, 165, 210
cats, 82–84, 183, 209
causal: links, 102, 135–140; network, 95, 101; relations, 112, 189, 217; transactions, 129, 133, 215–216
causal-historical, xi, 3, 5, 55, 72–74, 80, 85, 86, 88–90, 94, 96–97, 108, 124–128, 133–134, 135, 137–140, 145, 206, 208, 212–213, 216
chain, 72–75, 80–82, 89, 95, 133–140, 212, 217
chalk, 35
champagne, 141
characteristic sentences, 121
chemist, 210–211
circularity, 67, 69–70, 74, 80, 86, 127–230, 207, 223
claims: collecting, 115, 118; entry, 130
classification, 4, 108, 118–122, 127, 184–185, 194
clergy, 94
closet, 218

collecting: claims, 115, 118
colonists, 212–213
commensuration, 111, 114–116, 121, 124, 127, 131–133, 184, 194
communal: norms, 194, 196; sense, 115–117, 119–122, 124–125, 130–132, 217
communicative, (events, exchanges, links, transactions), 72–74, 80–82, 86, 89, 126, 133, 135–136, 138–140, 145
compressible fluid, 174
conclusions, 160, 164, 176
confirmation, 170, 175
confluence: of use, 111–114, 116–117, 119–123, 127, 130
conjunction, 118
connectives, 164, 167, 195
connotation, 72
consecutiveness, 185, 190–191
consequences, 176, 190, 192
consilience: of communal practices, 194; of epistemics, 112
constants, 29, 146, 158, 202
context, 94, 96, 100, 192, 194, 204
contingency, 11, 13
contradiction, 161, 178–180, 218–220. *See also* absurdities, antinomies
contradictory beliefs, 150–152, 155, 158, 220. *See also* inconsistency
contraries, 188, 220
contrarieties, 189, 197
conventions, 60, 206–207, 222–223
convergence: of idiolectic senses, 111–112, 114, 116, 121, 125
convergent: epistemics, 185, 194; realism, 171
conversation, 113–134, 125, 137
conversational implicature, 60
copula, 118

General Index

correctness, 194
correspondence, 99, 102
cosmological world-story, 173
counterfactual, 7–9, 14, 19–22, 35, 51, 67, 70–71, 87, 208
creatures: Humean, 183–195, 215, 220, 223; ratiocinative, 192, 194–195, 221, 223; rational, 185–186, 189, 192, 221
criteria, of individuation for names, 35, 51, 144, 205
cross-cultural identification, 213–214

d-chains, 80–82, 212
D-relations, 161–178, 197, 220
deduction, 153–154
deductive relations, 161
deliberation, 186
demons, 6–7
demonstrations, 163–164, 166
demonstratives, 4, 82, 84, 115–116, 184, 215
denotation, 3, 55, 72
deontic logic, 164, 166–167, 175
derivations. *See* S-*derivations*
descriptions, 47, 57, 59, 61–62, 68–71, 77, 80, 87–88, 95–97, 104, 107, 128–129, 132, 141–143, 145, 167, 172, 204, 206, 209, 212, 217
descriptive: content, 125–127, 140–141, 144; contexts, 128–129, 133, 144; ignorance, 184, 194; terms, 166, 213
descriptive indicative sentences, 110, 115, 118, 120–122, 128, 130–131, 214
Descriptivism, xi, 3, 57–58, 66–72, 74, 85–86, 88–89, 94–96, 104, 108, 124–125, 127, 132, 142–143, 184, 207

designation, 43–44, 53–55, 209–210. *See also* rigid designators
designators, 1, 7–9, 28–55. *See also* proper names, rigid designators
detective stories, 139
diachronic, 115, 124–125, 129
dilemma, 105
direct reference, 52, 55, 205
disconfirmation, 170–171
discursive context, 94, 96, 100, 144
disquotational principles, 40, 148–149, 155, 218, 220
division of linguistic labor, 114, 142
dogmas, 9, 214
dogs, 183
dolphins, 183
dot-quotes, 118–120, 215

Earthlings, 24
egg, 17
element, 19–22
elf, 97, 106
elm, 114
elucidating, 193, 195
empirical epistemics, 112–113, 116, 127, 129, 133, 189, 193–194
empiricism, 1–3, 9
English names, 51–53
entailment, 161
entry claims, 116, 130
environment, 184
epicycles, 216
epigones, 2, 44
episodes, 62–66, 75
epistemic: authority, 165, 168–169, 171–172, 181; picture of proper names, 125–130, 132
epistemics, 110–116, 125, 127, 129–133, 184, 188, 193–194

epistemological fault finding, 155
epistemology, 4, 9–10, 13–14, 22–23, 26–27, 133, 135, 137–138, 158, 188–189, 192–193, 201, 215, 218; of logical analysis, 159ff; of natural science, 169–176, 180–182, 193–194; normative, 155; of speaker's reference, 140, 145
equations, 173–174
equivalence of names, 121–122
essentialism, 1–2, 6, 11–22, 24–25, 200
ethics, 182, 196, 221
events, 165
evidence, 13, 22–23, 189, 191
exhibited tokens, 117–120, 122
expectations, 175–176, 185, 187, 196
experiment, 170. See also thought-experiments
expertise, 114, 142
explanatory: appeals to intentions, 62–66, 74–75; contexts, 129–130, 216; epistemology of natural science, 172–176, 180–182, 193–194; spiral, 207, 222
expressing: vs. reporting, 191, 221
expressive: resources, 164, 167, 177, 193–196; role of logical particles, 191, 193–196
extension, 65
extensional contexts, 128, 214
extensionalist strictures, 1

fiction, 89–90, 96, 99–104, 112–123, 126, 211–214
fictitious story, 68
fish, 95
fixed point, 115
flaccid designators, 45, 47

folk semantics, 98
fool's gold, 19–20, 25
fool's water, 25
formal: logic, 28–30, 192; systems, 3, 30, 101, 146, 199, 202. See also logical calculi
formalisms, 3, 44, 57, 147, 168–169, 175, 181
formalizing, 160, 167. See also symbolization
formation rules, 161, 166, 177, 197
formulae, 29, 146, 161–164, 178, 197, 220
foundationalism, 200
functional classification, 118–119
furniture of the world, 165
fusion, 115–116, 131–132

gases, 169, 173–174
generalities, 197
generality, 188, 192–193
generalization, 185, 188
geocentric, 173, 216
gold, 6–7, 10, 19–22, 24–25, 200
grammar, 159
grammatical: form, 100, 105, 159; subject, 110, 120–121
graphite, 35
groundings, 80–81, 214–215

hard-core, 168–169, 171, 177, 219–220
hardness, 178
hearer, 73–74, 81, 125–126, 133, 141
heliocentric, 173
historical: inquiry, 91–94, 110–111; Jonah, 96; Robin Hood, 91, 93, 96; saint, 73

General Index 233

Humean creatures, 183–195, 215, 220, 223

I-relations, 160–163, 165, 167–169, 176, 178, 186, 190, 197
ice, 11–15, 201
idealizations, 131
identity, 28–49, 57, 163–164, 219
idiolectic sense, 110–117, 119, 124–125, 129, 132–133, 184–185, 194
illusion, 6, 200, 204
illustrating devices, 118
imaginative act, 99, 102–103
implication, 160–161, 167, 186
implicature, 60
incompatibilities, 187, 190–193
incompressible particles, 174
inconsistency, 151–152, 160, 167, 178, 186, 218. *See also* contradictory beliefs
inconsistent triad, 193
incorrigible, 207
indeterminacy, 9
indexicals, 130–132, 184, 216, 220
indicator, 23
indices, 145
indiscernibility, 219
individuation of linguistic items, 35, 51–53, 144, 205
induction, 175, 221–222
inference, 160, 162; principles, 186–192, 215, 222
inferential: commitments, 187, 189, 191–193, 195–196; conducts, 183, 196; relations, 103, 186, 190–191, 197–198, 222. *See also* I-relations
inferential relations, 4.121, 8.215, 8.224, 8.233
ink, 35

inner episodes, 62–66, 75
inscriptions, 35–36, 51–54, 203, 215, 222
inscrutability, 9
intentional: discourse, 189, 191; relations, 63–65, 104, 207; stance, 186, 192, 221
intentionalist, 199
intuitionist logic, 167, 175
intuitions, 22–27, 43–46, 71, 79–80, 83–85, 127, 132–133, 160, 167–169, 176–178, 180–182, 196, 198, 201–202, 206, 208–210
intuitive test, 44–48, 204
isomorphic limit senses, 131
isomorphism, 164, 167
isonymy, 121–123, 128, 215

jade, 202
judgments, 192–194
justification, 189–190, 193

kinetic thermodynamics, 169, 173, 219

language-games, 198
languages, 3, 159, 199, 202, 215, 219, 222–223
laws, 129, 221–222
legend, 90, 96, 126, 213
limit senses, 131–132
linguistic conventions, 206–207, 222–223
linguistic labor, 114, 142
logic, 3–4, 28–30, 57, 97, 99, 151–154, 179, 199, 219–220. *See also* formal logic, logical calculi, symbolic logic
logical: acumen, 151–155, 218, 220;

234 General Index

logical (*cont.*)
  analysis, 159–160, 163–167, 169, 171–172, 175, 177, 180–182, 195–196, 198, 219; anomaly, 176, 178, 180; calculi 146–147, 160–169, 175, 177–178, 181, 197–198, 199; form, 26, 100–102, 106, 109, 158–159, 163–165, 169, 182–183, 196–198, 219; intuitions, 167, 176–178, 180–182; particles, 166–167, 182–183, 187, 191, 193–196, 222; space, 189–190, 197, 220; truths, 9, 162; vocabulary, 191–192, 196

martini, 59, 61–62
material inference principles, 187–188, 192, 215, 222
mathematical logic. *See* formal logic, logical calculi, symbolic logic
mathematics, 199, 213
maxim, 187
measurements, 22, 170, 173–179
mechanics, 173, 209
memory, 78–79, 117, 133, 209
mention vs. use, 33
metalanguage, 148
metalinguistic: conditional, 41–43; expression, 49; intentions, 75–76
metaphor, 204
metaphysical necessity, 1, 19, 22, 49
micro-entities, 173
Millianism, 55, 72, 205
minimalism, 121
mistake, 59, 63, 82–83
modal intuitions, 22–23, 25–27, 43, 181
modality, 49
molybdenum, 114, 142
monkeys, 183

monolingual, 150, 155
moon, 173
myth, 90, 96, 112–113, 126, 213

names, 3–5, 28–56, 58–60, 67–96, 99, 101–127, 129–133, 135–146, 158, 184, 194, 203–204, 208–213, 215, 217
namesakes, 144–145, 217
natural kinds, 24–26, 189
naturalism, 2, 55, 66, 104, 126–127, 207, 217, 223
naturalistic fallacy, 221
necessity, 4, 9–11, 15, 21, 25–26, 28–43, 49–50, 200, 219
negations, 187, 193
Newtonian mechanics, 173, 209
NL-arguments, 160–169, 171, 181, 196–197
noncircularity. *See* circularity
nonnatural meaning, 199
normative authority, 189
norms, 114, 181–182, 184–189, 194, 196; epistemic, 152, 154–156
novels, 112, 211
numerals, 213

observation categorical, 188
observations, 22, 173–174, 177–178, 182
obstacle, 179–180
omniscience, 27, 152, 154, 156, 196; creative, 137
ontological: commitment, 3; import of theories, 165, 172–175; relativity, 9; status, 55
ontology, 64–65, 104, 127, 217, 219

General Index   235

operators, 49, 99–103, 164
origins, 11–19

pain, 179
paradox, 176, 178–181
parameters, 170–171
partial (designation, truth), 83–85, 209–210, 212
particles, 174. *See also* logical particles
pepperoni pizza, 221
perception, 23, 81–82, 116, 129–130, 133, 184, 189, 214–215
perspectival limit senses, 130–132
perspective, 27
phenomena, 172–176
phenomenal natural kinds, 24–26, 202
phenomenon, 178–179
physician, 210–211
physicist, 69, 71–72, 88, 210–211
picking out, 184
pizza. *See* pepperoni pizza
planets, 173, 203
positivism, 174
possible worlds, 1, 7–22, 30–44, 48–54, 68, 200–204, 219
practices, 194
pragmatic distinction, 60
predecessor theories, 174–175
predicate calculus, 163–164
predication, 92–93, 95, 118
prediction, 170
prescriptive, 129
presuppositions, 128, 140, 143–145, 157
pretense, 99
privileged access, 157, 207
Procrustean bed, 177
proofs, 167

proper names, 3, 28–56, 58–96, 99, 101–127, 129–133, 135–146, 158, 184, 194, 203–204, 208–213, 215, 217
propositional form, 183–184
prose: Kripke's, 203
puzzle about belief, 147*ff*, 205, 218, 220
pyrites, 19–20

quantum leaps, 223
quotation marks, 35, 51–53, 205

ratiocinative creatures, 192, 194–195, 221, 223
rational creatures, 185–186, 189, 192, 221
realism, 171, 174, 217, 219
reasoning, 160, 163, 166–168, 171, 176, 178, 181, 185–186, 197–198, 199, 221
reasons, 179, 189–191; as reasons, 190–191
reference: borrowing, 81–82; determining, 133, 140, 143; fixing, 74, 80, 128–129, 138; preserving, 80, 128–129; transmitting, 74
referential use, 59–64, 80, 107, 141, 196, 206
reflective equilibrium, 181, 196, 198
regress, 68
regularities, 187, 190
regulative ideal, 115, 132
relations, 104–105, 108, 117, 127, 133, 207, 219. *See also* D-relations, I-relations
relevance logic, 167, 178
reliable indicator, 23

repeatability, 192, 194
reporting, 191, 221
representation: *in absentia*, 73, 116, 184, 194, 215, 220, 223; theory of, 105, 199
representations, 64–66, 82, 191–192, 198, 220, 222–223
reticence, 149, 156
rigid designators, 1, 7–9, 28–55, 57, 144, 202, 204, 213, 219
Rival, 10–16, 20
romance novels, 136
rules, 160–161, 166, 222

S-derivations, 161–162, 164, 168, 178
sailors, 78–79, 85
saint, 73, 89, 95
salve veritate, 9
satisfaction, 94, 104
scientific theories, 98–99, 216, 222
scope, 46–48, 204
semantic: ascent, 40; descent, 39, 41; reference, *see* speaker's reference; theory, 98, 101, 211
semantics, 2–4, 29, 33, 90, 105–106, 118, 141, 145, 199, 219
sensations, 184
sense: communal, 115–117, 119–122, 124–125, 130–132, 217; Fregean, 72, 77; idiolectic, 110–117, 119, 124–125, 129, 132–133, 184–185, 194; limit, 131–132
sensory capacities, 23
set theory, 146, 163, 199
sheep dog, 187
shrew, 114
situated, 4, 55

skeleton, 218
slip of the tongue, 62
smoke, 185, 190–191
Socratic method, 193, 195, 222
space and time, 130–132, 216
speaker relativity, 143
speaker's reference, 58–63, 66–67, 79, 107–108, 111–112, 116, 120, 123, 135, 137–140, 142–144, 147, 158, 195, 206–207, 209, 222
sperm, 17
star-quotes, 118, 215
stipulations, 8–21, 200, 203
stories, 68, 75, 77–78, 82, 91–92, 94–96, 99–100, 102–103, 112
structural: classification, 118, 122, 144; rules, 160–161, 197
structures, 207, 219
substitution, 121, 128
successor theories, 174–175
surface irritations, 184
symbol: manipulators, 194–195; processing, 196
symbolic logic, 159–160, 162, 219. *See also* formal systems, logical calculi
symbolization, 160, 162–164, 166, 168, 177, 197, 218. *See also* formalizing
syncategoremata, 166
synchronic, 125, 129
synonymy, 9, 108
syntactic mileau, 195
syntax, 146, 156, 218

tags, 52, 55, 72
telescopes, 8, 15
theorem, 29, 163
theoretical identification, 26

General Index 237

theories, 98–99, 169, 173–178, 189, 197
theorizing, 1, 22–23, 145–146, 222
thermodynamics, 169, 173, 219
this-such, 132, 184
thought-experiments, 6–27, 70, 84, 152, 154, 198, 200, 202
titanium, 114
tokens, 66, 73, 83, 96, 100, 108, 117–120, 122, 194, 206, 212, 215
transformation rules, 161, 166, 177, 197
translation, 148–149
transparent, 128, 214
transportability, 192, 194
transworld identification, 117–118
truth, 98–99, 101–104, 219
Twin Earth, 23–26, 202

uniformities, 187
uniquely satisfying, 57, 86, 97, 104, 129, 141, 213
uniqueness conditions, 68–71, 125, 132, 194
univocal accounts, 96, 99, 104

validity, 160, 162, 181
variables, 29
verbs, 165, 221
verdictive authority, 165, 168–169, 171, 197
vole, 114

well-formed, 161–162
word-world relations, 104–106
world-stories, 172–174, 216

XYZ, 23–26, 202

yellow, 6–7, 10, 200

NAME INDEX

Achilles, 179, 220
Alexandria, 136
Anscombe, G.E.M., 221
Aphrodite, 213
Aquinas, 168
Aristotle, 143
Armani, 59

Barkley, Victoria, 136
Batman, 123, 221
Bealer, George, 211
Begriffsschrift, 214
Bennett, Jonathan, 221
Bible, 68, 92
Big Valley, 136
Blackburn, Simon, 217
Blum, Katarina, 90, 211
Böll, Heinrich, 211
Bonanza, 136
Bowes-Lyon, Lady Elizabeth, 17–18
Brahe, Tycho, 173
Brandom, Robert, 192–193, 195, 221–222
Bruno, 63

Carroll, Lewis, 179, 220
Cartland, Barbara, 136–139
Cartwright, Barbara, 135–140
Cartwright, Ben, 137
Catiline, 69–70, 128–129
Cato, 82–84, 209
Chastain, Charles, 215
Chomsky, Noam, 219
Christie, Agatha, 137, 139
Christmas, 97, 213
Cicero, 69–71, 88, 128–130, 139–140
Clemens, Samuel Langhorn, 120, 122–123
Costner, Kevin, 91, 93

Davidson, Donald, 159, 163–166, 200, 218
Dennett, Daniel, 186, 220
Descartes, René, 27
Devitt, Michael, 61, 80–85, 91–92, 94–95, 98–99, 101–104, 204, 206–212, 214–217, 220, 222–223
Donnellan, Keith, 58–60, 77, 80, 107, 141, 206
Dumas, Alexandre, 91, 93, 144

Name Index

Egypt, 68, 136
Einstein, Albert, 70
Eli. *See* Jum Eli
Elizabeth II, 16–19
Evans, Gareth, 212

Feynman, 69, 71–72, 88, 139–140, 143, 210–211
Fidel, 45
Field, Hartry, 209
Fielding, 100
Fitzwaters, 91, 211
Flynn, Erroll, 91, 93
France, 147, 150, 153
Frege, Gottlob, 27, 72, 101, 103–104, 165–166, 214

Gawain, 117
Glyph, 212–213
Gödel, Kurt, 70–71, 97, 99, 139–140, 208
Gorbachev, 221
Gracie, 135–140, 157–158
Greene, Lorne, 137
Greta, 109–112
Grice, H. Paul, 60, 199, 206
Gutch, John Matthew, 211

Harman, Gilbert, 200
Hegel, 2
Heidi, 75–78, 82, 84–85, 88, 119
Helmut, 75–80, 82, 84, 88–89, 107, 116–119, 139–140, 143, 157–158, 208–209
Hercules, 112–114
Hesperus, 27, 30–42, 48–54, 120–123, 203, 215

Hilbert, David, 45
Hitler, 45
Hode, Robyn, 91, 211
Holmes, Sherlock, 90, 112–114, 211, 214
Hood, Robin, 90–96, 211
Hopper, Hedda, 144
Houde, Ruben, 91–94, 96
Humphrey, 45
Huntingdon, 91

Israelites, 68
Ivanhoe, 91

Jacques, 59, 61–62
Jemima, 82–84, 209
Jonah, 91–92, 95–96
Jones, 59–61, 141; Tom, 100
Jorg, 112
Jum Eli, 102–104
Jupiter, 213
Jutta, 112

Kaplan, David, 205
Kent, Clark, 123
Koch, Anton, 217
Kripke, Saul, xi, 1–5, 6–61, 66–75, 80–81, 85–89, 91, 94–96, 108–109, 124–126, 128, 130, 133–135, 139–158, 168, 181–182, 199–208, 211, 213, 216, 218–220

Lancelot, 117
Leibknecht, 209, 217
Leibniz, 27, 185, 190, 219
Lewis, David, 204
Locksley, 91

London, 147–157
Londres, 147–149, 151–154
Lycan, William, 203, 205

Madagascar, 212
Marcus, Ruth Barcan, 208, 211–212
Marian, Maid, 91, 93, 211
Mele, Alfred, 211
Merry Men, 93
Moses, 68, 87, 143, 210
Munday, Anthony, 211

Nana, 82–84, 209
Napoleon, 73, 76, 217
Neurath, Otto, 75, 78–80, 82, 84–85, 89, 107, 116–119, 122, 139–140, 143, 208–209
Nile, 136
Nineveh, 95
Nixon, Richard, 45–48, 201

Paderewski, Jan, 109–112, 114
Parsons, Louella, 144
Petra, 109–112
Phosphorus, 27, 30–42, 48–52, 203
Pierre, 147–158, 195, 205, 218
Piers Plowman, 91
Plato, 2, 87, 106
Putnam, Hilary, 23–26, 202

Quine, W.V.O., 1–3, 9, 108, 164, 188, 200, 220

Reinhold, 75–78, 82, 85
Russell, Bertrand, 27, 115, 141, 214, 220

Santa Claus, 73, 89, 95, 97, 99, 104, 106, 211, 213
Schlick, Moritz, 75–80, 82, 84–85, 89, 107, 116–119, 139–140, 143, 208–209
Schmidt, 70, 208
Scott, Sir Walter, 91, 93
Sellars, Wilfrid, 35, 118–119, 193, 215–216, 220–221
Sheriff of Nottingham, 93
Sherwood Forest, 90, 93
Simmons, Keith, 201, 204–205
Smith, 59–60, 141
Socrates, 87, 106, 210, 222
Stanwyck, Barbara, 136–137, 139
Stewart, Rod, 144–145, 217
Superman, 123

Tennyson, Alfred Lord, 91, 93
Torquata, xv, 200
Tortoise, 179, 220
Truman, Margaret, 16
Twain, Mark, 120, 122–123

Venus, 35, 37, 53, 120–123, 203, 213, 215
Vienna, 75

Wayne, Bruce, 123
Wittgenstein, Ludwig, 198, 217

Zeus, 213
Ziff, Paul, 45–46, 48, 115, 214

OHIO UNIVERSITY LIBRARY
Please return this book as soon as you have finished with it. In order to avoid a fine it must be returned by the latest date stamped below. All books are subject to recall after two weeks or immediately if needed for reserve.

DEC 1 5 1995